The El Questro Story

The EL QUESTRO Story

Meg Hornabrook

A Cataloguing-in-Publication entry is available from the National Library of Australia

ISBN: 978-0-646-58079-1 (pbk.)

Reprinted 2013

Cover design and typeset by BookPOD

Printed and bound in Australia by BookPOD

Dedication

This book is dedicated to two brothers: Torrance MacMicking, a drover, who in 1958 consolidated several leases into the holding he named El Questro.

And John, whose generosity in sharing information gained during his years in the Kimberley has proved invaluable in the preparation of this book.

Acknowledgements

Many people have generously contributed to the contents of this book and others have assisted in its production.

Norma and Bob Wainwright, Keith Wright, Ronnie and Will Atkins, Mandy Smith, Dick Daniels, Ian Sinnamon, Jack and Ian Trust, Susan Bradley, Geoff Warnock, Tom and Patrick Birch, Michelle and Mark Poulson, Derek Goodard from Agriculture WA, Michael Beh, Ambrose Mungala Chalarimeri and Roderick Woodland are amongst the Kimberley folk who assisted me with information or verification of details.

Finding Doug Harrison on one of my tours was a great bonus. Doug worked on El Questro in the early 1960s, and on discovering that I was seeking historic material relating to the Station he gave me copies of his letters and the relevant chapters of his book of recollections from those exciting days. Cathie Clement, Helen Bunning and David Mills provided snippets of information, as did Dr Darrell Lewis and Patsy Millett. I acknowledge also the assistance I received from the willing and helpful staff at Western Australia's Landgate, the Battye Library and Public Records Office in Perth. Your contributions have both validated and enhanced the content of my book.

The following owners, managers and contractors of El Questro have all provided information or photographs for the book: Morris Marshall and his son and daughter – Chris and Lee, George Lansell, Des and Charles Lougoon, Edgar Pickles, Denis Wells, Digger Flohr, Craig Lorimer, Jim Ranken, Helen Ohrt, Margaret Hudson and the Salerno family, Celia and Will Burrell, Geoffrey Pie and Alan Emblin. I am indebited to you all.

My sincere thanks to employees past and present: Jo Broderick, Micko Bass, Simone Field, Phil Slade, Lyn Fontainini, Maria Tomasi and Bridget Parish. Particular thanks go to Pete (Brownpete) Guggisberg and Tobie Hynes for access to their photographic collections. Also to Zak Dragic from Explorers Australia Pty Ltd who at the last minute stepped into the breach to create the relief map of El Questro.

Endeavouring to trace ownership of El Questro country from early European settlement to the present time, and interpreting records in the archives section of the Department of Lands, has been challenging to say the least and I am most grateful to Shirley Threlfo for unravelling many of the lease details.

Just as I thought the end of the book was in sight, I revisited the museums at Wyndham and Kununurra. At the latter I made the acquaintance of Andrew Barker, the president of the Kununurra Historical Society. Andrew enthusiastically embraced my quest for information and opened the door to another dimension of research which yielded some colourful and valuable material.

My gratitude also extends to friendly wordsmiths, Angela Berry, Carmela Stefanidis, Judy Smith and Patricia Rust, for their significant assistance with the manuscript for the book.

Had Torrance MacMicking still been alive when I arrived to work at El Questro I feel certain there would have been more valuable anecdotes included in this book. I have been more than compensated by my fortuitous introduction to his brother John McMicking who for more than a decade generously shared his knowledge of life in the East Kimberley with me. In countless ways John contributed to the El Questro story and endeavoured to 'keep it honest'. It was 'Johnny Mac' who patiently cajoled me into bringing this book to its conclusion and my debt to him knows no bounds.

To my friends and family, who have supported and encouraged me through this seemingly endless project, I offer my heartfelt gratitude. And last but not least, my appreciation goes to Christina Mowle for her patient and good-natured editing work and to Sylvie Blair at BookPOD and Dalida Boustead for transforming my manuscript into the book we see today.

I sincerely thank you all.

Contents

Postcript

Introduction

The beauty of the vast unobstructed landscape and unsurpassed natural wonders of Western Australia's remote Kimberley region is beyond adequate description. The Kimberley is a land of worn and timeless horizons encapsulating the spirit of the country; it is a moving experience. To know it is to love it and to be humbled.

Situated in the far north-west corner of the continent, with plateaux and fertile plains crossed by more than a hundred rivers, the Kimberley's possibilities as grazing country were recognised by early European settlers in the mid–19th Century.

Thus began a journey of discovery and development as, undaunted by its challenges, a succession of adventurers risked all in order to gain a foothold on the 'promising' land. They braved rocks and ravines, murders and mayhem, development and destruction – it is a fascinating and uniquely Australian story, some of which is chronicled here – however, the primary focus of this book remains El Questro Station. Internationally recognised, it is one of the extraordinary jewels in the Kimberley crown.

The story begins with the geological origins of the ancient and remarkable landscape. It continues through the arrival of man, to European exploration and settlement, to the present day and the phenomenally successful tourism destination of El Questro.

My introduction to El Questro came about by fortuitous coincidence. Prior to 1996 my work life had been immersed in the travel and tourism industry, including operating my own small touring company. After a series of personal financial setbacks, coinciding with a downturn in the economy in the late 1980s, I found myself as a mature-aged job seeker with few prospects. A radio program extolling the delights of the Kimberley caught my interest and as I began to investigate employment prospects there, a colleague from the travel industry suggested my qualifications would be well suited to a tourist destination with an exotic name – 'El Questro'. To my delight, my application as a tour guide was successful and I soon found myself packing my life into a suitcase and heading out of Melbourne into the great unknown.

The El Questro Story grew out of research I undertook when, as a new guide with no previous knowledge of the area and with merely one page of reference material, I was asked to compile an information manual for the use of El Questro's new Rangers. Keen to expand my limited knowledge, I set about the task of research and discovery. This was the beginning of my love affair with the land, for the deeper I delved, the more intrigued I became with its natural wonders and fascinating history. The extraordinary landscape, the awe-inspiring expression of the power of nature and the forces that formed the land, the myriad creatures of every kind, and the diversity of human characters I encountered comprised an opportunity I could not resist.

Enslaved by my compulsion to continue documenting the provenance of this remarkable country, I continued to collect and record additional material until I found the manual had become the embryo of this book. Every effort has been made to seek out and verify the truth of material included here, but truth can be fickle and recollections differ according to individual perceptions or interpretations. I have drawn much of the material from written memoirs and have also used anecdotal material from local residents or former owners, managers and employees of El Questro, most of which is impossible to verify. If I have inadvertently misrepresented anyone, I offer here my sincere apologies!

The El Questro Story has been a labour of love for me. It is not intended to be a literary masterpiece; rather it is my effort to share some of the knowledge gained and the delights experienced during my wonderful 11 seasons at El Questro. I was quite unprepared for the effect this magnificent, rugged landscape and its people would have on me and how much I would enjoy the work and play of life at El Questro. It proved to be an enduring affair.

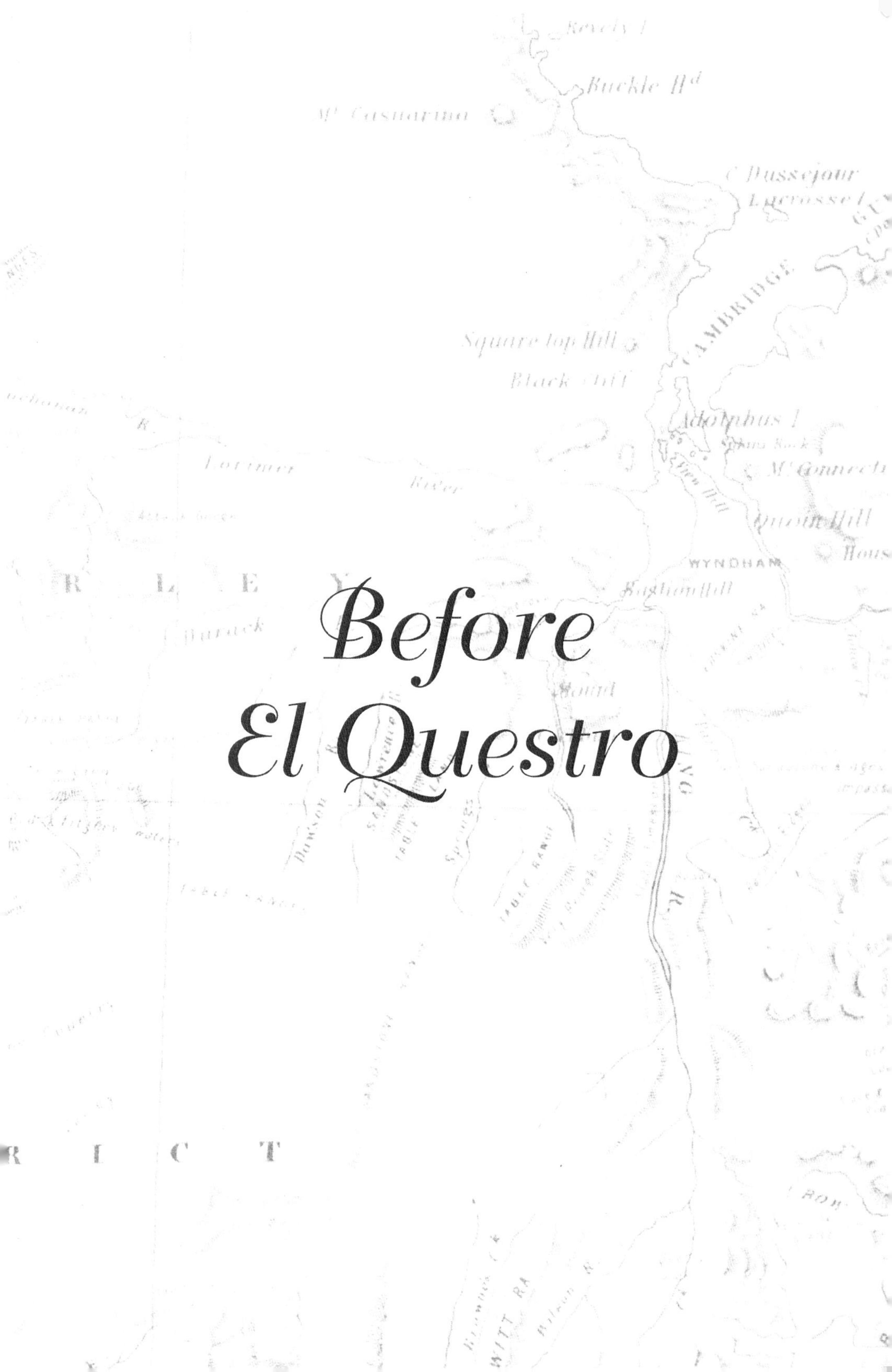

Before El Questro

The Pentecost Falls. Photo by Brownpete.

Genesis

And God called the land Earth. Genesis 1:10

'That's a load of rubbish,' came a voice from somewhere behind me as I brought the vehicle to a standstill. Naturally I was taken aback, but I was confident of the facts I had provided during the drive to Emma Gorge, a beautiful resort at the foot of the Cockburn Ranges.

As the visitors alighted from the 21-seater bus after their day of exploring in the Wilderness Park, an American stepped forward and denounced my explanation of the origins of the geological features we had seen along our 28–kilometre drive from the Station Centre. It was my first encounter with a Creationist, and on reflection the experience served me well, reminding me of the many Creational beliefs held by others.

Throughout the Kimberley, time is expressed geologically. The ancient horizons, the rust red rocks and the worn and weathered landforms inspire contemplation of their formation and evolution. The First Australians have their myths explaining how their land was created, commonly known as The Dreaming. Earth scientists have geological explanations for the unique landscape dating back two billion years to the Proterozoic era when the earliest rocks were formed and the story of El Questro really began.

Visitors to the Kimberley cannot fail to be touched by the vastness and antiquity of the topography. It is an ancient land of spectacular features and diverse origins and its geographic boundaries encompass some 423,000 square kilometres above the 20th parallel. Although this area only represents around 16 per cent of the state of Western Australia, it is significantly larger than the Federal Republic of Germany and is similar in size to the state of California, USA. The Kimberley is bordered to the south by the Fitzroy River with the Great Sandy Desert beyond, the Ord River to the east, and a rugged coastline to the north and west.

To appreciate the diversity of the landscape throughout the region, one requires an elementary understanding of its origins.

When the surface of the Earth cooled sufficiently to form a solid crust, the convection currents within the hot magma in the mantle below it fragmented the crust into tectonic plates and caused them to move around the globe. This process is known as Continental Drift and it continues today, with some plates shifting up to 15 centimetres each year.

The general acceptance of the Theory of Continental Drift by Earth scientists in the 1960s opened the door to the Theory of Plate Tectonics and the more recent understanding of Earth's crust as consisting of a number of mobile plates on which the continents ride. The continuous movement of the tectonic plates has a major impact on the global climate and the evolution of life. Additionally, it can create mountains, open new oceans and change large continents.

During the past three billion years the plates have merged and drifted apart, carrying the continents with them. It is believed there have been at least four occasions when most of the landmasses amalgamated to form a 'supercontinent'. Thus, over time, the configuration of the continents has changed, sometimes adopting blocks of earlier supercontinents – these ancient embedded fragments are referred to as cratons.

Less than two billion years ago when the supercontinent Rodinia was breaking apart, the Kimberley Craton, a stable but independent portion of the continental crust, broke away from a larger continent to the north and slowly drifted towards the northern section of continental Australia. It is believed a mountain range comparable to the Andes in South America was formed along the southern and eastern margins of this craton. The eventual collision around 1,830 million years ago (Ma) caused major fractures and upheavals in the Earth's crust along the southern perimeter of the Kimberley region. This fault-bounded zone of highly deformed and heat affected rocks, known as the Hall's Creek Fault, extends for 850 kilometres from Darwin to the Great Sandy Desert. Over ensuing millions of years, this distorted and tortured area was eroded to its present remnant levels and immense loads of the resulting sediments were deposited in the centrally located Kimberley Basin. Major river systems flowing from the north brought additional sediments to the Basin.

The prolonged period of deposition built thick beds of sandstone, interlaid with mudstone, shale, dolomite, pebbles and boulder conglomerate up to five kilometres in depth in places. Over time the sedimentary layers have metamorphosed by heat and pressure into predominantly sandstone rock, as can be seen in the stratified cliff faces where an area has uplifted and subsequently eroded.

This elevated area is known as the Kimberley Plateau. It covers 160,000 square kilometres and dominates the central Kimberley region with impressive sandstone tablelands and flat topped mesas almost 800 metres high at its centre.

El Questro Wilderness Park, comprising almost 400,000 hectares – one million acres – is located on the eastern fringe of this plateau. Here the spectacular twin plateaux of the Cockburn Range and the nearby Pentecost Range and the 125–kilometre–long Elgee cliff line are a part of the vast Kimberley Plateau.

There are no fossils to be found in the ancient rocks of this elevated complex for its origins were some 1,800 million years ago (1,800 Ma) in Pre-Cambrian times when only primitive, multi-celled forms of life were beginning to emerge in shallow seas.

Mount Wells, in the Durack Range to the south-east of the Wilderness Park, is the tallest of the Kimberley peaks. Reaching 983 metres, its slopes give birth to the mighty Ord and Fitzroy Rivers in addition to other watercourses that over time have carved their way through the Kimberley Plateau. The Chamberlain River, the longest of the four rivers to dissect El Questro country, rises in the foothills of this peak and extends for 236 kilometres before merging with the Pentecost River.

Corrugated ripples on the surface of flat rocks frequently attract the attention of visitors. This captured moment in geological time is the imprint of shallow water flowing over a sedimentary mud flat or sand bed surface which, over millennia, was transformed into sandstone rock by heat and pressure. The spectacular russet colouring of the escarpments and other rock surfaces indicates the presence of iron amongst the many minerals found in the region and, like a long abandoned horseshoe, prolonged exposure to the elements has caused the iron to oxidise and rust. In some instances intense pressure and heat have fused the rough granular sandstone in the strata and converted it to smooth-surfaced quartzite. Alert fossickers may detect white and clear quartz crystals, geodes of agate and violet-coloured amethyst in pockets on El Questro.

Between 200 and 100 Ma the plateau was uplifted, and again between 70 and 50 Ma, while the relentless elements continued to shape the surface. A multiplicity of rejuvenated watercourses began to carve slender incisions through the ancient sediments, drastically dissecting the plateau and creating deep gorges, waterfalls and other dramatic land formations. In places, small pockets of alluvial silt have collected in valleys and estuaries, providing the nutrients for grasses and woodlands to proliferate.

In other enclosed pockets, sheltered from the ravages of fire and protected from the hostile sun and other destructive elements, remnant tropical rainforests of dense trees and primeval palms survive in small refuges. Growing in cool moist conditions beneath the tree canopies, several species of enchanting ferns, vine-thickets, native Lasiandra and other sensitive tropical vegetation cling to a fragile existence and delight the human senses.

The topography of the Wilderness Park is remarkably diverse. Divided by the Gibb River Road, the alluvial floodplains of the Cambridge Gulf lowland country in the north are bordered by the Erskine Range to the east and dominated by the picturesque Cockburn Range with its apron of scree and shale. The remains of stromatolite structures with their disputed Pre-Cambrian origins are found in this northern sector of El Questro.

An extensive survey made in the 1990s of the North and South Cockburns by botanists and naturalists from Western Australia's Department of Environment and Conservation revealed a fascinating diversity of flora and fauna, many of the species either endangered or endemic to the mesas. Little wonder the government was anxious to take control of this pristine plateau rising starkly from the surrounding lowland of stony plains and mudflats, and designate for future use as a national park.

The balance of the Wilderness Park lies in the Southern Kimberley Ranges Province where the rugged terrain comprises rocky ridges, rounded hills, cuestas and structural sandstone plateaux associated with the Durack Range. Stony soils and deep red sands support eucalypt woodlands, spinifex and mixed tropical grasses. It is indeed a diverse and wondrous landscape. Visitors are privy to waterfalls and wetlands, wildlife and wilderness, caves and chasms, grasslands and gorges, lush springs and steep escarpments. With few exceptions, these varied and contrasting features have in one way or another been shaped by water.

Elsewhere in the Kimberley other elements have played a part in fashioning the ancient landscape. In the area cradling the southern margins of the Kimberley Basin the Earth's crust has been subjected to intense stress. The resulting faulting in the adjacent King Leopold and Halls Creek Mobile Zones led to intermittent periods of volcanic activity, with igneous intrusions creating the tortured and rugged country we see today. More recently, 600 Ma, glacial conditions caused ice sheets to cover much of the region, leaving tillite deposits and other telltale footprints upon the land.

Even more recently, in the Devonian era approximately 350 Ma, warmer temperatures caused a rise in sea levels and the central plateau was surrounded on three sides by warm tropical seas. These conditions were ideal for the formation of a limestone reef extending for almost a thousand kilometres. Later the reef was lifted above sea level and now remains as a broken chain of limestone ridges visible in part in the Napier and Oscar Ranges in the west and the Ningbing Range to the north-east of Wyndham.

Thus, over millennia, forces sometimes cataclysmic and at other times barely discernible shaped the land for the arrival of mankind in the Kimberley. Fluctuations in climatic conditions are reflected in sea levels that in turn govern our coastline. The last glacial maximum peaked a mere 15,000 years ago when sea levels were 130 metres lower than at present. The Kimberley had wide coastal plains that extended almost to the edge of the continental shelf and significantly reduced the distance to neighbouring islands.

The succeeding deglaciation drowned these plains once again and in many places pushed the coastline inland to the ramparts of the Kimberley Plateau, giving us the spectacularly rugged coastline we enjoy today. Elsewhere great river valleys were flooded, creating the expansive waterways of King Sound in the western Kimberley and the Cambridge Gulf to the north of El Questro.

The tropical monsoonal climate in the Kimberley varies considerably across the region with short transitional periods separating the two dominant seasons.

The summer months from October to April are hot and humid as the sky increasingly fills with fluffy white cumulus clouds heralding the approach of seasonal rains and storms. The rainy season, known colloquially as 'the wet' is the time when maximum temperatures in the East Kimberley hover around 40°C and humid monsoonal conditions prevail. Towering cumulonimbus thunderclouds appear; these dramatic moisture-laden clouds form huge vertical pillars extending to 15 kilometres in height and are known to some as the King of Clouds. They are largely responsible for the mean annual rainfall of 816 millimetres in Kununurra, with the annual falls ranging between 400 and 1,000 millimetres. Approximately 90 per cent of the annual rain falls during the months of December, January, February and March. Tropical cyclones and low pressure systems are often experienced in these months. The wet season is the time of rapid growth and regeneration of the region's wide variety of vegetation.

A hot transitional period during March and April is when the swollen streams and rivers begin to subside and eventually diminish to dry or sluggish watercourses, and the tall grasses start to brown. From May to August the south-east trade winds provide welcome relief from the oppressive heat and humidity of the wet. Each day an orange sunrise gives way to the bluest of clear blue skies and the temperature ranges pleasantly between 16°C and 32°C. Warm days and cool evenings leading to chilly nights are the norm over six weeks in June/July. It is during these months ever increasing numbers of visitors come to explore the magic of the region and escape the cold of the southern winter. At day's end, spectacular sunsets of changing hues provide the cue for the planet Venus to be the first of the myriad celestial bodies to fill the firmament. This awesome effulgence of heavenly light, sadly unfamiliar to many urban-dwellers, is just one of many humbling experiences in the Kimberley outback.

El Questro: A diverse landscape

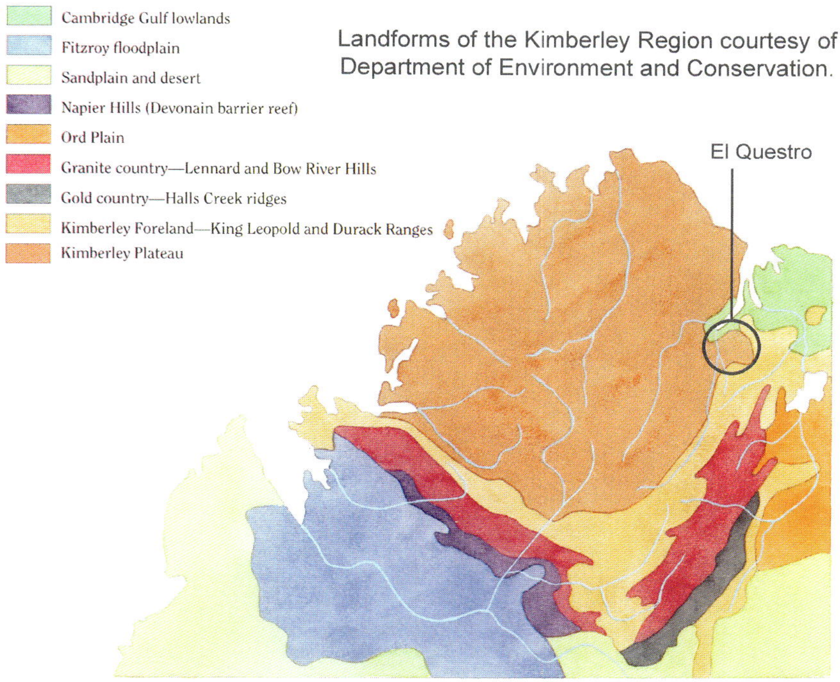

Landforms of the Kimberley Region courtesy of Department of Environment and Conservation.

Stromatolites on El Questro in the Cambridge Gulf lowlands.

Natural and polished agate stones and an uncut violet amethyst.

Rippled rock surfaces betray ancient water movement.

Above: Rock falls create new scars in the scree slopes following Cyclone Ingrid in 2005.

Below: Tidal marshland at Gullibidgee Swamp. Photo by Brown Pete.

Left: The outlook from a cave mouth at Lost City. Photo by Tobie.

Right: A slender chasm entrance dwarfs its visitors.

Below: An area of gibber on the northern plains.

Opposite Page
Top: Grassland and flood flats. Photo by Tobie.
Middle: Catacombs among stratified rocks. Photo by Tobie.
Below: Sunset over the tidal reaches of the Pentecost River.

Top: A wetland along the Karunjie Track. Photo by Brownpete.
Below: Glimpses of wilderness. Photo by Brownpete.

Left: Overlooking El Questro Gorge. Photo by Brownpete.
Middle: Grassland and a seasonally dry watercourse.
Below: Fire near Emma Gorge.

Opposite Page
Top: Tropical rainforest in El Questro Gorge.
Middle: View from the ridge at Pigeon Lookout.

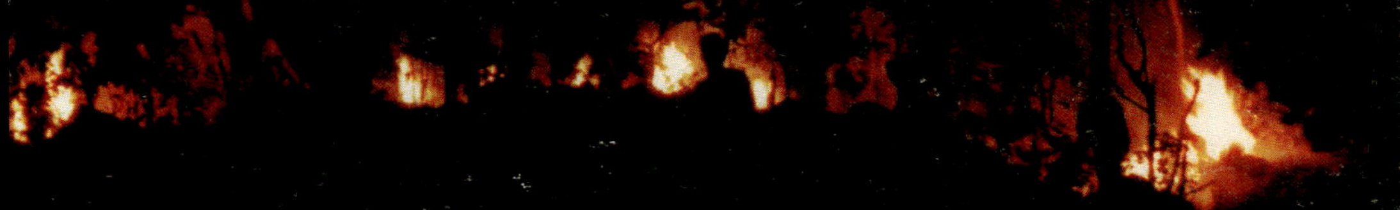

Emma Falls in the wet season. Photo by Brownpete.

Opposite Page
Top: The western face of the Cockburn Range. Photo by Brownpete.
Middle: The extensive mudflats.
Below: The Durack Range after fire. Photo by Brownpete.

Overleaf
Top: Debris in the tree indicates the flood level of the King River during the wet.
Bottom: Flowering boab trees indicate the approaching wet seas

Human Migration

The appearance of the *Homo* genus on our planet approximately 2.5 million years ago is utterly insignificant compared with Earth's 4.5 billion year existence.

Research on the neighbouring island of Java found evidence of *Homo erectus* dating back 1.2 million years and *Homo sapiens* at 100,000 BP (years before present). Despite the close proximity, our continent was at no time linked to Java or any other south-east Asian island or land mass; there has always been a water barrier of at least 50 kilometres. Any migration to the Australian continent would have necessitated a sea crossing and the distance covered would have depended on sea levels at the time.

During the Pleistocene Epoch 1.8 million to 10,000 years ago, under the influence of the Great Ice Age, Earth's climate and temperature fluctuated between long and severely cold periods and the warmer times of the brief inter-glacial periods. It is thought by some there were 17 glaciations during this period when the mean annual temperature dropped 10°C below those presently experienced. These were times when the oceans froze into immense polar ice sheets, lowering sea levels and exposing vast expanses of the Australian continental shelf.

It is generally agreed that the greatest sea level drop most pertinent to the colonisation of Australia was during the last glacial maximum some 24,000 to 15,000 BP when the level fell 120 to130 metres. There is dissension among archaeologists as to exactly when the maximum drop took place. Research suggests the sea level between south-east Asia and continental Australia had fallen to about 100 metres below present level by about 24,000 BP. However, archaeological evidence reveals that prehistoric man had already crossed this water and reached Arnhem Land, most likely during a previous glacial period around 50,000 BP.

The anthropologist Joseph Birdsell in 1977, proposed that two of the five possible sub-routes of early migration from south-east Asia involved a sea journey of less than 100 kilometres during Pleistocene times. One route was through Timor to north-west Australia and the other via Sulawesi to north-west New Guinea.

Sahul, the combined landmass of Papua New Guinea and Australia, was created when the waters in Torres and Bass Straits dispersed, forming

Greater Australia with a continuous land-link stretching from Tasmania to Papua New Guinea. Early humans created a migratory route using the island chains of the Indonesian archipelago as stepping stones from south-east Asia to the enlarged Australian continent. In other parts of the world, past migratory phases of *Homo sapiens* have largely been governed by opportunistic environmental conditions affecting food resources and living conditions, rather than through use of cultural and technological evolution. Conversely, in the case of Australia, the significant water crossing required some degree of technical and communication skills.

Humans arriving on the Australian landmass during the time of the megafauna would have found a vastly different land to their place of origin. The familiar giant elephant, tiger and monkey were replaced by an entirely different range of prehistoric beings: *Procoptodon goliah*, a 2.5 metre high kangaroo; *Megalania prisca*, an enormous goanna-like carnivore weighing up to 600 kilograms; a giant flightless bird, *Genyornis newtonii*, and our largest marsupial, a huge wombat-like *Diprotodon optatum* of hippopotamus proportions. At the top of the prehistoric food chain was the carnivorous marsupial lion *Thylacoleo carnifex*. This predator was the continent's largest known mammal and was comparable in size to a female lion or tiger today.

Bones of giant animals found at archaeological sites alongside tools and other remains of Aboriginal occupation indicate that humans coexisted with the megafauna for thousands of years. Some more recently extinct animals are featured in ancient rock paintings while others are recalled in legends. The reason for the extinction of these giant creatures has been a contentious and hotly debated issue for many years. Climate change leading to ecological collapse is considered to have been the principal cause of the loss of most species prior to 130,000 years ago.

It is now thought the demise of most of the remaining species on the continent by the time of the last glacial maximum approximately 20,000 years ago was due to a combination of vegetation change along with human's predatory activities. Australia is known to have some of the most fire-prone landscape in the world and recent research by the University of New South Wales reveals there was high fire activity across the continent between 60,000 and 28,000 years ago attributable to the climatic conditions.

The nomadic people with their primitive tools and clever use of fire as a hunting technique are believed to have significantly affected the vegetation over most of the continent. Their burning practices caused the then much less fire-adapted landscape to give way to fire tolerant vegetation, dominated by the Eucalypt and palatable to very few species of fauna. However, the greatest human induced fire activity came after the arrival of European colonists in 1788.

More than 40 large mammal species were lost after humans arrived. Most of these extinctions occurred about 45,000 BP with the loss of the last megabeast around 20,000 BP.

The two most recent departures of prehistoric mammals from mainland Australia are the flesh-eating Tasmanian devil and the Tasmanian tiger or thylacine (*Thylacinus cynocephalus*). Artistic representations of thylacines have been found amongst Aboriginal rock paintings at sites in Arnhem Land and the Kimberley. Their disappearance is attributed to the arrival of the dingo, *Canis lupus*, in the mid-Holocene era. In recent years there has been much discussion about the time of arrival and origin of this species on the Australian continent; ongoing research continues to produce changing views. Currently it is generally accepted that the dingo was imported from Asia between 4,000 and 5,000 years ago. At the time of European settlement it was the top land predator on the continent, but eradication programs by humans and the dingoes' hybridisation with the domestic dog mean the pure bred dingo is now threatened with extinction.

The last glacial maximum was a time of changing climatic conditions when our continent experienced excessive dryness and increased aridity. The processes of aeolian erosion peaked and much of the continent was covered by wind blown dunes. The dramatically lower sea level presented an opportunity for humans to cross the narrow water barrier between the islands to the north and Arnhem Land and the Kimberley; this may well have been the period of greatest migration.

Deglaciation was underway by 14,000 BP and the Pleistocene epoch abruptly gave way to the present interglacial Holocene epoch some 13,000–10,000 BP. Sea levels rose rapidly around the globe and inundated approximately one-seventh of the Greater Australian land mass, pushing occupation into more marginal and previously uninhabited areas across the continent. Population numbers varied according to the availability of natural resources, which were in turn governed by the availability of water and other environmental factors.

Unlike other inhabited continents where advances in agriculture and urbanisation were emerging, Australia's Aborigines retained their hunter-gatherer ways and lived according to the availability of natural resources. Indeed, there was little need for change and very few adaptable plants or animals suitable for domestication. Instead the small population of Indigenous Australians lived in harmony with nature and the land. They enjoyed sufficient leisure time to develop a rich cultural and spiritual life, much of which is reflected in their artistic expression. The land with its unique features was the spiritual home of the Indigenous population for tens of thousands of years with minimal change to their traditional ways until historically recorded time.

Earlier visits to the Kimberley coast by Indonesian and Chinese fishermen over the centuries had little or no effect on the Indigenous Australians. This was not the case with the arrival of Europeans on the continent in 1788. Their arrival commenced the dispossession of the Aborigines, separating them from their land, decimating their culture and their beliefs, and tragically reducing their population by introducing diseases from which they had no immunity.

While there are no definite figures for the Aboriginal population at the time of European settlement, 750,000 is considered a reasonable minimum estimate. Some researchers believe the population across the country at that time consisted of approximately 600 clan groups speaking 250 languages.

The term 'the Dreaming' has romanced the imagination of many non-Indigenous folk. It not only refers to the creation period and the time when the cultural heroes established the laws, it is also the time beyond living memory. The term was coined by anthropologists Baldwin Spencer and Francis Gillen in 1904, in an attempt to translate the Arrernte word 'altyerrenge'.

Many clues to the story of early humans in the Kimberley are found among the rocks where evidence of changing cultures from the first societies through to recent times is recorded in stone. The north-western area of the continent contains one of the world's richest repositories of remnant rock art and stone artefacts, and the earliest paintings found at Carpenter's Gap, dated to a minimum of 39,700 BP, are believed to be among the oldest. It will take many more years of research to unravel the intricacies of the distinctive cultural, technical, and stylistic changes that have taken place over thousands of years and are reflected in the remnant art and stone work.

Rock Art

The term 'rock art' encompasses engravings, paintings or any marks intentionally carved, imprinted, drawn or stencilled on rock surfaces by humans. In essence, it gives voice to the past.

During my first season working as a Ranger at El Questro I had the good fortune to meet Grahame Walsh. Little did I realise at that time the effect this boldly individualistic rock art researcher would have on my life. Hearing him speak passionately on the subject close to his heart opened my eyes to a new and enduring interest. For more than a decade thereafter until his untimely death in 2007, I travelled annually to Queensland in the wet season to work for brief periods at the Takarakka Rock Art Research Centre, assisting with archiving his field notes, sketches and photographs. In addition to his own research material, Walsh's extensive reference library was crammed with the most interesting and authoritative books and contained the work of two earlier researchers who had entrusted their collections to him. These were fascinating times for an amateur in my position.

The thoroughness and diversity of Walsh's research methodology made him a leading researcher in his field, but this self-taught man attracted much criticism from within contentious academic circles. Nevertheless, foremost among the academic awards his acclaimed publications earned him was an Honorary Doctorate (D. Litt) from The University of Melbourne – a remarkable achievement for one who failed Year 10 and had no tertiary education. His final achievement came only weeks before his death when Griffith University granted him a Ph.D. for his thesis on the methodology of rock art research and the interpretation of cultural and environmental histories.

Walsh's remarkable natural visual memory served him well during more than 30 years of field work at countless art sites throughout Australia. In 1977 he was introduced to the art treasures of north-western Australia and they became his focus and obsession. Fortunately, at the time Walsh commenced his research in the Kimberley there remained a scattering of Aboriginal elders with knowledge of the remnant mythology and traditional customs. These ageing men, sensing the decline of their culture, were anxious to entrust their information to him and he accompanied them to many cultural locations where he recorded the images and associated mythology.

Not long afterwards, he found the politics of land claims and political correctness compromised the integrity of this research into the more recent art period so he switched his efforts to unravelling the mysteries of the prehistoric rock paintings in the region. In doing so, he was largely responsible for bringing the Bradshaw or Gwion Gwion figures to the attention of a fascinated art world and general public.

It was clear the Kimberley art spanned an extensive period of time and incorporated many identifiable schools of conforming art. By studying these established styles and painstakingly recording the superimposition of one stylistic variation over another, Walsh succeeded in breaking Kimberley rock art into a sequence. The evidence of distinct major changes in Aboriginal culture and ideology over a period of time prompted him to designate three art epochs: Archaic, Erudite and Aboriginal, each separated by a period of artistic disconformity and further divided into periods according to the stylistic characteristics of the art.

The Archaic Epoch

The oldest art was generally found in shelters suitable for habitation. Walsh divided this epoch into two periods.

A small panel of cupules.

The Pecked Cupule Period features panels of multiple small cupules about 30 millimetres in diameter, pecked or abraded into the surface of the rock. These cup-shaped depressions of unknown purpose are considered to be the earliest surviving expression of art in the Kimberley and some panels contain thousands of cupules. They are found across northern Australia and have been recorded on other continents as well.

The Irregular Infill Animal Period (IIAP) refers to the depiction of outlined animal images with random dashes or elongated dots infilling important body parts such as the head, legs and tail. Hand prints and stencils of hands and weapons also feature during this period, as do images of humans and yams to a lesser extent. The IIAP provides us with the earliest surviving example of Kimberley rock painting. The majority of IIAP images found on El Questro feature macropods with broad random dashes within a cleanly outlined naturalistic form. Images of reptiles have also been found. Faint hand stencils, some with partially amputated fingers, may be found at many ancient sites and a study of weapon stencils gives a realistic glimpse into the size and form of early man's tools of survival.

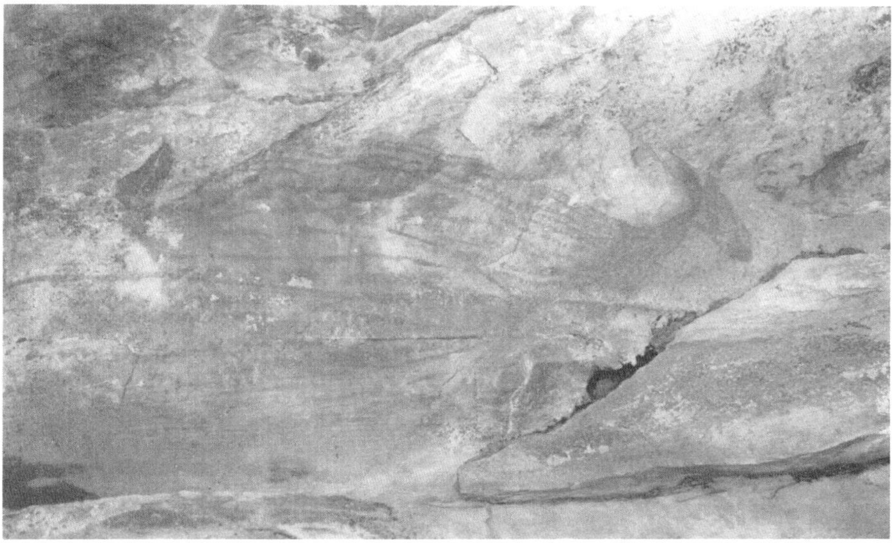

An Irregular Animal Infill Period depiction of a macropod.

Without dating or a scale of measurement, it is difficult to know if any of these early naturalistic animal depictions represented megafauna.

The Erudite Epoch

The remarkable Erudite Epoch emerged prior to the early stages of the last glacial maximum. This epoch of aesthetic form and superb brushwork featured the human body in a wide variety of naturalistic ceremonial stances and attires. There is no evidence of the evolution of this significant stylistic change and its apparent introduction as an existing culture caused Walsh to speculate on the possibility of a new cultural peopling of the area. The competence of the artisans and the focus of their subjects indicates a population living during a time of abundance when resources were bountiful and survival easy, providing plenty of leisure time for cultural pursuits.

The enigmatic figures in this style were first discovered and recorded by Joseph Bradshaw during his expedition to the Prince Regent River in 1891. Subsequently, all early Kimberley art came to be known by the Bradshaw name. Early researchers found these figures had no association with the contemporary culture of the Kimberley Aborigines who laid no claim to their creation at that time, believing instead the elegant human figures were painted with blood by a small bird using its bleeding beak or a tail feather to create the fine artwork. The Sandstone Shrike-thrush, known to the Aborigines of the area as Gwion Gwion or Bramba-bramba, features in the mythological explanation of the art and is often found at rock outcrops or on ledges close to the art sites, giving the art its Aboriginal name.

Walsh divided the Erudite Epoch into the Bradshaw Period and the later Clothes Peg Figure Period. The former was broken into numerous groups and sub-groups covering the many changes to the style and decorative elements depicted in the paintings. Of these, the most prolific is the aptly named Tassel Bradshaw Group, featuring anthropomorphic figures wearing tassel adornments and other decorative accoutrements. It is followed by the Sash Bradshaw group with the profile of an elegant three pronged sash extending from the hip. Another Bradshaw Period group, depicting unadorned human figures going about the normalities of secular life, provides a window into this ancient civilisation. Walsh called it the Elegant Action Figure Group.

A life-sized Sash Bradshaw figure.

The predominantly decorative and sometimes frivolous Bradshaw Period was followed by a radical change to the simple Clothes Peg Figure Group. As the name suggests, the austere depictions of static unadorned human figures were not dissimilar to old fashioned wooden clothes pegs and were generally painted in plan view. Of the prehistoric Kimberley art sequence this group is amongst the most prolifically represented, and it certainly dominates the Erudite Epoch art found on El Questro Wilderness Park. Figures from this period often display an interesting range of weaponry comprising spears, spear-throwers and a variety of boomerangs.

This remarkable artistic style disappeared around 18,000–14,000 BP when the acutely dry conditions of the last major phase of aridity created great stress for flora and fauna. Possibly it was a shortage of resources that led to the partial abandonment of the Kimberley area for as long as 10,000 years and resulted in a cessation of the art tradition. During this period of minimal habitation there was major discontinuity in the rock art sequence.

Clothes Peg Figure with boomerangs.

Little is known of the materials used by the early artists. Most images from the first two epochs remain as stains impregnated in the rock. Sadly there is little remnant organic residue to assist with analysis and dating. Inspection of many of the prehistoric paintings found on vertical rock walls and overhead ceilings indicate the use of a fine brush capable of dispersing highly refined ochre in unbroken strokes up to 150 millimetres and occasionally exceeding 500 millimetres in length. The remains of the work of these skilled artisans are still found mostly on the hard and stable surfaces of King Leopold and Warton sandstones while in many other places in the Kimberley it has faded or totally disappeared. It is likely the ancient art has been preserved by a thin protective skin of silica and oxalates left as a residue from a succeeding environmental period.

There is great interest in determining the age of the earliest work, but despite rapid advances in technology there is still no definitive answer to this intriguing question. The lack of retrievable material used in the production of paint for the earliest works together with the hard texture of the rock makes conventional laboratory analysis and dating methods ineffective. Research continues and some time frames have been established through the dating of mud nests built by wasps over pre-existing art. The optically stimulated luminescence dating (OSL) of sand particles taken from a wasp nest overlying a mulberry-coloured human figure suggested a minimum age of circa 16,400–23,800 years, indicating the painting was completed at or prior to the height of the last Ice Age some 20,000 BP.

The Aboriginal Epoch

Temperatures improved and sea levels rose at the conclusion of the Ice Age, and by 10,500 BP the Holocene period heralded the re-occupation of the Kimberley and the beginning of the Aboriginal Epoch. The ensuing rock art utilised different technology and was significantly different from any previous style. It is directly linked to the forebears of the Aboriginal people of today.

With the Indigenous population scattered in tribal groups across the continent there was little uniformity of culture and belief systems and this is reflected in the art. Early examples of Kimberley rock paintings from this last epoch were rudimentary and had no formal artistic tradition. However this began to change as recurring themes emerged, depicting outlines of decorated hands, compartmentalised anthropomorphic and zoomorphic figures, and combinations of the two, giving birth to the distinctive Clawed Hand Period.

The figures were rendered in a simple broad red outline. Devil figures and the first instances of genital depiction and sexual themes appeared in Kimberley rock art during this period. Advances in tool technology some 5,000 BP saw the introduction of the small tool tradition when stone spear points and small stone blades were deftly flaked from fine-grained rock. Using resin as glue, these were skilfully bound to handles, creating spears and axes.

Perhaps the most visually impressive works of the Kimberley rock art sequences are the spectacular Aboriginal Period figures that followed the Clawed Hand Period. These static, larger than life anthropomorphic representations, with their big black eyes staring from an expressionless

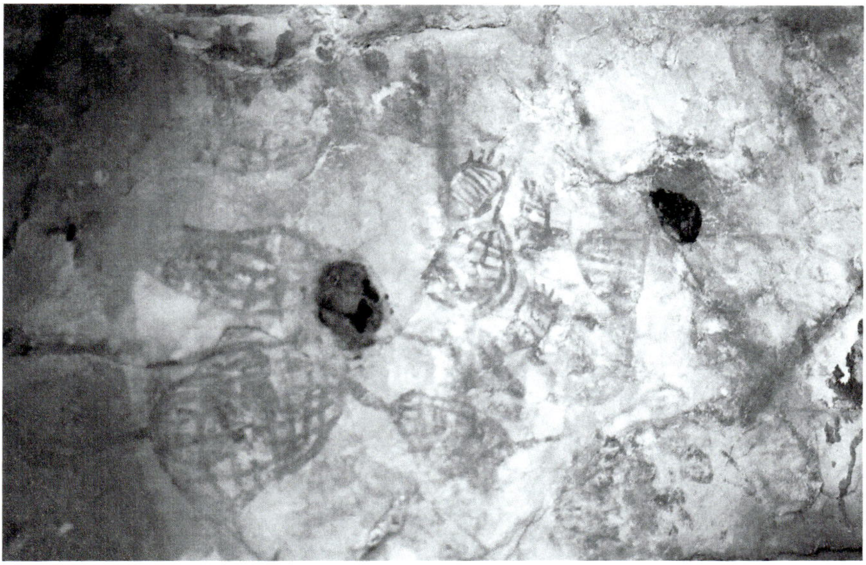

Two wasps' nests over a possible Clawed Hand Period panel.

whose mouthless face, have become a contemporary icon of Indigenous art in the Kimberley region.

Readers may recall the Wandjina figures featured in the opening ceremony at the Sydney Olympic Games in 2000. Traditional Aborigines believe the Wandjina to be supernatural Ancestral Beings represented in human form; they are the spirits of the towering rain-bearing cumulonimbus clouds and they control the seasons, fertility and all meteorological elements. They are the creators of the land, its features and all living things. In short, the Wandjina are the Ancestral Heroes of the Aboriginal people of the north and west Kimberley. The images are usually painted using red, yellow or black pigment on a brilliant white background. Wherever possible the white was prepared from the rare huntite mineral giving luminosity to the panels during the wet seasons.

Theories abound about these remarkable figures whose origins are obscure. It is generally accepted the Wandjina cult had its origins in the Kimberley's north-west where the rainy season is at its most potent. It is a time when cyclones and other powerful forces dominate the lives of the inhabitants of the area today, just as they would have during the lives of their spiritual and superstitious ancestors. Is it a coincidence that the form of the early

Wandjina figures.

Wandjina figures resembles the towering thunderhead clouds that dominate the skies during these months?

The Wandjina cult and belief system originally belonged to the people of the large Ngarinyin, Worora and Wunambal tribes in the north and west of the Kimberley where legend recounts how supernatural beings came from the sea and began their travels on land, creating its features and giving law to the people. Intricate mythology developed along their paths and actions. When their time on Earth was finished the Wandjinas died, leaving their shadows on the rock in paintings representing the spirits of the principal characters featured in the myth.

Wandjina sites and their associated mythology were of great importance to the local custodial Aborigines. In order to keep the spirit of the Wandjina alive and effective, it was customary for the painted image to be ritually retouched as required. Walsh found the thickness of the pigment on some panels measured seven millimetres from frequent repainting. Recent analysis of a 600-year-old Wandjina's eye revealed it had been repainted 89 times.

Over time the Wandjina images underwent significant changes. Progressive repaints saw full length standing representations truncated to the waist and then further reduced to a bust, and eventually only the face and halo were painted with minimal elaboration. Recent dating of an Early Wandjina Simple Head depicted in beeswax indicated an age of 3,700 BP.

At many art sites the more recent works have faded to oblivion, leaving only the prehistoric work of earlier epochs. Future research will reveal whether it was the climatic conditions or the materials used during the Aboriginal Epoch that compromised the durability of the art from this period.

To a lesser extent the Wandjina influence and mythology extended into the south Kimberley and east as far as Pine Creek in the Northern Territory. It appears the spirit of Ungud, the mythological snake, held sway in the eastern Kimberley from the Forrest River region to the middle Ord and it is probable that both mythological groups were contemporaneous. Like the Wandjina spirit, Ungud was believed to influence the rain and other weather conditions as well as being responsible for the fertility of all species and the dreaming of 'child spirits'.

At the time of early anthropological field work in the north-west, most Kimberley Aborigines had little knowledge of reproduction; they believed the Wandjina controlled the distribution of the spirits of children, which lived in certain pools of water. Men would visit these pools and 'dream' the baby spirit and later the dream would be passed on to the mother. The resultant child would be named after the Wandjina associated with the 'baby dreaming pool' from whence it came.

New spiritual beliefs and practices began to filter into the Kimberley from the southern desert area and there began a general degeneration of the accomplished rock art that had been practised throughout the Kimberley over thousands of years. By the mid-1900s most of the traditional initiation had been displaced by the influence of the desert cults. The 20th Century also saw the end of a Stone Age culture. The consequences of European settlement banished many of the Aborigines from their traditional Kimberley homelands, bringing many of their long-established ways to an end. Cultural beliefs were diluted and in most part displaced at the missions through the introduction of Christianity. Tragically, this was the end for the rock artists of the Kimberley.

While the East Kimberley is not as richly endowed with rock paintings as the West, El Questro's numerous cultural sites contain evidence of stone tool manufacturing and representative art from all the major stylistic periods with the possible exception of the Clawed Hand Period.

In recent years there has been significant commercial interest in Indigenous art and today many Aboriginal communities have developed their own art centres where local artists paint and their work is sold direct to visitors, collectors or art dealers.

In October 2006 Walsh was diagnosed with a brain tumour. Following the diagnosis, efforts were doubled to complete an ambitious publication on the Clawed Hand and Wandjina periods which he saw as the remnants of a living culture. Sadly this was not to be and he died in 2007. Today the Kimberley Foundation Australia Ltd provides funding for ongoing research into complex questions about environmental changes and early habitation in the region.

Early Exploration

During the first half of the 15th Century the island of Timor had been visited by Chinese naval expeditions, and by 1516 a Portuguese colony had been established on that island – a mere 500 kilometres from north-western Australia. It is therefore strange there should have been no recorded sighting of the Kimberley coast prior to 1644 when the Dutch navigator Abel Tasman passed by on his expedition between Cape York and Carnarvon on Australia's west coast. Further exploration of the general Kimberley coast followed.

However, our interest lies in the East Kimberley where the first known inspection of the coastline in the vicinity of El Questro was carried out by Captain Matthew Flinders in *HMS Investigator* during his 1801–1803 circumnavigation of the Australian continent. Flinders is recognised as one of the most successful navigators and hydrographers of his time. A footnote in his book *A Voyage to Terra Australis* states he found the name 'Australia' more agreeable than 'New Holland' as given to the continent by early Dutch explorers and he was indirectly responsible for the change of name.

In 1819, Lieutenant Phillip Parker King in command of *HMS Mermaid,* continued the coastal survey work done by Flinders. Included in his brief was the search for a river likely to lead to an interior navigation of the great continent. King entered the Cambridge Gulf and named it after the Duke of Cambridge. However, with time and fresh water running short, he ignored an estuary to the east which was later found to be the mouth of the Ord River. Instead, he named View Hill on the northern point of a small isthmus separating the East and West Arms of the gulf and explored directly southward. He investigated the King River to the east of an impressive tabletop range which he named Cockburn after Sir George Cockburn, the Lord Commander of the Royal Navy. It was Cockburn who transported Napoleon Bonaparte to exile on the small island of St Helena after his defeat by the British at the Battle of Waterloo. A rock painting of a ketch-rigged vessel has been reported at a site at the southern end of the Chamberlain Gorge. If such a painting exists it could attest to an incursion into the Cambridge Gulf by these early coastal explorers.

The presumption that land across the continent of Australia was available for annexation prevailed from the earliest days of colonisation; it was merely an extension of the centuries-old European program of colonial expansion.

The settlers had no idea of the Aborigines' spiritual connection with the land and its significance to them, and British perceptions of primitive civilisations made it inconceivable that a society could survive without an identifiable political structure or representatives capable of negotiating an agreement.

The first attempt to explore the then unnamed Kimberley was a British expedition led by 25-year-old Lieutenant George Grey. The instruction given to him by the Colonial Secretary, Lord Glenelg, was to explore the country south of the Prince Regent River and hopefully gain evidence of a river supporting the theory of a Great Inland Sea in the centre of the continent. The Prince Regent River had been named by Phillip Parker King who took a whale-boat upstream beyond Kings Cascades. The coastline where Grey and his party disembarked from the *Lynher* in December 1837 had earlier been independently charted by both Lieutenants Matthew Flinders and Phillip Parker King.

On 9 December, not long after establishing a base camp near the entrance to Hanover Bay, a British flag was hoisted and Grey formally took possession of the territory. During the following four months the heavily equipped expedition covered little ground. The tough country and the seasonal heat and rains took their toll on the goats, sheep and Timor ponies; all were succumbing daily. Aborigines posed a continuous threat and during one conflict an Aborigine was shot and Grey was injured by a spear. With the painfully slow progress, the expedition was close to failure when they unexpectedly came across a major river which Grey named 'Glenelg'.

Shortly afterwards, in the remote reaches of the Glenelg River, the party came across two galleries, featuring paintings from the most recent Kimberley rock art period. This was the first documented European discovery of the distinctive Wandjina paintings of the Kimberley. The discovery was even more remarkable because at that time, no other prehistoric cave paintings had been recorded. These anthropomorphic images became internationally known by way of the sketches and descriptions Grey included in his published journals. It was not until forty years later in 1879 that the discovery of the Paleolithic Cave Art of Northern Spain came to public attention, with similar discoveries in caves at Lascaux in France and elsewhere following some years later.

During the time Grey was exploring the area around the Glenelg and Prince Regent Rivers, Lieutenant Lort Stokes onboard *HMS Beagle* – earlier of Charles Darwin fame – had been engaged in coastal exploration in nearby Collier Bay and Camden Harbour to the south and west. During this time he discovered and named the Fitzroy River, but was unable to navigate this promising river.

It appears that neither Stokes nor Grey was any judge of pastoral country, for both men were greatly influenced by the beauty of the area and its harbours, and their enthusiastic reports ultimately contributed to a failed attempt to establish the North West's first settlement in 1864.

By the 1870s pressure for new land had become critical in the eastern states, prompting the Western Australian Government to send Alexander Forrest and seven men on a survey mission to the North West in 1879. Aware that several large rivers flowed into the Cambridge Gulf, the intention of the expedition was to learn where they originated and to explore the country through which they flowed, assessing the potential for settlement and pastoral development.

Forrest and his party travelled by ship to De Grey station on the northern fringe of the Pilbara district where they commenced their expedition. Using horses, they followed the coast to the north until they reached Beagle Bay on the Dampier Peninsula. From there they travelled inland in a north-easterly direction until they came upon the Fitzroy River which they followed upstream through fertile country for 240 miles to its junction with the Margaret River. Here they crossed the Fitzroy River and headed north. Forrest named the Oscar, Napier and King Leopold Ranges; the latter proved to be an impenetrable barrier that prevented them from following instructions. Instead the expedition turned east and found its way back to the Fitzroy. With sickness in their party, dwindling supplies and horse losses they struck out heading for the Overland Telegraph Line in the Northern Territory. In doing so, they discovered the headwaters of the Fitzroy and Ord Rivers. The latter they named after the governor of Western Australia. Despite some daunting experiences, Alexander Forrest's expedition uncovered millions of acres of good grazing land along the flood plains of these rivers.

Forrest returned to Perth from the Territory with glowing reports of reliable rainfall and an estimated twenty million acres (8,093,712 hectares) of good, well watered country, suitable for grazing and agricultural purposes. He described the northern country as a 'cattleman's paradise'. In addition to deeming the country appropriate for both cattle and sheep, he suggested it was capable of supporting tropical agriculture and pastoral development.

Alexander Forrest named the 420,000–square–kilometre region 'Kimberley' in recognition of John Wodehouse (1826–1902), the first Earl of Kimberley, a prominent English statesman who amongst other offices had been Secretary of State for the Colonies. Elsewhere in the British Empire, Lord Kimberley's name was given to an area in South Africa where diamond mining had begun in 1873. More than a century was to pass before the coincidental discovery of diamonds in the Australian area of the same name and the creation of the world's largest diamond mine.

News of Forrest's discovery created widespread interest among opportunistic graziers and city investors alike. In 1879, Patsy and Michael Durack left the family holdings in Queensland and travelled by sea to Perth to interview Forrest and obtain more information about possible opportunities in the North West. Forrest declared the Kimberley to be 'without doubt the coming pastoral land of the continent' and added 'this river, which I have named the Ord in honour of our Governor...is probably the same observed by Phillip King to enter the Cambridge Gulf a little to the western side of its head'. Forrest advised the Duracks of the course he felt the river would take to reach the Gulf. He surmised that the Ord flowed into the West Arm of the gulf in a north-westerly direction from its known junction with the Negri River. This conjectured course passed diagonally through today's El Questro country to the junction of the then unnamed Salmond and Pentecost Rivers.

Later, in response to the increasing speculative interest in the region, Alexander's brother, John Forrest – also an explorer and now the Surveyor-General and Commissioner of Crown Lands, with a seat in the Executive and Legislative Councils, organised the first large-scale survey of the Kimberley district in 1883.

The Durack Expedition

The Durack family arrived in New South Wales from Ireland in 1853, and by 1867 had expanded their cattle enterprise into unsurveyed land in south-west Queensland. In 1879 Patsy Durack, in partnership with Solomon Emanuel, was amongst a group of graziers interested in the prospect of the newly discovered pastures in the Kimberley. Following their meeting with Alexander Forrest and anxious not to miss out in the rush for land, the Durack brothers joined other 'map graziers' and secured tentative selections of the fabled country before returning to Queensland. In total the combined Durack–Emanuel allotments covered approximately two and a half million acres (1,011,716 hectares). Tom Kilfoyle and several other interested associates also secured unseen land on the map. All of the adjoining 50,000-acre (20,234-hectare) allotments through El Questro country were allocated to a speculator named D.J. O'Neill.

Seaborne parties from the eastern states brought prospective settlers such as Panton, Osmond, the MacDonalds and the Duracks to explore the area, with the latter deciding to mount an expedition to establish the true course of the Ord River from the Cambridge Gulf to its previously established junction with the Negri River.

The party of six men under the leadership of Stumpy Michael Durack comprised John Pentecost as surveyor, geologist and bushman Tom Kilfoyle, Sydney Emanuel, James Josey and Tom Horan. With 27 horses, almost 800 kilograms of provisions and equipment, they travelled from Sydney to Port Darwin in the steamship *Vortigen*. Here the Larrakia Aborigines or 'saltwater people', Pintpot and Pannikin, joined the group and travelled with them from Darwin on the 110–tonne schooner *Levuka*. Leaving the Timor Sea, the party arrived in the Cambridge Gulf in August 1882 and, in accordance with Alexander Forrest's belief, proceeded down its western side, unaware the mouth of the Ord River lay concealed in the East Arm of the gulf. The horses and provisions were unloaded to the north of The Gut, in an area now known as Nulla Nulla, almost due west of where Wyndham was established two years later.

It was from this point they set out on their search for the Ord River. The party named the first river they crossed the Durack. Marvelling at the unbelievable colours of the spectacular Cockburn Range, they continued south-east through hard country now known as Home Valley. Stumpy Michael wrote of the landscape:

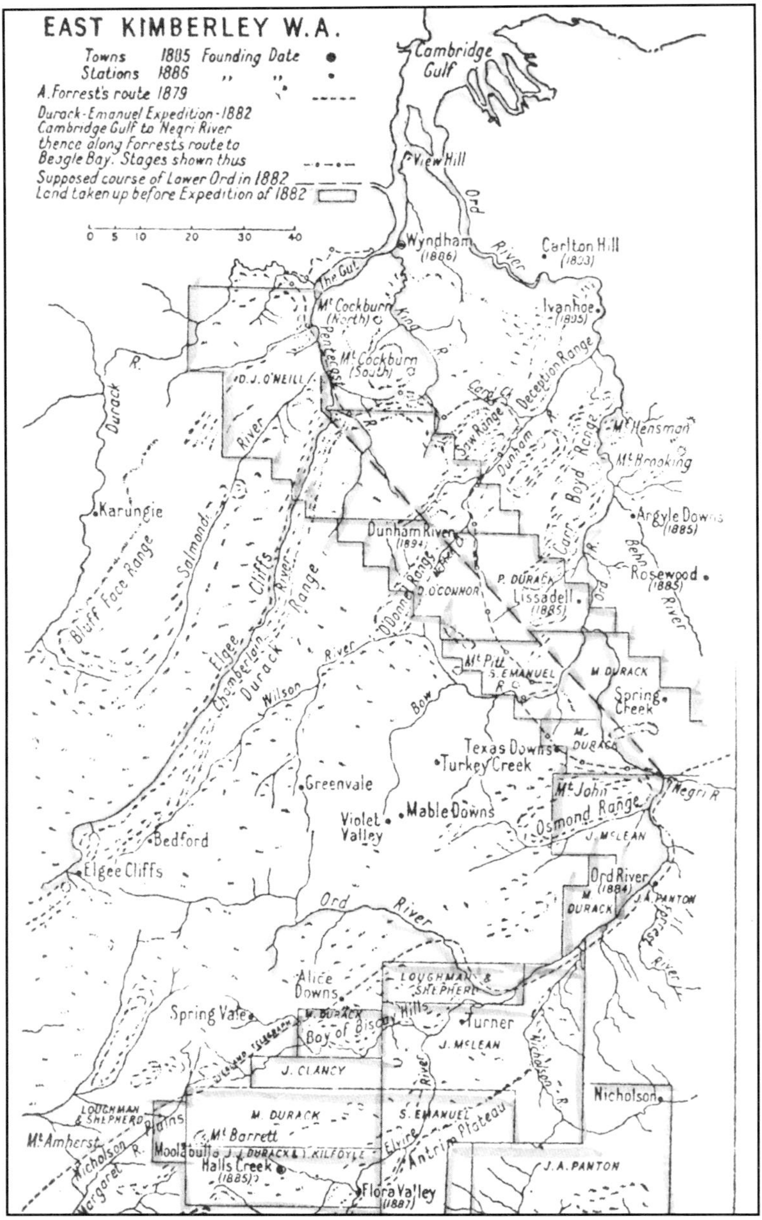

This illustration from *Kings in Grass Castles* by Mary Durack shows the provisional allotments taken up along the presumed course of the Ord River and the route of the exploratory expedition led by Michael Durack through El Questro country in 1882. Courtesy of the Durack Collection.

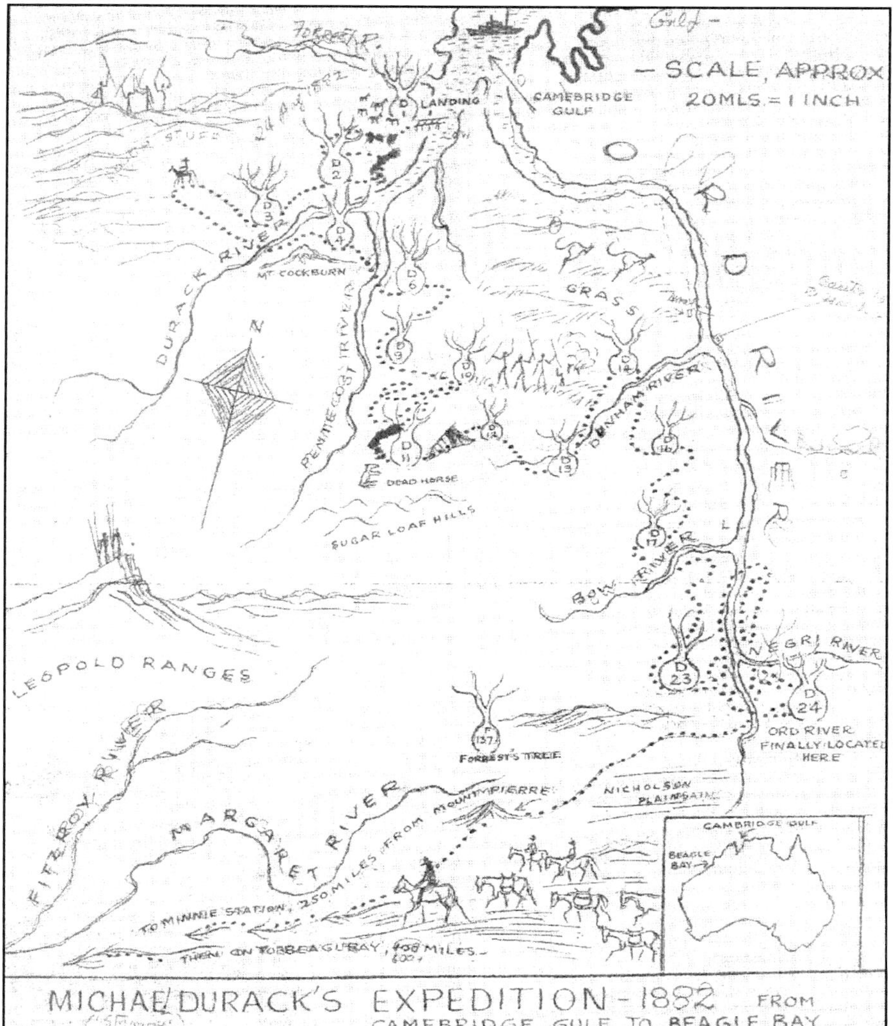

Durack exploration solving the riddle of the Ord River. Drawn by Elizabeth Durack. Courtesy of the Durack Collection. J.S. Battye Library of West Australian History.

> If one were to paint this country in its true colours, I doubt it would be believed. It would be said at least that the artist exaggerated greatly, for never have I seen such richness and variety of hue as in these ranges and in the vivid flowers of this northern spring.

Pushing on into the country that is now El Questro, the party travelled some 25 miles along a river which once they discovered it was not the elusive Ord, they named Pentecost after the surveyor in their party. Possibly, the Salmond River was sighted, but it was not examined or named at that time.

Close examination of a large boab tree located on the bank of the later-named Chamberlain River close to its junction with the Pentecost River, reveals a 'D' carved into its ancient trunk. The letter denotes the route taken by the Durack expedition. This was the sixth of their twenty-four camp sites along their trek to the Ord River. Unfortunately the customary camp number engraved beneath the 'D' is barely distinguishable.

The Durack Tree where the expedition camped in 1882.

From this point, the Durack party travelled along the southern side of the Cockburn Range to the King River and beyond. With horse losses mounting, and despairing at the inaccuracy of the conjectured course of the Ord

River, the men pushed on. They named the Bow and Dunham Rivers before encountering the broad reaches of the Ord River only six miles short of its junction with the Negri River. Then with the Fitzroy River and Beagle Bay on the west coast their destination, the party struggled on. Once their mission was completed, they made the sea voyage from Derby to Fremantle where they arrived on New Year's Day in 1883, some six months after leaving Queensland.

In Perth they modified their land holdings, releasing the tentative allotments in the inferior country along the conjectured course of the Ord River – land which 80 years later would be named El Questro – in favour of approximately three million acres of more promising Ord and Fitzroy River country. The Duracks were to take approximately one and a half million acres along both sides of the Ord River near the Northern Territory border and the Emanuel leases extended over a similar acreage of flood plains and desert margins in the Fitzroy region of the west Kimberley.

This was the beginning of a huge land grab in the North West and soon more than 51 million acres (21 million hectares) of pastoral leasehold country had been taken up.

The emblazoned 'D' on the Durack Tree overlooking the Chamberlain River.

Joseph Bradshaw

The selected extracts from the Journal of Joseph Bradshaw (31 January–6 June 1891) included in the following pages relate to El Questro country and Bradshaw's recording of the rock paintings in the area of the Prince Regent River that later would carry his name. The extracts are taken from records on microfiche held in the Battye Library in Perth.

In response to Alexander Forrest's disclosure of great pastoral opportunities in north-west Australia, Joseph Bradshaw formed a small syndicate and took up twenty blocks of 50,000-acre allotments along both sides of the Prince Regent River. Bradshaw left Melbourne in January 1891 determined to make a personal inspection of the country in order to satisfy himself of its suitability for pastoral settlement. In the company of his brother Frederick, his cousin Aeneas Gunn, Mr Allen and two Larrakia Aborigines, Bradshaw sailed from Darwin on *S.S. South Australia* arriving in Wyndham on 9 March 1891, where only two days prior almost half the fledgling town had been destroyed by a severe cyclone.

During his brief stay there, Bradshaw bought rations sufficient for eight weeks, and 11 additional horses at an average price of £11. Being unfamiliar with the nature of the country Bradshaw anticipated reaching the Prince Regent River in a week, but it took 17 days and food was very short towards the end of the expedition.

The following excerpts are taken from his diary as he and his party of six made their way through the northern sector of El Questro country and beyond to what he believed to be the vicinity of the Prince Regent River. From his description of the country near his destination, it is apparent that Bradshaw was on the lower tidal reaches of the Moran River and not the Prince Regent River. A later expedition by Brockman in 1901, found a tree emblazoned by Bradshaw which proved this to be so.

> Saturday 14th March. Left Six Mile and camped at Palm Springs or Chinaman's Garden for first night. Travelled in single file along a stony ledge between the King River and the steep gravelly hills. Sighted a tree marked by the explorer Gregory in 1857. Crossed the King River at a gravelly place and camped under a shady Boab and a Cabbage Box.
>
> Skirted the base of Mount Cockburn for 18 miles and camped on a creek. Met up with the Pentecost River – wide and deep. Found a low rocky place to cross a few miles further. Plentiful supply of fish.

> From our camp at sunset the rugged sides and perpendicular escarpments of Mount Cockburn presented a most unique picture; it must have been an island when the surrounding country was the bottom of a mighty tide river ocean millions ago.

The expedition continued westward on its way to their 'pastoral territory' in the vicinity of Prince Regent River. Averaging approximately 20 miles in a day, they encountered 'wild black fellows' as they travelled but there was no conflict between them. It seems they were on the Roe River near its junction with the Moran River when in April 1891 Bradshaw's party found Aboriginal stone arrangements – a circle of ceremonial stones placed around a large stone monument or 'charlalar' as it was known in the local language and only days later they discovered numerous Aboriginal paintings in a secluded gorge.

> 16th April. Further on there was a great pile of immense rocks on the west side of the river. In the secluded chasms of these rocks were numerous Aboriginal paintings which appeared to be of great antiquity and I do not attribute them to the present representations of the black race.
>
> 17th April. Decided to return to Wyndham, but prior to doing so made some sketches of the native drawings – over one of which 'the white ants had made a main road'. The tribal name of the local natives in that area is 'Woolyami'.
>
> 4th May. Recrossed the Pentecost River at camp 4 and travelled 2 miles upstream to camp under a luxuriant sycamore.
>
> 5th May. We took a N.E route early today and came through the Cockburn Pass. The mountains presented a grand appearance in the morning sunlight with its perpendicular escarpment towering high aloft! We seemed to be travelling under its very shadow and then up a rocky gorge, where for a few minutes we had to lead our horses along a narrow gravelly ledge with rocks below and rocks above, and then a few paces over a stony saddle and we found ourselves on the watershed of the King River. This was about 1pm, but it was 4pm before we reached the river and camped. Made a damper from the last of the flour and divided it amongst the men. The last of the sugar sweetened the tea tonight, by noon tomorrow we hope to secure a days rations from the Chinaman at the Palm Camp. We travelled 8 hours today and did about 20 miles over very rough stony country.
>
> Wed 6th May ...after passing camp No 2 where we recrossed the King R. and after a journey of 12 miles we reached the Palm Springs, the first outpost of civilization. Ah Sure the Chinaman living there supplied us with a days stock of necessities on which we pitched camp at our old camp No 1.

Bradshaw, on his return, released the allotments previously held in his name and instead secured a one-million-acre lease over country to the north of the Prince Regent River, bounded by the Indian Ocean to the west and the Roe River to the east.

Before leaving Melbourne to take up this land, Bradshaw presented a paper to the Victorian Branch of the Royal Geographical Society describing his travels and the art he had discovered. Later, in 1938, the German Frobenius Institute conducting anthropological research in the Kimberley was to call the art after Bradshaw.

In 1891 in partnership with others, Joseph Bradshaw established a settlement and named it Marigui. They shipped horses and 4,000 sheep from Wyndham but the country they settled was quite unsuitable and the venture was a disaster. It was subsequently abandoned. In 1894 the dismantled buildings and plant were shipped around to the newly acquired Bradshaw's Run on the Victoria River on the Northern Territory side of the West Australian border. The remaining sheep were shipped back to Wyndham and overlanded to the station.

Frederick Drake-Brockman

Frederick Slade Drake-Brockman was another explorer to traverse El Questro country as leader of an expedition in 1901. Although the family name was Drake-Brockman, Frederick styled himself Brockman.

Prior to the expedition Brockman was employed in the Department of Public Works. As surveyor-in-charge of roads and telegraph he worked in the Ord River area where he was commissioned to select a practical route for a road from Wyndham to Halls Creek, and a telegraph line through the same country. In 1891 Brockman transferred to the Lands and Surveys Department and became Chief Inspecting Surveyor in 1894.

In an effort to fill a vast gap in the geographic knowledge of north-west Australia, and to provide opportunities for new mineral discoveries and the opening of more pastoral land, the government funded Brockman's 1901 expedition. The expeditionary party of 13 included the botanist Dr F.M. House and the government geologist Andrew Gibb Maitland, with Charles Crossland as second-in-charge and Dickey, an Aborigine. It was an exceptionally well equipped expedition. Brockman understood the importance of good equipment and adequate provisioning, and had 55 pack animals to carry the five and a half tons of provisions, 13 saddle horses and three extra. Nine of the pack horses carried thousands of horseshoes with small steel plates on the toe to counter the rough stony conditions.

The party camped for several nights at the junction of the Pentecost and Chamberlain Rivers before travelling south along the Chamberlain for 11 days. We have F.S. Brockman to thank for naming this river, although there is some uncertainty after whom it is named. Joseph Chamberlain in London being the Secretary of State for the Colonies at the time of the expedition makes him the most likely contender.

Leaving the Chamberlain valley travelling west, the expedition travelled through the Leopold Ranges to Walcott Inlet and returned along the Drysdale River. They covered an estimated 1,425 miles (2,300 kilometres) in six months and 18 days, and successfully mapped vast tracts of previously unexplored land. Many watercourses and geological features were named and numerous unique natural history specimens collected, documented and photographed. It is not surprising that we find House among the scientific names of some of the Kimberley flora and fauna.

The expedition found many remarkable panels of Aboriginal art on the mainly sandstone rock surfaces. However they encountered very few Aborigines and, regardless of their distance from European settlement, those they saw carried axes and chisels fashioned from white man's iron.

The following extracts are from the official and unofficial diaries of Frederick Slade Brockman's Kimberley Expedition of 1901. The passages have been selected for their connection to El Questro country and surrounds. As was the custom for explorers to mark their trails, Brockman emblazoned his initials and the camp number on trees along the route thus: FB2 (for his second campsite).

> 3 May 1901. Arrived at Wyndham from Fremantle to start provisioning. Bought extra horses, now a total of 71.
>
> 10 May. Followed the Halls Creek telegraph line to Spring Creek.
>
> 11 May. South West approximately 10 miles to a small pool in a creek near the King River. . .

From the King River onwards they were exploring unmapped country. Brockman rode out to a trig station placed on Mount Cockburn about 12 years prior by a Government Surveyor. He writes (unofficial diary, 13 May 1901):

> ...the most noticeable mountain range on the shores of the Cambridge Gulf ... a precipitous sandstone range about 900 ft in height, 700 ft of the top being a sheer wall of red stone with only one break away, by which we climbed to the top.... This is the finest mountain I have seen in the district.
>
> 14 May. Travelled approximately 13 miles W.S-W to a small creek running northerly. Camped about 4 miles SW from extreme west end of Cockburn Range ...
>
> 15 May. Travelled 4 miles SW over very rough ground to the Pentecost River. Difficulty getting down steep face of the hills on the east side of the river which in places rises perpendicular for about 300 feet. The river valley from the cliff top appears very narrow and flanked on both sides by rugged ranges.
>
> 16 May. Camped at Pentecost River, shoeing horses.

Gilly, another Aboriginal member of the party, absconded during the night with a new, loaded Colt revolver (unofficial diary):

... a prisoner under sentence for murder and who while in prison was guilty of a savage and murderous assault – armed is a menace to both the wild Aborigines and any white man he may meet.

17 May. Explored 1 mile down river. 50 per cent through very rough gorge.

18 May. Continued down river approximately 11 miles and from a rise picked out the course of the river towards the inlet at its mouth. All country travelled, very rough and poor.

Sunday 19 May. Returned via Cattle Creek to camp at FB2.

(Unofficial diary)

The western wall is about 500 feet perpendicular, it is perfectly regular without a flaw or breakaway for about ten miles.

20 May. At FB2. These sandstone ranges with their gentle slopes from one side and bluff faces on the opposite side are most difficult to negotiate.

Over time, the bed of the Chamberlain River is modified by agents of erosion and climatic events. At the time of Brockman's expedition it was very different to the way we find it today.

22 May. Travelled along the gorge of the Chamberlain River about 6 ½ miles – crossed the river 4 times. Twice came to a cul-de-sac and had to turn back. The river a nice running stream but the bottom is covered for a width of about a quarter of a mile with huge water worn boulders alternating with slippery bars, it is in fact a series of rapids. The barometer showing that we are rising about 100ft in each 3 miles ...[at a crossing] after starting to cross, one of the pack horses slipped on a bar and turned a complete somersault into the pool below, he was not in the least hurt and scrambled out safely, but his disaster appeared to make the others nervous.

Dickey shortly afterwards emulated the feat of the pack horse and slipped into the same pool.

Several days later Brockman makes an interesting observation after encountering Aborigines:

These are the first we have met. I should be glad to find them more numerous as that would be evidence of better country. As a rule you may gauge the capabilities of country for pastoral purposes by the number of natives it supports.

25 May. Camped under the shade of a very fine Boab tree measuring 48'6" at the base.

With the only alternative being to return the way they had come, the expedition was obliged to continue south along the Chamberlain River valley 'flanked by the same unbroken ranges' – the 125-kilometre-long, as yet unnamed Elgee Cliffs had them pinned in. Visitors to El Questro taking a heli-scenic flight or driving to Explosion Gorge on the Chamberlain River may catch a glimpse of the northern end of this geographical phenomenon.

> 27 May. Looking for a break in the cliff line with prospects of being able to get away westerly soon. It is most aggravating to be forced so far south.

Shortly afterwards the expedition finds a small tributary offering a chance to exit the deep Chamberlain valley and, after the men cleared a track for the horses, the expedition was at last able to head west into the vast inhospitable tableland beyond.

Brockman later made the following observation in his diary:

> 17 Jun. Approximately 6½ miles from Camp 24. Cave paintings on the face of a sandstone rock protected by an overhanging ledge. The principal figures consisted of a group of 12 figures, 9 being head and busts nearly life size. Each bust having a tunic and sailors knot or pendant falling from the throat. The two central figures being full length clothed in tunic, pendant, waist belt and close fitting pants and showing the hands and feet. The last figure on the left hand end of the group being a head only, much larger than the rest and placed horizontally. The figures are exactly similar in character to those described by G. Grey on the Glenelg River.

The expedition continued for another six months with ongoing horse losses from accidents and from the then unknown 'Kimberley horse poison'. Many of the remaining horses were very weak and some were unable to stand with their packs on when at last they encountered their outbound route at the Pentecost River and returned to Wyndham through El Questro's northern country:

> 20 Nov. Returned to the Pentecost River from the west under North Mount Cockburn. Picked up traverse of 18 May (FB4), completing the circuit. Continued up river for about 2 miles above FB4.
>
> Travelled to south end of Mount Cockburn and on to the King River.
>
> 25 Nov. Arrived at Wyndham.

In 1915 Brockman was appointed Surveyor-General.

European Settlement of the East Kimberley

West Australia, with its minimal population, endeavoured to attract settlers and investors with inducements. Following George Grey's enthusiastic report on the area some 30 years earlier, attempts at settlement at Camden Harbour on the north-west coast commenced as early as 1864–65. Several land companies were formed in response to the government's terms offering periods of rent free leases in the north. Amongst these was the Camden Harbour Association, whose optimism attracted many investors particularly from Victoria. Within a short time settlers were on their way to the North West without any preliminary inspections taking place. The first ships bearing settlers and their flocks of sheep started to arrive at Camden Harbour in December when the heat was oppressive, the grass dry and lacking nutrition, and available fresh water could not be found within range of the ships. As man and beast began to die, many of the survivors abandoned their investments and departed on returning ships. By the time the ill-fated settlement was officially abandoned late in October, all of the stock had perished.

Encouraged by the reports from Alexander Forrest's exploration, the Western Australian Government in 1880 announced grants of generous acreage to settlers in the Kimberley and called for applications for the lease of pastoral land.

Alexander's brother, John Forrest, was amongst the pastoralists to bring sheep to the fertile Fitzroy River plains where he enjoyed greater success than the previous attempt by the Camden Harbour Association further north.

The first pastoral leases of the Kimberley were granted by the Governor under the 1882 Land Regulations of Western Australia, and by 1882–83 some 44,201,080 acres of land had been granted to 77 people throughout the Kimberley region.

The eastern side of the Kimberley was almost exclusively settled by cattlemen from Victoria, New South Wales and Queensland, who walked their cattle across the continent to take up their vast leases in the North West. The first mob of cattle arrived in June 1884, driven by the legendary bushman Nathaniel Buchanan. Nat and his younger brother William were amongst the most remarkable pioneers of the Australian pastoral industry. Their exceptional skills as horsemen, their innate powers of observation and their bush skills were well utilised in carving new routes and opening up the unexplored Top End – from Queensland across to the Pilbara – on the west coast of the continent.

Buchanan, with another brother Gordon, Bob Button and others, set out from Richmond in Queensland with cattle belonging to William Osmond and Joseph Panton from Victoria. Their destination was Ord River Station adjacent to the then unknown Bungle Bungle Massif.

The Duracks were one of several pioneering families to undertake the arduous task of walking their cattle across the continent from east to west to settle in the Kimberley. We are fortunate the experiences of many of the significant families in this remote region have been recorded and published as the challenges and adversity they faced make absorbing reading.

I have recounted here some of the remarkable Durack family story, so ably researched and documented by Mary Durack in her acclaimed books *Kings in Grass Castles* and *Sons in the Saddle*. Similarly, extraordinary achievements by other pioneering families such as the Emanuels and the MacDonalds were responsible for opening up country on the Fitzroy River plains.

The latter, brothers Charles and Will MacDonald, having found ample pasture and good water during their preliminary exploratory inspection, returned to New South Wales where they put together a plant of two 4-wheel bullock wagons and 100 horses, and set out in mid-1882 with 1,000 head of cattle. The drove ran into appalling adversity in Queensland which was in the grip of a drought. Several of the men abandoned the expedition and many cattle were lost. The brothers struggled on, facing attacks from inhospitable Aborigines and crocodiles in tidal creeks. They reached Arnhem Land where Charles became ill with malaria and was taken to Palmerston roped to a horse. Will continued on alone, miraculously coming across fresh tracks which he followed until he met up with Michael Durack and his party and they continued together until they reached the Ord River. Recognising that he was too weak to reach his destination, he diverted to the Cambridge Gulf where he found assistance to complete the last leg to the Fitzroy Crossing. Three and a half years after his departure, with only 327 cattle and 13 horses remaining, he attained his goal and arrived at the junction of the Fitzroy and Margaret Rivers. The 3,480 miles travelled from Goulburn to establish Fossil Downs on the Fitzroy River must surely be one of the longest overland droving expeditions.

In June and July of 1883 the Durack family and their associates, including Tom Kilfoyle and Tom Hayes, left Queensland in four groups with a total of 7,250 cattle and 200 horses. All, including their wagons drawn by 60 bullocks, were bound for Western Australia. Held up by floods and bad seasons, it took almost two and a half years for the herds to walk 3,000 kilometres to their destination across some of the toughest country on the continent. The outbreak of disease also took its toll on the stock and over half the horses and cattle were lost on the trek. The total cost of the exercise was £72,000 – a huge amount in those days.

In September 1885 the Duracks and their depleted mobs arrived in the East Kimberley where they took up their 2,000,000 acre holdings on both sides of the Ord River, naming their properties Argyle Downs and Ivanhoe Station. Within a couple of years a house with red mud walls and thatched with grass, pandanus and spinifex had been built at Argyle. It had a verandah paved with river flagstones and inside the floor was a preparation of rammed termite mud. The final Argyle homestead was built in 1894 using local sandstone and mud mortar. Almost a century later, before the dammed waters of Lake Argyle flooded the station buildings, the state and federal governments funded the careful demolition, removal and reconstruction of the old homestead at its present site. The rebuilt homestead was opened to the public in 1971 and now serves as a museum and memorial to the Duracks and other pioneers of the Kimberley.

From 1883 to 1890, the Kimberley and the adjacent Pilbara and Gascoyne regions, or North West Australia as the area was then known, came under the governorship of Frederick Napier Broome who had been appointed by the British Government and after whom the coastal settlement was named.

Rumours of gold in the Kimberley had persisted since Alexander Forrest noted auriferous or gold bearing country during his expedition in 1879. Since then, prospectors following Forrest's route had found traces of gold in the Kimberley and Territory. By the conclusion of the wet season in 1885 the number of prospectors coming to the area was increasing rapidly and the East Kimberley was abuzz with anticipation.

Earlier, Patrick (Black Pat) Durack and Tom Hayes had left their overlanding cattle in the Territory and made their way to Darwin. Here they purchased stores and equipment and shipped them to Cambridge Gulf to supplement the arrival of the settlers and their cattle. The ongoing rumours of gold and the promising report from the government geologist Edward Hardman prompted them to include mining equipment as well as the general supplies required to meet the needs of other early settlers.

The stores were shipped to the Gulf and unloaded along the mangrove-skirted shores below View Hill where Durack established the first provisions depot in the East Kimberley. Amazingly this was accomplished within days of the first of the Queensland drovers reaching their destination on the Ord River. Almost immediately, a second store was established nearby by August Lucanus.

In August 1885 prospectors Charles Hall and Jack Slattery arrived in Derby with 10 ounces of gold. Found on the Elvire River, the discovery of this payable quantity of gold gave birth to the first gold rush in Western Australia in 1886 and to the township of Halls Creek.

John Forrest travelled to the Cambridge Gulf on board the *S.S. Albany* in 1886 to inspect the area and determine a site on the Gulf for the proposed new township. He was unimpressed with the location of the two stores at the base of View Hill and ordered Captain Anthon to proceed south along the shoreline for some fifteen miles to Bastion Hill where the vessel could be anchored within 15 yards of land. Here the party went ashore and from the hill gained a view over the surrounding open country. They also found fresh water in a small gorge nearby.

The new site for the settlement in the Gulf was gazetted by Forrest and officially named Wyndham. It was named after Major Walter George Wyndham, the younger son of the Governor's wife, Mary Anne Broome, by her first marriage.

Anthon's Landing served the settlement in the tidal Cambridge Gulf until the opening of the Port of Wyndham later in 1886. This new port facilitated the arrival of the first shipment of cattle and sheep to the Gulf and provided a timely gateway for hundreds of hopeful diggers who flocked to the area seeking their fortunes.

Most of the early miners setting out from the Bastion Hills followed the regular route to the goldfields via the clear open country and the Dunham River. Others travelled south-west from Wyndham, leaving the name The Diggers Rest at the King River crossing as their legacy.

Despite its location some six kilometres from the mouth of the King River, access to fresh water became critical for Wyndham township. With an eight-metre tidal variance, the river water was either salt or brackish for many kilometres upstream, and very soon the dwindling supply of fresh water from the gorge above the settlement proved insufficient. Fortunately the situation was resolved when springs were discovered at the eastern extremity of the Bastion Range some three miles from the Port. Here the government sank a well that became known as Three Mile Soak. This and several additional wells located in the area served the residents who were required to cart the water and store it in tanks on their properties. The sale of water for 4 pence and 6 pence a bucket indicates just how precious a commodity water was in those early days.

In November 1886 the government conducted an auction of 200 town lots and was successful in selling 63.

In its heyday Wyndham had five hotels and 12 trading stores. Amongst the mercantile traders were Denis Doherty and Francis Connor who, like the Duracks, were quick to seize the opportunity of supplying the goldfields. In 1897 Connor and Doherty were to join forces with three Durack brothers and create the company Connor, Doherty and Durack.

On the pastoral scene, as the first settlers were arriving in the Kimberley, government surveyors were still at work charting the country. In addition to the river flats and ranges, the surveyors were directed to gazetting smaller areas where there was permanent water with potential grazing land nearby. In Britain the Secretary of State for the Colonies, endeavouring to discourage speculation in the Kimberley region, set the rental at ten shillings for every thousand acres leased, with a proviso that within two years of being taken up the country must be stocked with two head of cattle or 20 sheep for every thousand acres or the lease would be forfeited.

Fencing the enormous holdings throughout most of the Kimberley was not an option and the open-range system of grazing that evolved generally remains in practice today. Without fences and designated watering points to control the spread of livestock, the more appealing pastures on the alluvial flats and river frontages have been subject to overgrazing. Today the resulting degradation and erosion continues to be of concern to the land administrators charged with the responsibility of maintaining long term pastoral productivity.

Following vigorous campaigning by the colonists a new constitution was drafted in 1887 providing the right of self-governance for Western Australia. After years of discussion and modification, in 1890 an act giving Western Australia its first Responsible Government passed both Houses of Parliament in London. John Forrest became the state's first premier and was to hold this position throughout a decade of rapid development and demographic change.

As an independent colony, Western Australia had its own parliament and the power to make its own laws. Alexander Forrest, having been the first Member for the Kimberley in the former Legislative Council, became the Member for the West Kimberley in the new Legislative Assembly and Francis Connor was elected unopposed to represent the East Kimberley in the new state government. Connor was largely responsible for gaining approval for the construction of a new jetty for Wyndham.

In the East Kimberley extensive tracts of good cattle country opened up along the rich black soil plains and river flats of the Ord River and its tributaries. This area, with intrusions of mountains and hilly country, extended for almost 300 miles along the border with the Northern Territory, and a wide variety of native grasses supported most of the stock in the district. However, along the western margins, the rough and rocky nature of most of the hilly country – together with the dramatic red sandstone ranges and spinifex country as found on most of El Questro – was deemed of little value for grazing. This poorer country was later settled by squatters who struggled on a 'strive and starve' basis. Many of the struggling properties, unable to adequately stock their land, mustered cattle from their wealthy eastern neighbours and these cattle, re-branded and earmarked, found their way to the port or meatworks at Wyndham via a system known as 'the Underground'.

Cattle duffing was outright theft and punishable accordingly, but the common practice of poddy dodging was not so clear cut. A poddy is a motherless and generally unbranded calf, often referred to as a cleanskin. Even today, with no proof of ownership these cleanskins are vulnerable to poaching.

Isolation and lack of communications between the East and West meant the two Kimberley regions developed separately and were governed independently from Perth. The regions were known collectively as The

Kimberleys until 1903 when the two electorates amalgamated, thereafter it was known simply as the Kimberley or more locally as the East and West Kimberleys.

Wyndham flourished under the influx of the diggers in the gold rush, and during the brief boom time as many as 16 ships were at anchor in the Gulf. The miners provided business opportunities for the pioneering families and a ready and convenient market for their cattle. In no time at all, six pubs and a couple of general stores were trading in the town and shantys and shacks were beginning to spring up around the port.

Urban settlement extended along the eastern perimeter of the Cambridge Gulf from the original site at the port in the shadow of Mount Bastion. Thus we find the Port of Wyndham to the north of the town and then the settlements of Three Mile, Six Mile and Twelve Mile consecutively strung several kilometres apart southward, along the road to Halls Creek.

The conditions encountered by the miners were appalling and there were many deaths from starvation and sickness. The route to the goldfield was rough and inhospitable, horses died and possessions were abandoned along the way. Numerous diggers failed to reach their destination while others died on the field. Malaria, typhoid, thirst, sunstroke, dysentery and scurvy all took their toll. The lives of some were taken by fellow diggers, and others were speared by Aborigines. Equipment and supplies were sold by teamsters at the goldfield charging vastly inflated prices. The traders slaughtered their working bullocks and sold the meat and other by-product for two shillings a pound. Sugar was similarly priced.

It is reported that at its peak there were 3,000 men on the field, but all too soon the gold petered out and by 1888 Halls Creek had become a ghost town. The drought years from 1889 to 1892, combined with the arduous and lonely lifestyle of the untamed country, failed to attract many settlers and the majority of the miners moved elsewhere. The drought forced meat prices down until by 1892 beef was fetching 4 pence a pound and sheep 3 pence. Wyndham's population fell away to a few government officials and a handful of men employed at the port.

In 1900, when Western Australia participated in the referendum for the Constitution Bill for Federation, there were only 61 men and women of voting age remaining in the electorate. The majority of Western Australia's

64,491 eligible voters were in the southern goldfields. The Overland Telegraph reached Wyndham in 1889. This link with the south was intended to reduce the isolation of the East Kimberley. However it was not long before the Indigenous community created communication problems when they discovered the porcelain from the overhead insulators made excellent spearheads. The subsequent pursuit of offenders by police resulted in the death and wounding of a large number of local Aborigines and the death of one officer and wounding of several others. There was little equality in the justice system at Wyndham and in 1893 four Aborigines were convicted for being in possession of telegraph insulators valued at a paltry 2 shillings and 6 pence. They were sentenced to two years' hard labour while the same magistrate sentenced a white man to six months' gaol for stealing goods amounting to six times the value.

From the outset of European settlement in the Kimberley, the establishment of pastoral and mining industries resulted in hostility between the station whites, the police and the Indigenous occupants of the land. Approximately half of the Aboriginal population in the East Kimberley is believed to have died during the first 50 years of white settlement. Disease and the Aborigines' efforts to defend themselves and their tribal land from the invaders resulted in their population declining to an estimated 60,000, and there were fears that they were 'a dying race'. Records of reciprocal massacres and other atrocious forms of reprisals are not so readily available.

Displaced Aborigines were moved to government feeding depots, missions, town reserves or onto cattle stations where tribes and bloodlines were thrown together, resulting in the loss of many languages or dialects and a breakdown in the strict rules of social interaction and kinship.

At the end of the 19th Century all the suitable land around the Ord River Basin had been taken over by white settlers and by 1939 many Aborigines in the East Kimberley were attached to cattle stations. The Aboriginal men and women took readily to the saddle and learned to competently control the stock, sink wells, and construct huts, fences and yards. Aboriginal women were employed to work around the house in a domestic capacity.

Some Aboriginal families voluntarily became incorporated into life on the cattle stations, while for others it was akin to enslavement. White workers were costly and hard to come by on the remote stations and the Aborigines, with their skills and innate knowledge of the country, were pressed into service. Entire families were retained for the sake of a few valuable workers.

The treatment of the Aboriginal workers by their white bosses varied from station to station but it was generally considered to be a good life. The boys grew up wanting to follow in the footsteps of their older relatives and become stockmen; it was the only life they knew. They were eligible to join the workforce from 14 years of age. Initially there was no pay. Employees were given a pair of boots, a hat, a shirt, a pair of trousers, a couple of blankets and a weekly stick of tobacco. Their families were provided with sugar, flour, milk and home-killed meat.

White men on the stations, deprived of the company of European women, frequently engaged in liaisons with Indigenous women but seldom took responsibility for the offspring resulting from these casual encounters.

Citing concerns for the wellbeing of mixed-race children in a world in which they belonged to neither race, and with a less widely publicised policy of racial assimilation, the government began removing these children from their families and installing them in church-based missions and as household labour. Under the management of the Aboriginal Protection Board the practice continued from 1909 to 1969. The children affected by this controversial government policy are known today as the 'Stolen Generation'.

The cattle mustering season usually started in March and continued for eight months. Horses were mustered in preparation and the unbroken ones handled and broken in. Each stockman had allotted to him three or four horses that required shoeing at the station before moving out to the stock camps to start the mustering. The camps were generally located on a bore or watering hole. Once the season started, the men rarely returned to the homestead, moving from one camp to the next as work was completed on each mob of cattle. They worked long hours, starting between three and five in the morning after the horses had been rounded up and brought back to the camp and, depending on the nature of the work, often not finishing until after dark. There were no portable yards in the early days; in the absence of any form of enclosure, the men exchanged their mustering mount for a 'cutting horse' that was quicker and more adept at separating the selected individual. Once the beast had been cut out from the mob, a stockman on a bronco horse or mule would ride amongst the cattle, lasso it and then drag it over to a constructed panel against which it would be pinned and branded and castrated as required.

The discovery of large deposits of gold at Coolgardie in 1892 and shortly afterwards at nearby Kalgoorlie-Boulder served Western Australia well and provided another market for Kimberley beef. The stakeholders in both the East and West were competing for the same market for their cattle. However, the manipulative West Kimberley cattle-growers, backed by the established and influential partnership of Alexander Forrest and Sydney Emanuel & Co. with their monopoly on shipping and marketing, were quick to take advantage of the situation and secured the lion's share of this trade. Around this time the developing cattle industry in the East Kimberley came under threat of infestation by the parasitic cattle-tick found in areas of Queensland and the Northern Territory. Quarantine restrictions were introduced controlling the movement of cattle in the area and creating further setbacks to the struggling pastoralists in the East.

Following Alexander Forrest's death, Emanuel bought the Forrest interests in 1901 and the next year, in partnership with Sidney Kidman and others, acquired Australia's largest pastoral company – Victoria River Downs in the Northern Territory.

Wyndham and the Meatworks

A new wooden jetty capable of handling Wyndham's 8.2-metre tidal range was completed at Anthon's Landing in 1894. It was constructed to allow for cattle to be loaded onto ships for the export market. The cattle approached the port from the far side of the hill behind the Town Hotel and, moving through a long race, skirted around the base of the hill, then went down the short jetty and onto the waiting vessel.

The tick problem was resolved within three years of its outbreak, enabling more than 7,000 cattle to be shipped annually from Wyndham to Fremantle and on to the goldfields and other southern markets.

As an alternative method of bringing cattle south, Alfred Canning was commissioned to survey and construct a stock route through the Great Sandy and Gibson deserts from Halls Creek in the Kimberley to the railhead at Wiluna, some 1,780 kilometres distant. Recognising his excellent skills as a bushman and surveyor, the government had previously commissioned Canning to assist with countering the rabbit invasion of Western Australia by surveying the course for the No. 1 Rabbit Proof Fence. The fence was completed in 1907. Extending over 1,845 kilometres, it became the longest unbroken fence in the world.

Alfred Canning & Co. worked on the stock route project between 1906 and 1910. The Great Artesian Basin was tapped for water to supply the 51 wells constructed along the route, one day's travel apart. The first use of the completed Canning Stock Route in 1911 was a disaster with all of the cattlemen killed by Aborigines. Understandably the route was not a popular venture; only eight mobs of cattle used the route and it fell into disrepair.

By 1929 the condition of the wells had deteriorated and Canning, now in his late sixties, was called upon to reopen the route. The improvements led to its regular use over the following 20 years until coastal shipping and road transport provided a better alternative.

Meanwhile the rapidly increasing cattle production in the Kimberley soon exceeded Western Australia's consumption and, in order to prevent this surplus from reducing prices, thousands of cattle were walked to the eastern states for sale. Despite the losses on the 3,500-kilometre trek, this was still more profitable than selling on the local depressed market.

Concern for the future of the industry in the Kimberley brought together the principal players and former rivals from the east – Durack, Connor and Doherty – and from the west – Alexander Forrest and Sydney Emanuel & Co. Their objective was to lobby government for the establishment of a cold-storage facility at Wyndham, from whence chilled beef could be shipped to foreign markets.

As early as 1907, rumour of a meat freezing works at Wyndham was creating interest amongst pastoralists in the Kimberley and across the border in the Territory. In 1909 The Bovril Australian Estates Company, after a successful flotation on the London Stock Exchange, bought Victoria River Downs from the Emanuel–Kidman partnership. Bovril anticipated the future development of a freezing works to service their needs, but meanwhile the company had a creative back-up plan: to build a floating and travelling abattoir whereby live cattle would be loaded onto a steamer at Wyndham, slaughtered and butchered during the voyage to Fremantle and delivered to their destination as frozen beef. At that time it cost up to £3 a head to ship live stock on this route.

The ensuing discussion and negotiations with both federal and state governments continued over a prolonged period. In the interim, shipping of live cattle extended to the Philippines, with cattle bringing up to £14 a head. The port facilities, capable of loading 500 head of cattle onto a ship in a three-hour period, handled nearly 25,000 head anually. This trade continued in an uncertain manner between 1910 and 1918, scarcely keeping the Connor, Doherty and Durack business afloat until the opening of the Wyndham Meatworks.

M.P. Durack bought a Model T Ford in Manila and, being the first car in the East Kimberley, it created quite a stir when it was unloaded in Wyndham.

By 1912 all money had disappeared from the town's economy and trade was conducted using promissory notes. The pioneering Durack family and their associates Connor and Doherty controlled most of the limited trade at that time.

Life was by no means easy for the early residents of Wyndham. As well as there being no ready access to fresh water for human consumption or for growing fruit and vegetables, there was no electricity and until well into the 20th Century, the primitive Coolgardie safe was the only form of household refrigeration in the relentless heat of Australia's hottest town. There was little protection for meat or perishable items once they were removed from the ship's cool rooms and it is small wonder that Wyndham's white population only numbered around 50 at that time.

After years of discussion the government's final agreement for the construction of an ambitious meatworks complex came in 1913, but the sourcing of materials and building construction were curtailed in 1914 by the outbreak of World War I. Although there was no conscription at the time, all eligible men volunteered for service, the majority joining the Light Horse Brigade in a war that was to cost 6,000 lives – ten per cent of Western Australia's young population. By 1917 few white men were engaged in the Kimberley pastoral industry; instead their place was taken by 803 male Aborigines and 560 females.

Construction of the meatworks commenced in August 1915. All building materials were delivered to Wyndham by ship and the resulting increased shipping traffic and more frequent delivery of fresh fruit, vegetables and other household provisions was a bonus for the town's residents.

Built on the flat land adjacent to the new wharf at the Port of Wyndham, the giant five-storey brick complex was completed in 1919. It became operational on 29 May and the heaviest beast killed on that day weighed 960 pounds. The average weight was between 761 and 764 pounds, or just under 350 kilograms. The main building was surrounded by smaller ones which were used for administration, staff accommodation and recreational facilities including sporting and entertainment venues.

The meatworks initially got off to a slow and difficult start, for not only was the price of beef low and the market uncertain, but it was further disadvantaged by wartime shipping restrictions and labour disputes. However once underway, the average seasonal kill of almost 30,000 cattle was vital to the town, and during the 16-week killing season it employed some 300 largely itinerant workers from the south. With the exception of Queensland's sugar industry, the meat works at Wyndham was the single largest employer in Northern Australia. Sadly, little of the vast complex at the Port of Wyndham remains today.

The season opened in April and, to ensure a continuous work flow at the meatworks, outlying stations were required to commit the number of beasts they would deliver on an agreed date months in advance. Thus mobs of cattle were regulated to arrive at Wyndham on average every three days. A telephone line was hooked up to a hut at Goose Hill, some 30 kilometres out from the meatworks, and a man was stationed there to keep in contact with the travelling mobs and report back to the works. The system was geared to deliver and slaughter the cattle without any delay or double handling. A day's kill might have consisted of several small mobs or part of a large one with the remainder of the mob held on feed while the first draft was being killed.

It was all good grassland between Goose Hill and Schemoolee, as the open country on the Gulf end of the Twelve Mile Plain was known. Here a dam provided water for the incoming cattle, making it possible for a delivery to be delayed or brought forward as required. A fenced paddock between the ranges allowed for holding any stock that happened to be lame or in poor condition.

Cattle approached the meatworks from the north of the Bastion Range – there was little or no grass beyond Schemoolee on this final stage. A small iron water tank of about 5,000 gallons (19,000 litres) was located around the hill a mile or more from the works. Water was pumped into it from the main supply and the cattle were watered there before being taken on to the yards which could hold a thousand head or more. Troughs were found only in the back yards as the stock had to be kept off water for eight hours before slaughter to facilitate the work of the butchers.

Every beast had to pass a health inspection before proceeding through the system. The last holding yard before the forcing pen that fed into the elevated race was a washing pen capable of holding about a dozen head of cattle. Sprinklers set in a stone floor and mounted overhead ensured the cattle were well washed before moving in single file onto a long ramp leading directly up to the 'knocker box' on the slaughter floor. The killing was generally done with a double ball peen spalling hammer. This long handled hammer had a rounded face and weighed a kilo or more. The knocker box had a tilting floor and after the beast was tapped on the head it was tipped out, washed and hoisted up by a hind leg onto a roller hook on the overhead rail. The beast was then stuck and left to bleed for a few minutes. This blood was processed and turned into powder.

Lined up along the rail at right angles to it were six cradles. When the carcass had been bled it was lowered on its back into a cradle, the head and hocks were removed and it was skinned down the sides. The carcass was then hoisted back onto the rail where the skinning was completed and the innards were dropped out into a barrow and wheeled to the by-products chute. The carcasses proceeded to the open slaughter floor where they were sawn in half down the centre by the swinging saws hanging from the roof. The sides were inspected at the entrance to the chillers and stamped on the shoulder and thigh, designating their class. They were then pushed along the rail into the refrigeration chambers where they hung for two or three days at temperatures a few degrees above freezing. After their nominated time in the chamber, the sides were cut into two pieces, the crops separated from the hinds and placed in stockinet bags, then stacked in the freezers awaiting shipment. Likewise the offal, hides, entrails, horns and hooves were placed into their designated stockinet and hessian bags prior to moving into the freezers. Nothing was wasted – even the tail switches were sent away to make brooms.

Boilers and a huge refrigeration wheel took up three storeys in the building and were located in the same area. Water flowed through the ground floor, washing the blood and other residue out into the gulf where crocodiles gathered for easy pickings.

The main building had an electric lift to the top floor or 'bag floor', where women known as 'baggies' cut stockinet and hessian from large bolts of material and sewed it into bags for the various cuts of meat and other products. The bags were stamped with a colour code, folded into bundles of 25 and dropped down the chute for use on the slaughter floor. In addition to the butchering process, the meatworks made their own boxes and had a cannery and fertiliser section.

When a ship docked, the frozen beef was hauled to the wharf along a single line railway track from the west side of the meatworks by two trains. Everything was done by hand and despite the heat the men wore heavy clothing: balaclavas, gloves and large boots wrapped in bags to keep them warm while they humped the frozen lumps on their backs from the freezer to the nets. The nets in turn were loaded onto the railway trucks for haulage to the wharf where they were hoisted aboard by cranes and swung into the ship's hold. It took about three weeks to turn a ship around.

The Wyndham Meatworks. Courtesy State Library of Western Australia, The Battye Library. 2580529PD by courtesy of Aerial Surveys Australia.

In May 1934 the first consignment of chilled beef left Wyndham for Great Britain and, according to its grade, beef was also exported from Wyndham to the Far East and to Australian ports.

The meatworks dominated the skyline and directly or indirectly influenced the economic and social wellbeing of most folk in the East Kimberley.

The separate Meatworks Institute was akin to a club and provided a social venue for the local and itinerant employees. There were sporting facilities with a regular program of activities, weekly open air films in the Theatre Garden and a large unlined hall for badminton and a variety of entertainments. Expectations were simple and easily satisfied; most people sang, others played a musical instrument or recited a poem or could spin a yarn. Dances and concerts were popular entertainment for decades and, in addition to the meatworks facilities, balls and gala events were held in the dining room at the Town Hotel.

After 48 years the Western Australian Government sold the meatworks to private enterprise and instead of relying on an itinerant workforce from down south many local residents were employed. The killing season was extended and the processing was converted to the chain system that facilitated the carcass remaining on an overhead rail throughout the entire operation.

In its time the meatworks endured fluctuating fortunes caused by a worldwide slump in beef prices and the waxing and waning of the local population. The distance from world markets and the competition of quality meat from overseas kept trade suppressed. Years of industrial disputes and a continuing reduction in demand for frozen meat saw the meatworks close in 1985. The last bullock was killed on 10 October 1985. It was a crippling event for the area. Unsurprisingly, governments and the private sector were reluctant to invest in the north, leaving the remote Kimberley region largely undeveloped for the first four decades of the 20th Century. By 1921 the 420,000-square-kilometre Kimberley region had a white population of little more than 1,000. It was a lonely life for the 945 white males and 186 females who lived mostly in towns like Derby and Broome.

With only rough tracks linking the settlements, horses, donkeys and camels provided the principal method of transport while elsewhere on the continent telephones and motor vehicles were becoming commonplace.

At this time the population of Australia was less than seven million with almost a third living in Sydney and Melbourne. The North West with its sparse population was considered vulnerable to seizure by nations to the north where, only a few hundred kilometres away, there were more than 40 million people on the islands of Java and Madura alone.

A survey by the government indicated the Kimberley could support a thriving pastoral industry and a massively expanded population. Both Commonwealth and Western Australian Governments, anxious about the area's vulnerability to foreign invasion, investigated programs to develop and populate the area. Proposals were explored to exploit the mineral resources and to develop tropical and sub-tropical agriculture on small to medium sized holdings, but little action was taken.

During the depression years a scheme was proposed to settle thousands of young British and Australians on small farms and, later, there was a proposal to settle 100,000 Maltese in the area. But Western Australia with its population of less than half a million had no funds with which to pursue development. In summation: inaccessible terrain, freight costs, lack of finance and the depression impeded any progress.

As persecution of Jews and anti-Semitic violence escalated throughout Europe, there was another little known attempt to populate the North West. The obscure Freeland League for Jewish Territorial Colonisation, formed in London in 1935, was seeking a sanctuary where the Jews could practise their religion without fear of persecution. Their Utopia required a sparsely populated area with fertile soil, a tolerable climate and good rain and water supply where they could establish new industries and develop business and trade. Their charter was to investigate areas for possible settlement, and to negotiate with the governments concerned.

In 1936 the Australian Commonwealth Government under Joe Lyons agreed to the entry of a limited number of Jewish refugees from Germany. Two years later Dr Isaac Steinberg, a Russian-born former People's Commissar of Justice in Vladimir Lenin's government, and later the co-founder of the Zionist-based Freeland League, began dialogue with Michael Durack who was looking for a buyer for the Connor, Doherty and Durack properties, totalling almost three million hectares on both sides of the Western Australian and Northern Territory border.

The pursuit of a Homeland brought Steinberg to Australia in 1939 where he remained throughout the war. Steinberg's persistence and energy kept the proposal alive in Canberra for four years and there were times it seemed the goal was within his grasp. The ACTU and many church leaders were behind the scheme and in 1944 a Gallup poll found 37 per cent of Australians also favoured it. However, the Zionists and other Jewish organisations opposed the scheme and the general community's dislike of immigrant group settlements, together with the government's fear of the settlement eventually becoming an autonomous state, were major factors in Prime Minister Curtin's government rejecting the proposal in 1944.

Thus instead of being part of a historic movement, Connor, Doherty and Durack eventually sold their properties, Argyle, Newry, Auvergne and Ivanhoe Stations, to the Peel River Land and Mineral Company in 1950.

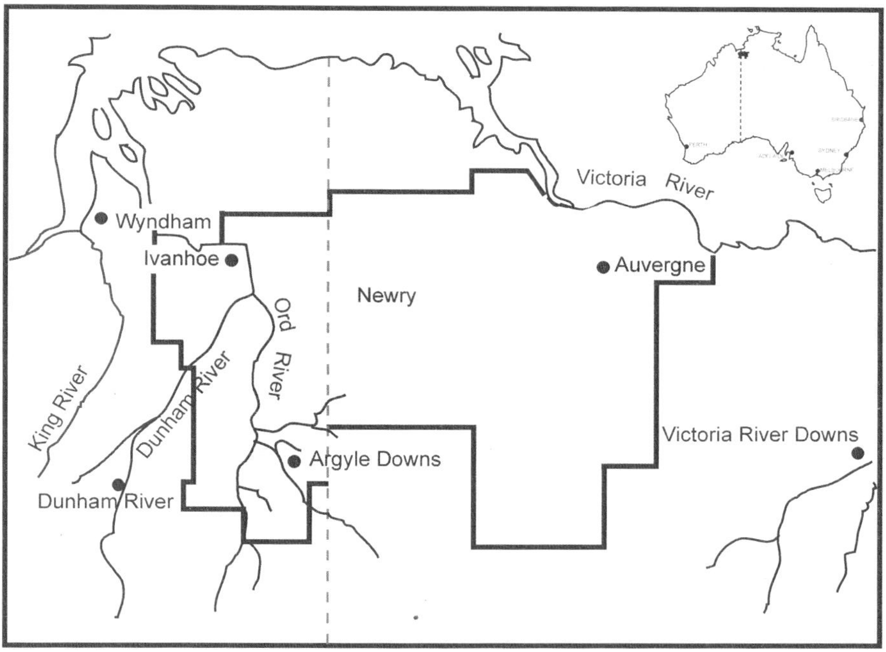

The Connor, Doherty and Durack properties on offer for proposed Jewish Settlement.

Transportation and Stock Routes

The remoteness of the North West required all supplies to be brought to the settlements of Derby and Wyndham by coastal shipping. Most of the stores and household goods were then transported from the port to the outlying stations. Some of this long distance haulage across rough country was done by pastoralists using pack horses but the bulk of it was handled by the Afghan community.

Using camels, the Afghans traversed vast tracts throughout the Kimberley. When horses and camels were the only means of transport, the route taken varied according to the seasonal availability of feed and water but invariably avoided rough stony ground. In the East, one of the routes used by 'the Ghans' ran from Wyndham along today's King River Road to The Diggers Rest and from there to the north of the Cockburn Plateau and thence via Yarrabar Creek to a ford on the Pentecost River. Once over the river the track continued south-west to the homestead at Karunjie Station. From here it made its way to other 'high station' homesteads on the Kimberley Plateau.

Some old maps show stock routes as they were gazetted by the Lands Department and in most cases they coincide with the routes used by the drovers. Other routes were designated sight unseen and marked by Perth-based government surveyors along the most logical route.

The early days saw stock routes numbered ↑22256 and ↑17421 gazetted and excised from the El Questro area. In 1918 prior to the opening of the meatworks, the second route was surveyed and pioneered by Neal Durack on his return from the war where he had served with the Australian Light Horse. This route is shown on maps as emerging from between the North and South Cockburn ranges and crossing the Pentecost River a short distance downstream from Branko's Lookout. It continues along the Salmond Valley to the Afghan camp in Moonlight Valley. Durack's role is recognised by a small elevated area on El Questro named Neal Knob. Much of the rugged country it traverses was later described by its owner, Torrance MacMicking, as 'the mountains of the moon'. It was very rough and far too stony for cattle or soft footed camels to travel; consequently this route was never used and Sahanna the Afghan accessed his country by way of Menmuirs Paddock. Instead, the Ghans and drovers from Tableland, Glenroy and Mount House Stations in the high country followed the Wood and Durack Rivers to join the Gibb River Stock Route at the Chapman Junction, then north-east to the New York Jump-up where there was an abrupt change in the gradient. This was the only place in the range where Wyndham-bound cattle could descend from the plateau area on Karunjie Station.

In those early days the lease on Karunjie was held by Dave Rust and Scotty Salmond who had served together in the Middle East with the Tenth Light Horse. They took up the lease in 1926 under the Soldier Land Settler scheme.

Taking cattle down the winding vehicle route from the second level of the New York Range to the valley floor was a hazardous operation. Had the cattle taken the descent en masse and got a run on, they would have ended up in a heap at the bottom.

To simplify this, Dave, Scotty and a team of men set about working on a shorter track. Using gelignite, they blew some slabs of cap-rock off a ledge and with their crowbars levered the slabs down to the slope below. The slope was excavated to form a terrace that provided a narrow track for the cattle to traverse. Hand placed stones, stabilised with gravel that had been carried to the site in greenhide bags, reinforced the entire structure. This created a steeper but shorter track allowing drovers to hold the cattle on the flat area above, where they could not see the descending bullocks that were being led a few at a time down the track to the comparatively level area below.

Years later, in 1946, the Public Works Department working with Rust, Salmond and the Karunjie boys went to work on the New York Range to build a road to follow the bullock route straight over the top. This was a shorter and more convenient route than the one the vehicles had followed until then, but it required a lot of hand placed rock work. For some reason the job was never completed to a stage where it could be utilised and a massive amount of work went to waste. Up until the 1970s this was the only place a vehicle of any kind had been able to get over the New York Range and there were very few other places that a pack animal could navigate.

Although it is now bypassed by the Gibb River Road, the fact that the terrace of stonework has withstood decades of wet season ravages is testimony to the commitment and ingenuity of the men of those early days and their remarkable feat of engineering. The incongruous name originated from a throwaway remark by Rust or Salmond who, when asked where they were going – retorted in a matter of fact manner 'I'm off to New York' – and the name stuck.

Cattle from the more westerly Gibb River area came in over North Creek and followed the well established wagon route along Chapman River valley to the north-east, until the two routes converged on the Durack River.

Bindoola Creek rises in the New York Range and flows close to the Jump-up, passing over the Oomaloo Falls into a valley known as Menmuirs Paddock from whence it continues for about 80 kilometres to the Pentecost River Crossing. Water along this route was all natural except for one bore on Bindoola Creek at Home Valley homestead where there is a permanent waterhole that was difficult to access with a mob of cattle. Some time around 1960 a bore was sunk there and once it was equipped, life became a lot easier for the drovers and folk living there as well.

Once over the Pentecost River they were on El Questro country and, providing there was water at Yarrabar Creek, the cattle travelled parallel to the Karunjie Track on the Barclay Stock Route to The Diggers Rest and the Pumping Station on the King River. After crossing the river they travelled alongside it to a cutting where the steep mangrove-clad riverbank comes to within six metres of a cliff face, creating a difficult bottleneck on the King River Road. This was the greatest hazard on the entire stock route and the remains of the iron railway fence erected by the Public Works Department to prevent cattle from falling down the steep slippery bank into the tidal river below are still visible today. From here it was a short distance to the holding arrangements at Parry's Lagoon prior to the cattle taking their fatal walk to the abattoirs at Wyndham, 19 kilometres distant.

Fresh water was only available early in the season at Yarrabar. When this dried up, cattle bound for Wyndham took the rough alternative Stock Route between the North and South Cockburn Range. The Public Works Department tried to resolve the water situation on the Karunjie Track by sinking bores, but the water they found was salt and their best effort was to sink earth tanks along the creek on the Track. Historic maps show an Old Well located on the bank of Yarrabar Creek.

The camel drivers, despite coming to Australia from a variety of countries, were known collectively as Afghans or Ghans and were almost without exception single men planning to return home with their new found wealth. A few remained in Australia and several married Aboriginal women.

The Ghans lived a life apart from the general community, observing Muslim rituals and practices, and spending the wet season in their settlement in the Four Mile area at Wyndham. It was here they built their tiny corrugated iron mosque with a gable roof, about the size of a small garage. Today little remains of this settlement, however visitors may inspect the Afghan cemetery where modest mounds and sandstone heads mark the last resting place of ten or more Ghans from India and Afghanistan who worked and died in the area between 1919 and 1942.

These cameleers would transport all imaginable goods with the exception of pork or anything coming in contact with it as it was against their religion. From time to time station people yearning for the taste of bacon would have the storekeepers carefully wrap this taboo meat and conceal it amongst other goods in the hope it would travel unnoticed. Occasionally the bacon fat melted in the heat and dripped through the load, causing the entire pack to be discarded by the disgusted Ghan. Cheese Tin Creek on the Great Northern Highway near to its junction with the Gibb River Road was named when an Afghan cameleer delivering goods from the Port of Wyndham to Dunham Station mistakenly offloaded tins of cheese at this point, believing them to contain pork. The error was uncovered by the station storeman at the destination.

The first camel to be introduced to the continent was brought to South Australia from the Canary Islands in 1840. More were imported in 1860 and over the following 40 years it is estimated 10,000–12,000 camels were brought into the country. They were put to work as beasts of burden carrying supplies to outback stations and mining towns or assisting with exploration. These single hump dromedary camels, accustomed to hot desert conditions, were ideal for transporting heavy loads over long distances. A bull camel can carry up to 600 kilograms and smaller camels between 300 and 400 kilograms – equal to six or seven pack horses. Additionally camels have the advantage of requiring little food or water.

Today the camel population in Australia is estimated to be in excess of one million. With the exception of a few animals used recreationally, the rest live a feral existence in the central and western desert areas of our continent.

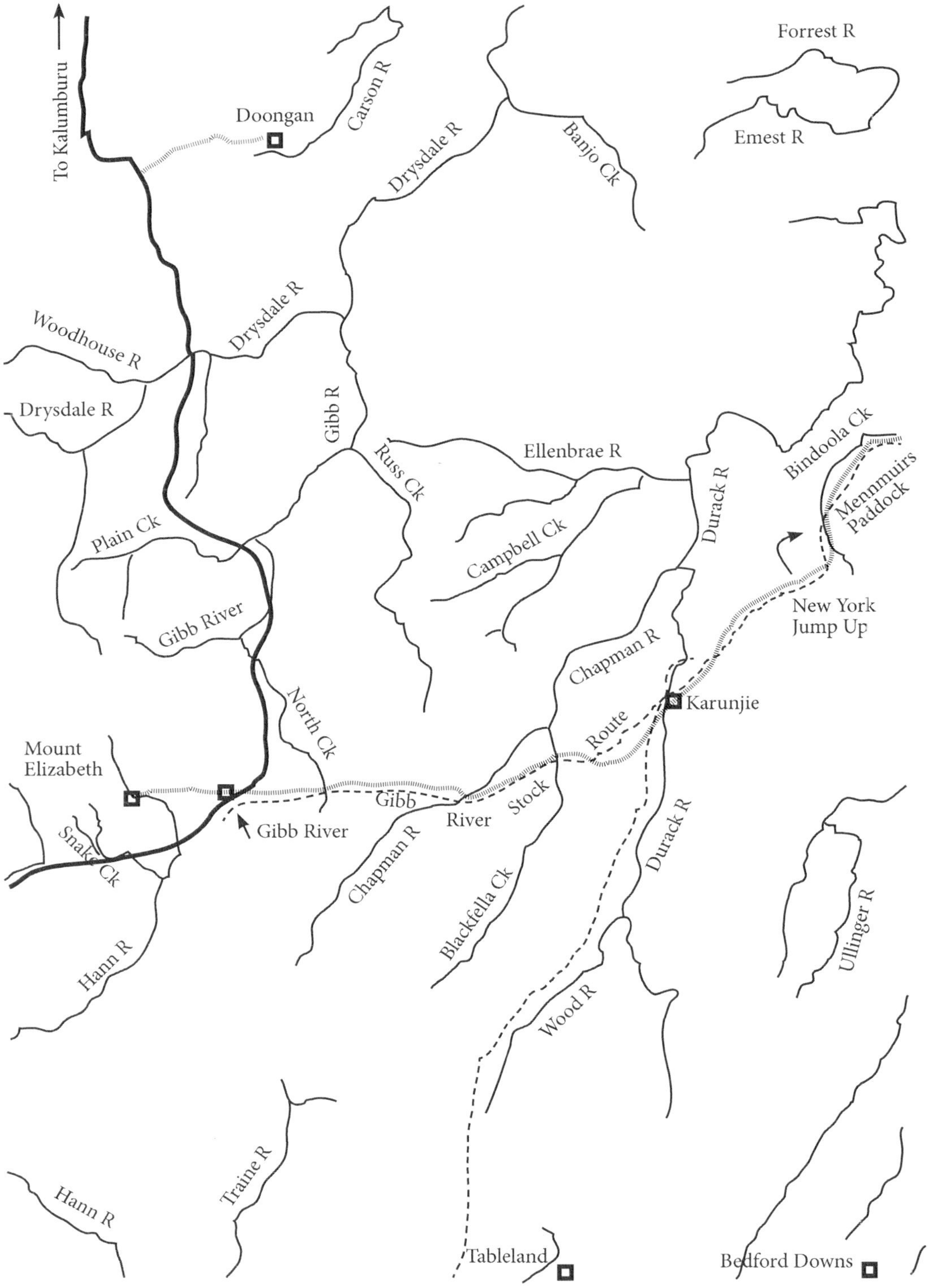
To Kalumburu
Doongan
Carson R
Drysdale R
Banjo Ck
Forrest R
Emest R
Woodhouse R
Drysdale R
Drysdale R
Gibb R
Russ Ck
Ellenbrae R
Bindoola Ck
Mennmuirs
Paddock
Durack R
Campbell Ck
Plain Ck
Gibb River
New York
Jump Up
Chapman R
Karunjie
North Ck
Route
Mount
Elizabeth
Gibb
River
Stock
Gibb River
Snake Ck
Chapman R
Blackfella Ck
Durack R
Ullinger R
Hann R
Wood R
Traine R
Hann R
Tableland
Bedford Downs

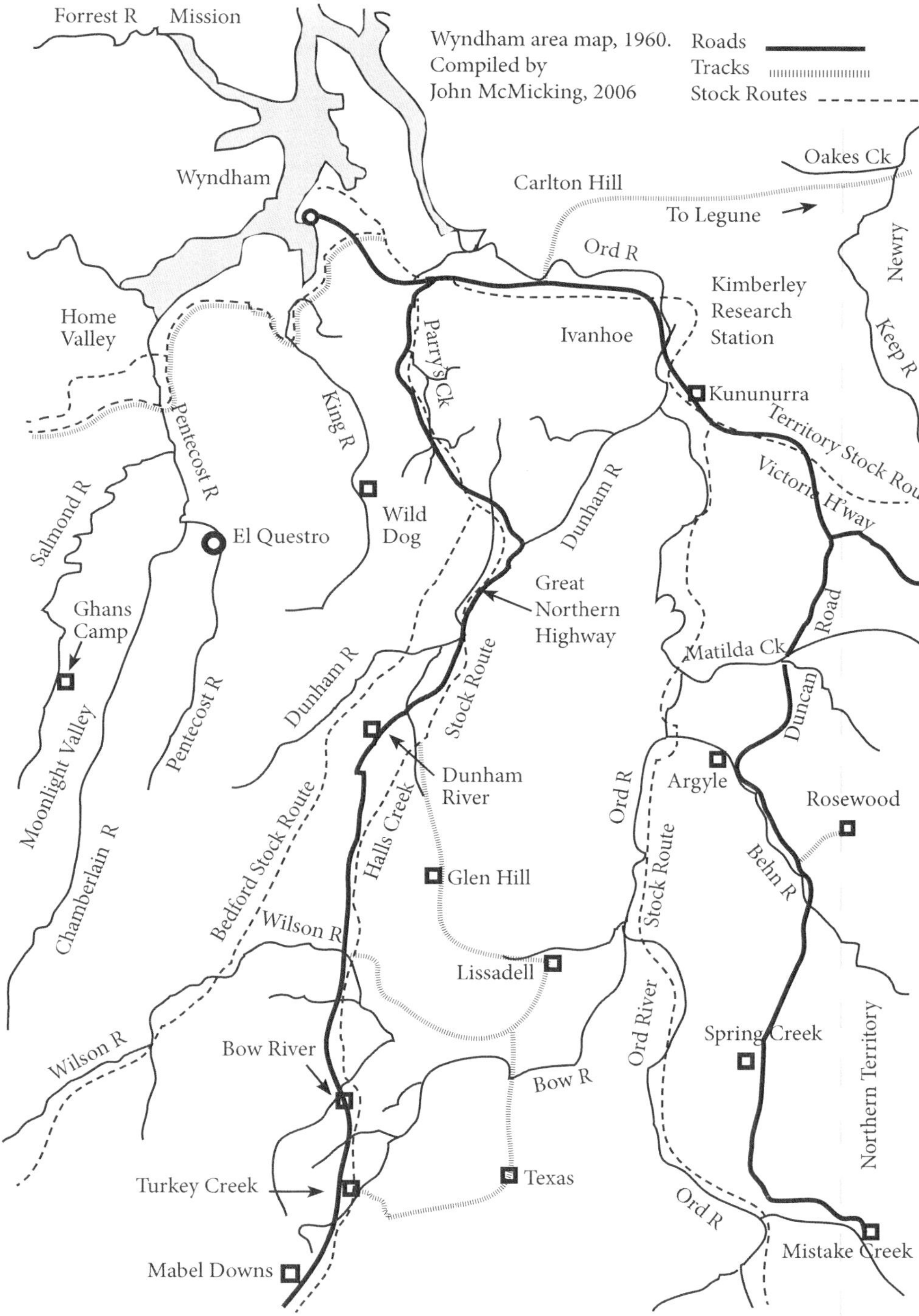

Early roads, tracks and stock routes. Compiled by John McMicking. 2006.

Rapidly increasing numbers are endangering outback vegetation and the population is being reduced by culling.

Donkeys were also used for transport in the early days and locals recall teams of 40 to 50.

In the 1950s police patrols were still carried out on horseback. Usually consisting of a white trooper, a tracker, a 'horsetailer' and possibly a cook or other offsiders, the plant would comprise six or eight mules as pack animals and 15 to 20 horses or riding mules. As with droving or mustering, the work took its toll on the animals; in order to maintain their condition the men were allocated three mounts each and changed them regularly.

Laurie Shaw was the last trooper to be based in Wyndham. His patrol took in Karunjie, Gibb River and Mount Elizabeth Stations, then north to Kalumburu (formerly Drysdale Mission) and returned via the Forrest River Mission (now Oombulguri). The circuitous trip took three months or more and was completed in the dry season. Any prisoners were kept under close scrutiny and generally kept in chains for most of the time. Aboriginal prisoners were walked back to Wyndham in neck chains until 1958.

The Prison Tree is a point of interest marked on tourist maps on the King River Road. This old boab tree with its bulbous girth may be seen close to the western bank of the King River near to the crossing. In former times it was called the Hillgrove Lockup and from time to time patrol officers bringing Aboriginal detainees to Wyndham confined their charges inside its cavernous trunk. Trooper Laurie Shaw was the last man to use the tree for this purpose. The hollow tree is capable of holding at least ten men – media reports claiming up to 30 are certainly exaggerated!

The beginning of the 20th Century saw the dawn of motor transportation with America leading the field in design and manufacture. Although vehicle ownership was slow to catch on in Australia, the sturdy body and high clearance of the Model T Ford made it ideal for the rough conditions of the rural roads. It quickly became the popular choice of the imported cars, leaving the sales of Dodges and Buicks lagging far behind.

During the 1920s the motor car became a feature of everyday life in the populated areas of Australia and by the middle of the decade large car manufacturers in America could see value in establishing plants in Australia. By 1929 it is estimated there was one car for every 11 people.

When early motor transport found its way into the Kimberley the only formed roads in the East went from Wyndham to Darwin and to Halls Creek. Few other vehicular roads existed until the late 1950s.

Perceiving a commercial opportunity, an enterprising resident of Wyndham shipped a large Model T Ford from Perth and in 1929, on payment of five shillings, Hanna Nicholson was granted a licence to operate the town's first taxi service. However, motor vehicles are known to have been shipped to Wyndham prior to this. In addition to the early Durack vehicle, *The Northern Territory Times & Gazette* reports that the Northern Territory Director of Mines shipped a government motor car to Wyndham with the intention of driving to the Tanami goldfields in May 1917. The *Gazette* also reported that in October 1918 Mr 'Cock' Brown was 'the first man who has been game enough to tackle the road from Wyndham to Katherine in a motor car.' The article concludes: 'Hats off to "Cock" Brown in recognition of his pluck and skill and may his considerable shadow never grow less.'

The early settlers forged tracks considerable distances across the country to their stations, enabling them to get trucks and tractors out to their homesteads. The region was criss-crossed with a network of rough bush tracks and by the time Dave Rust and Scotty Salmond took up the lease on Karunjie Station, vehicles were able to make their way from the east as far as Gibb River Station in the central Kimberley. Rust and Salmond are reputed to have driven their tractor and trailer to Derby to collect the supplies for Karunjie some 500 kilometres distant. In 1948 they drove a 4-wheel drive Ford V8 army blitz from Karunjie Station to Wyndham, taking almost four weeks as they were required to clear and make the track as they travelled.

Prior to mid-1950 there was no recognised road between Wyndham and Kalumburu Mission or Derby. Supplies for the mission were transported around the coastline by barge from Wyndham, and any cross-country journeys by police patrols or other Europeans were accompanied by Aboriginal guides who with their innate sense of the land travelled comfortably through the Kimberley wilderness.

With roads little more than dirt tracks, trucks and motor cars were the exception rather than the rule and cattle continued to be moved on the hoof until the situation changed in the 1960s. The sparse European population living in the North West was accepting of these pioneering conditions and hardly aware of the exciting developments that were taking place elsewhere in the world. Australia played its part in man's remarkable conquest of the air during the 1920s and 1930s – achievements that linked many remote areas with cities across the continent.

Aviation

The eight-metre tidal range in the Cambridge Gulf created vast areas of marshland and mud flats over which the King River meanders for 35 kilometres to its mouth. Bordered by mangroves, the marsh is otherwise without vegetation and in early years this flat land provided a convenient landing and refuelling stopover for early aviators on their pioneering flights.

As early as 1919, General Sykes, the British Controller of Civil Aviation, recommended that Wyndham should be the first Australian port of call on flights between London and Melbourne. The suggested route was via Cairo, India and Singapore to Wyndham, thence to Normanton and along the railway line to Melbourne.

Wyndham became quite an aeronautical focal point in the early days and was not without incident. In 1929 Charles Kingsford Smith – one of the world's great pioneering aviators – and Charles Ulm failed to arrive at Wyndham during their attempt to break the Sydney–London flight record. Flying in the famed Fokker aircraft *Southern Cross,* Kingsford Smith became lost during a heavy storm and made a miraculous landing on a tributary of the Glenelg River in the West Kimberley, several hundred kilometres off course. The mishap made national headlines during the ensuing search, and the four crew members with scant provisions other than some sandwiches, a flask of coffee and half a bottle of whisky, were fortunate to survive until they were located 12 days later. The incident became known as the Coffee Royal Affair. Kingsford Smith was to succeed with his record breaking mission in 1931, reducing the time to 8 days, 4 hours and 44 minutes. He again transitted Wyndham in 1933 when he further reduced the flight time from England to Australia to 7 days, 4 hours and 43 minutes.

Amy Johnson, the first woman to fly 11,000 miles solo between England and Australia in her De Havilland Gypsy Moth *Jason (1),* stopped at Wyndham in 1930 to refuel.

Likewise, English aviator Charles Scott piloting a DH.60 Moth, *Gipsy II,* departed from Wyndham in 1931 to smash the solo record between Australia and England, taking 10 days and 23 hours to complete the journey. In the previous month Scott had made world headlines when he broke the record flying eastbound on the same route. These were the first of many prestigious records he was to set. A remarkable character in many ways,

Scott left the R.A.F. in 1926 and emigrated to Australia where he worked for the fledgling Qantas, first as an instructor and then a commercial pilot – a brilliant and colourful pilot who had the distinction of being sacked and later reinstated by the airline.

The first airmail service between the Netherlands and Australia was pioneered in May 1931. A Fokker aircraft operated by KLM flew from Amsterdam to Batavia (Jakarta) where the mail was transferred to a second Fokker aircraft called *Abel Tasman* and flown to Wyndham, Brisbane and Melbourne.

Many of the pioneering aircraft on these long distance international flights landed at Wyndham, others flew via Broome or Darwin. These were dramatic times in the field of aviation and in May 1932 two German aviators, Hans Bertram and Adolph Klausmann, on a goodwill flight to Australia, encountered a violent storm while flying their seaplane named *Atlantis* between Timor and Darwin. They were blown hopelessly off course and, uncertain of their location, landed on a remote section of the Kimberley coast 160 kilometres west of Wyndham. The men somehow managed to survive for 53 days until they were miraculously found and rescued by Aborigines from Kalumburu mission.

In April 1932 the *Northern Territory Times & Gazette* reported on a response to a question on notice in Federal Parliament relating to Commonwealth Government expenditure on aerodromes at Darwin and Wyndham: A total of £4,149 had been spent at Darwin to prepare for the arrival of Charles Kingsford–Smith, but to prepare the dry weather landing ground on the marsh at Wyndham, a mere £9 was outlaid and furthermore it was deemed there was 'no justification for the provision of an all weather aerodrome – it meets all the requirements of the very occasional overseas flights.'

Despite this, by 1932 Western Australia Airways, Australia's first commercial airline, had extended its mail-runs to include Wyndham and in 1934 the first passenger service began.

The tidal mudflats continued to provide an unformed airstrip without mishap until 1936 when, using picks and shovels, an official airstrip was manually levelled on the marshland adjacent to the Six Mile section of Wyndham. This year also saw a base for the Flying Doctor service established in Wyndham.

The formation of the new runways met the demands of heavier and more sophisticated aircraft conforming to the recognised standards of the day.

In 1949 Air Beef Proprietary Limited commenced regular use of the airstrip at Wyndham. The revolutionary Air Beef Scheme was established by three Blythe brothers in partnership with MacRobertson Miller Airline Services (MMA) and Australia National Airways (ANA) and others. The enterprise involved the construction of a large abattoir on Glenroy Station capable of killing 60 bullocks a day and provided an alternative to droving the cattle along the lengthy route from the Blythe's three isolated stations to the ports of Derby or Wyndham. The cattle from Mount Hart and Mount House Stations located in the King Leopold Ranges joined those being slaughtered at Glenroy. They were walked the comparatively short distance between the stations with little loss of condition. The chilled carcasses were transported in a converted DC3 aircraft to the meatworks in Wyndham where they were packed, frozen and shipped to markets in the United Kingdom. In 1959 the chilled carcasses were flown to Derby instead of Wyndham. This scheme continued until 1965 and accounted for the movement of more than 15 million kilograms of chilled beef.

Road Development

The original Halls Creek Road out of Wyndham did not follow the Great Northern Highway as we now know it. The former route lay to the east and traversed some low lying country where for several kilometres the single lane track was neatly lined with square blocks of rock, laboriously hewn from local sandstone and intended to keep the gravel on the road. When the stones were meticulously laid in place in the late 1930s there were few vehicles using the roads. It could not have been foreseen that heavy army vehicles, trucks and road trains would be testing the skill of the early road workers. Today curious drivers travelling to Wyndham may experience the Old Halls Creek Road by leaving the Great Northern Highway shortly after the turning to the Grotto and then following the remnant road through a Nature Reserve, passing close to the Ramsar Wetland at Parry's Lagoon before rejoining the Great Northern Highway close to Wyndham.

Until 1939 no more than five per cent of the Western Australian Main Roads budget was allocated to the North West and the roads remained little more than dirt tracks, infrequently used in the dry season and almost impassable in the wet. It was the impending war and the threat of the Japanese advancing from the north that helped to change this and focus attention on the Kimberley, and by the end of the war some 25 per cent of the Main Roads Department's 1944/45 budget was expended on the region.

The Department had been given responsibility for the construction of several military aerodromes, many of them in isolated parts of the North West, and after the war the Army agreed to contribute towards the reconstruction of many of the roads and old tracks that had been badly damaged by the movement of their heavy equipment.

Greater interest was focussed on the Kimberley generally and a government appointed committee looked into ways of developing the region, examining ports, roads, water supplies, primary production, mining and oil prospecting options.

Workers maintaining the gravel roads in the remote area led a lonely existence. Away from home for months grading the corrugations and repairing general damage, their tool of trade was the grader and their rig consisted of a trailer of supplies and fuel, and occasionally a vehicle in tow. One of these men acquired his nickname when he lost his trailer of supplies in a flood; among the items requiring replacement was a grease gun. When ordering it over the radio, the operator in Wyndham had difficulty hearing and only caught the word 'grease', so the exasperated roadman spelled out 'gun': 'G – Jesus, U – onion, N – pneumonia'. He was known as Greasegun thereafter.

The arrival of Gascoyne Traders prior to the end of the war marked the beginning of the end of the donkey and camel days. Other motorised operators soon followed, with Paddy Flinders, an Aborigine from Turkey Creek, driving for Bill Flinders Transport, and Greasegun behind the wheel of a 6-wheel drive ex-army truck for local businessman Bert Sharp.

In 1949 the Commonwealth Government announced its intention to construct an all-weather road between Wyndham and Nicholson to service the centrally located Vestey property, some 250 miles distant.

Most of the driving at that time was on rough, randomly graded wheel-rut tracks. Wainwright and Wills started East Kimberley Transport in 1957 and were kept busy with deliveries to and from 'cattle baron' Lord Vestey's stations over the border in the Territory.

By the 1960s most large stations had their own road trains capable of carting 150–170 head of cattle. It was a progressive time in the Kimberley. New bores, tanks and fences on most stations, together with the introduction of generated electricity and improved communications, brought an appreciable change to the lifestyle. Under the state Liberal Country Party, significant funding was being allocated by both state and federal governments to develop roads in a project known as The Beef Roads Scheme. This was part of a strategy to provide all-weather roads to facilitate the transport of livestock and increase the nation's export earnings.

The future Premier of Western Australia, Charles Court, in his capacity as Minister for the North West and Industrial Development, was a driving force in the changes. Under his influence ports, airfields and roads were expanded or upgraded. He is recognised for his staunch support of the Ord River Irrigation development and for resource development in the area.

Court secured approval for the development of the Beef Roads across the Kimberley. Initially the scheme targeted upgrading the Great Northern Highway between Wyndham and Halls Creek and the road from Wyndham to Kununurra and beyond to Nicholson. Bridges over the Ord and Dunham Rivers in the vicinity of Kununurra were also planned and ultimately formed part of the Victoria Highway. Progressively a network of roads spread across the Kimberley enabling cattle to be transported – initially by truck and later by road train – with little loss of condition.

The road train is a trucking concept used to move freight efficiently in remote areas; it consists of a prime mover hauling two or three trailers. These vehicles first appeared on Australian roads in the 1930s and are also used in the Argentine and North America. Australia currently has the largest and heaviest road-legal vehicles in the world with a triple combination measuring up to 53.5 metres.

With the absence of an extended rural rail network in Western Australia, the state is largely reliant on road transport and the road train has become an essential method of conveying fuel, livestock, mineral ore and general freight. Today these trucks are the kings of the highway in the low population areas of the state.

In the Wyndham East Kimberley Shire at the end of the first decade of the 21st Century only 476 kilometres of road were sealed. The multiple wheels of a road train raise vast clouds of dust on unsealed roads and tracks, and consequently the transport of livestock by road train over the remaining 1,474 kilometres of unsealed road is generally restricted to doubles – a prime mover towing two semi-trailers – to prevent risk of the stock suffocating in the dust.

The Gibb River Road

The Gibb River Road is one of the two major roads to dissect the Kimberley region. The second is the northern section of Australia's longest highway, known as the Great Northern Highway. It extends for 3,204 kilometres linking Perth with the state's most northerly port, Wyndham.

Today the Gibb River Road is a formed two-lane gravel road with many concrete floodway crossings and increasing bitumenised sections. Even though it is still regarded by some as a remote and challenging route, it is a far cry from its early beginings when it was a rough track between Wyndham and Gibb River Station in the east and from Derby to Mount House Station in the west.

In the early days of white settlement in the East Kimberley, this wagon track and stock route was used by the cattle stations from the high country located to the south-west of El Questro. From Wyndham it passed to the north and west of the Cockburn Ranges and after crossing the Pentecost River went from station to station using the homesteads as depots.

Similarly in the West Kimberley there was a rough track from Derby as far as Mount House Station used only by bullock or donkey teams; it was known as Mount House Road. Beyond this point, the early stations on the Plateau relied on mules and horses for the delivery of their supplies.

Access to the Benedictine Mission at Kalumburu in the north was by horse or coastal barge. Change was on its way when in July 1954 John Morgan and a party of surveyors and road makers, under instruction from the Western Australian Surveyor General's Office, commenced the initial work on the road north from Gibb River Station to the Mission at Kalumburu. The early onset of wet season conditions at the end of that year made the road impassable in places, and with great difficulty a bulldozer was eventually delivered to the Mission.

Aboriginal author Ambrose Mungala Chalarimeri, who spent his childhood at Kalumburu, recalls the surveying and bulldozing of the route to the Mission at that time. In his book *The Man from the Sunrise Side* Ambrose writes about surveyors selecting the route and marking the trees with ribbons or white paint. The bulldozer, grader and trucks followed a day behind as part of a second team led by Scotty Salmond. The completion of the project gave the isolated Mission its first road access from Derby.

The information in the following paragraphs has been provided by John McMicking who worked throughout the Kimberley between 1951 and 1990 as a drover, a driver and predominantly a stock inspector. During this time McMicking witnessed many changes in the region. Perhaps the most dramatic was the introduction of the motor vehicle which eventually displaced the drover. The days of the working horse and the lifestyle associated with it rapidly evaporated and John, like many before him, was reluctant to see it disappear entirely. To this end, he has generously provided a great deal of information for this book and in places he is quoted verbatim.

In his written records of *The History of the Gibb River Road*, McMicking writes:

> The only way by road from Wyndham to Gibb River Station was by travelling out past the King River pumping station, around the north of the Cockburn Range and over the Pentecost River at the head of the salt water where the Gibb River Road crossing is today. From there the road climbed over the Pentecost Range into what was known as Menmuirs Paddock, a valley forty five kilometres long, through which the Bindoola Creek flows.
>
> The road played noughts and crosses with the creek all the way up to Oomaloo Falls, at the south end of the paddock which ended at the New York Range. (The term 'paddock' has nothing to do with fences; they were unknown in this area at that time. It was a natural paddock fenced only by hills and was far from stock proof). This range would have been named by Scotty Salmond.
>
> Up until 1951-52 the country north of Gibb River Station was accessible only by pack horse. The main members of the team who put the first motor road through from this station to Kalumburu were: -
>
> Trooper Laurie Shaw, with the Wyndham Police pack horse plant. Howard Gatenhof, Main Roads surveyor. Ron Duncan, Main Roads engineer, Roy Young, contractor. Ron 'Push-em-up' Eastoff, dozer driver.
>
> All of the country was in Shaw's regular patrol area so he was the obvious man to guide the machines north from Gibb River Station. The track from Wyndham to the Gibb homestead had been used by motor vehicles for some years and the road gang touched it up on their way out. Thereafter they had to pick their way as they went north under Trooper Shaw's guidance.
>
> Roy Young had a D6 cable operated dozer, a Cat 12 grader, a Jeep and an Austin truck. His loader was probably his old Hough. Not a big one, but good. What other machinery and men he had with them I do not know. The

> old road over the Pentecost Range, through Karunjie to Gibb would not have been conducive to transporting a dozer but Youngie and Pushemup were no strangers to rough country. Between them they could climb over anything. There would have been little need for a low loader on the way out as there was plenty of work to keep the D6 busy on the ground but they would need it coming home. His low loader was on an ex-army 6x6 wheel Studebaker, which took a bit of stopping. I knew that rig as I drove it when I worked for Roy. It would have been able to climb over the range empty, but they would have had some work to do on New York Jump-up to get it and the old Austin up. Still, that is what dozers are for.

Aborigines, Sandy Rivers and Albert Mindiging from Moola Bulla Station were also part of the team that worked on the road to Kalumburu. They had been seconded by Dave Rust and Scotty Salmon who also took some station horses to use for the roadwork.

Pushemup drove a bulldozer for the Main Roads Department and gained his nickname when his foreman asked him to form a large pile of gravel. The foreman returned four days later to find a 'mountain' of gravel and Eastoff still hard at work adding to it.

In the 1960s more government funding became available and the Beef Roads Scheme was expanded by the Main Roads Department. Among the new projects was the challenging construction of a road from Derby through the King Leopold Ranges to Glenroy Station in the West Kimberley. The new road was opened to road trains in 1962, bypassing Mount House Station and providing a more economical transport alternative to the enterprising Air Beef Scheme, leading to the closure of the abattoirs at Glenroy Station.

By 1963 the vast majority of the cattle were being transported by road and Western Australia's beef exports exceeded the previous year by 60 per cent. In 1965 the Beef Road from Derby was extended beyond Glenroy to Gibb River Station, opening up vast areas of additional pastoral country in the centre of the Kimberley and giving the route its present name. The Gibb River is reputed to have been named in recognition of Andrew Gibb Maitland, the government geologist and member of Drake-Brockman's 1901 expedition.

Although now an Aboriginal-owned station, Gibb River, was originally taken up by Fred Russ in 1921 with 50 breeding cattle. At that time the station stores were brought in by bullock wagon as far as Mount Hart and continued the rest of the way by pack horse or mule. The iron for the homestead roof and occasionally other supplies were transported by camel from Wyndham, 440 kilometres distant. It took Russ three weeks to drove his cattle to Derby for sale.

Russ built the airstrip at Gibb River by hand in 1938 and brought the first truck from Derby over the Phillips Range to the station the following year. This operation entailed manually clearing the track from Mount House as they progressed.

Jack Trust recalls working on the eastern end of the road from Wyndham to Gibb River in 1957. As part of a team of six, he was a truck driver and part-time cook. Other members of the team were Roy Young, another truck driver, Jack Scanlan who drove a D4 Dozer, and Laurie Johns drove the grader. Duncan Ward was the surveyor and Trevor Nelson his assistant. Two trucks, a Blitz and a Chevrolet, were provided by Young, with the Main Roads Department supplying the earth moving equipment and a Landrover. The work took almost six months to complete. Trust and Scanlan were left to walk the Dozer back to Wyndham. Their routine for this slow task involved Scanlan taking the morning shift on the Dozer while Trust drove the fuel truck with their stores to a suitable midday camp. After a break, they exchanged places to complete the next leg to their evening camp.

In 1964 Doug Escott and partners took up Ellenbrae Station to the west of El Questro. Escott was the first to take a vehicle up the New York Range at Bamboo Creek. He named it Roley's Jump-up after his ex-army Humber 4-wheel drive battlewagon with its Rolls Royce engine. Road access to Ellenbrae in the early days was out to Karunjie and north across country to the base camp at Campbell Creek. Escott drove his truck to Wyndham once a year to pick up a load of fuel for the station and in those early days it would take him a week to drive back to Ellenbrae.

In 1963 the Wyndham council graded a track into El Questro from the Wyndham-Halls Creek Road. Later, using a bulldozer and grader the council cut a single track on through El Questro as far as the Pentecost River where it would have linked up with the Karunjie track and stock route.

In 1967 McMicking drove out this way en route to Kalumburu. It was the stock route in those days and it took his party two and a half days to reach Gibb River homestead.

McMicking's informative recollections continue:

> It has long been my intention to some day write about my first trip into the North Kimberley. Despite my diary and log book going up in smoke years ago it is all still clear to me. My memory is good and I continued to travel in that country for 25 more years. I was only a lad of 36, born and bred in a Murchison drought and weathered more since then. Apart from three years at high school in Geraldton I have never been out of the bush.
>
> My first trip out along the Gibb River Road was in 1967. John Armstrong, the Kimberley's only Government Vet, came with me in my Land Rover and John Morrell, Halls Creek's stock inspector, brought his as well.
>
> None of us had ever been past the King River Pumping Station. We left Wyndham at seven in the morning with plenty of tucker on board, mainly the tinned variety as we had no refrigerators and the Eskys were of little use without ice. Armstrong was reliant on a 'city slicker' type of tucker box based on spaghetti and meat balls; like me Morrell had been around the bush for a while and we packed cooked meat, plenty of flour for dampers and Johnny cakes (very appropriate on this trip as we were three Johns) and some dry salted beef. Tin dog is only emergency tucker for a bushman but we took a fair whack of that too. We could not be sure how long we would be on this sparsely inhabited road. Fishing lines are a necessity as there are plenty of bream in that country.
>
> The going was slow but not rough until we got past the marsh and plain country sandwiched between the Cockburns and the Gulf. Then we came onto rockier ground as we approached the crossing of the Pentecost River. The crossing itself was wide and comprised of rocks, all large and larger. They were very slow to crawl over but not a hazard.
>
> It was only a few miles on downstream from the crossing to Harold MacNamara's Home Valley homestead on the bank of Bindoola Creek, where we called in to say gidday and have a mug of tea. They did not get a lot of visitors out there but knew we were on the road somewhere as we had Traeger transportable radios in our Rovers and kept in touch with all stations on the regular schedules. Harold was at home with wife Harriet and their two sons, Raymond and Peter. Raymond would have been in his early teens about then. Harold did most of his travelling on horseback but had been to Karunjie with his tractor as well and gave us some idea of the road ahead. We did not tarry long at Home Valley as we wanted to get over the range before dark.
>
> The track up the range was rough and slow and down the other side was worse. A lot of bare rock layered out like terraces with many nasty steps between. Armstrong reckoned it was akin to 'driving down the steps of the

GPO'. It took a fair bit of time to negotiate, but at last we were down off the range, across a little creek called the Maitland which comes from the east and joins the Bindoola. We were now in Menmuirs Paddock and were more than glad to make our first night camp.

On our way out I had discovered why the Land Rover company had mounted the spare tyre on the bonnet. It wasn't there just to inhibit the driver's vision – which it does admirably – or to catch you like a mouse in a trap when you check the oil and water. If you wrap three big bottles of beer in a wet bag and put them in it in the afternoon you can have a nice cool beer when you pull up. We had not brought much beer with us. Morrell and I did not want to embarrass our city bred vet boss so we loaded accordingly. Reasonable drinking men would have needed a trailer on this trip and we did not have one. But we did have two Land Rovers.

It was just on sundown and we had done 80 or 90 kilometres for the day without busting a gut so we had a beer and camped for the night. On these jaunts you can afford to be flash first night out, so we probably had chops or steak. After that if you want fresh meat you have to shoot it.

There was no way we could get off on a wrong road – there wasn't one. Next day we continued on, following the Bindoola Creek which we had to cross several times until we came to the New York Jump-up. This is at the same place as the creek enters the valley at Oomaloo Falls. The road from the Pentecost River to New York Range is rough and up and down for over 60 kilometres.

Even as a bullock road it was bloody rugged and would have been hell on the poor old bullocks' feet. Feed was sparse and the skimpy holes in Bindoola Creek were not the best to water a mob in either, even early in the year. I pitied the poor man and beast that had to make the trip late in the season. A lot of cattle had come along that road in the early days but the numbers were down now. The Air Beef scheme on Glenroy which started up in 1949, and the advent of road transport to the West Kimberley, had greatly reduced the need for this old track.

After negotiating the jump-up the country flattened out and the ground was mainly sandy, which was a nice change. By midday we had made another 50 kilometres to the Karunjie homestead which was deserted, as expected. It had been abandoned by Tom Orley for some time. Apart from a couple of American-style gun belts left on a bunk there was little there. The road in this area was not easy to follow as it was not defined with rocks and it took us an hour to find the crossing over the Durack heading west. We were lucky there had been an Army survey team through not long before to give us some tracks to follow. All I had was a mud map in my head.

Sixty kilometres from there brought us to the Chapman River, which is not a large one and we made camp for the night. Early next morning we found the country was changing and the going getting better. The rocks were thinning out and the trees becoming taller and more plentiful.

Then we made a real discovery: the Derby to Kalumburu road. This junction was some 20 kilometres north of the Gibb Homestead.

It was here that we 'men of vision' began discussing the future of the country and its potential for tourism. 'Tourism' was still a rude word amongst the locals back then. Morrell, like me, was a very keen beer man and thought this road junction would be a good place for a tavern. I agreed with him, with reservations. I reckoned too many people would find it eventually. He suggested we call it the Gibb Inn but I amended that to the Nebber Gibb Inn, which was agreed to unanimously as being more positive. Many years later I got around to building the place in a poem, called Drive On.

We turned south to Gibb River and called in to see the Russ family, which was rather a large one. Fred had four sons and at that time they were still all on the station.

The Derby Stock Inspector, Tom Ingate, was at Gibb having driven up to join us on the trip. After a good yarn with the Russ family we travelled over to the neighbouring station, Mount Elizabeth, which was only 20 kilometres to the west and made contact with the Laceys. The homestead there was a small one of white-washed stone, close beside the Hann River. When we arrived there were a few of the younger family members swimming in the pool close by. Frank had two sons and a daughter or two. One thing I noted was how close he had built his stock yard to the house. It was only about 150 yards from it, at the most.

Although it was advisable to spend a bit of time with the cattlemen on our route while we were there, with the distance we had to cover, time was of the essence and we had dust clouds to raise. Before long we were headed back to Gibb and the road north to the Mission. The only other two stations north of us were off our road. Doongan was over 20 miles to the east and uninhabited. Theda, further on, was also to the east of the track – we would check on that one when we got to Kalumburu.

The track was now all good level going on light loam to sandy soil through country that was fairly heavily timbered, mainly with grey box trees that grow nice and straight – good looking but bloody useless as timber.

Kalumburu Mission was of the Benedictine Order with its home base at New Norcia. On arriving there at about midday we made ourselves known to Father Sanz and met with several of the other Mission people.

We were taken on a guided tour of the place in the afternoon and after a long and very conversational afternoon tea, Sanz gave us a guide named Geoffrey, to show us our way around the beaches to the north and the old Pago Pago Mission site. There were big mobs of black fringe oysters out among the reefs, such as I had not seen since I used to go picking them at Nooria, when I was on Mardie Station ten years before.

We camped there over night and made our way back to the Mission early next morning and prepared for a good start on the road home. I would have to come back up here early in the season to get their cattle camp started on the pleuro eradication programme.

The manager of Theda and his wife were at the mission while we were there. I cannot recall their names. They were a pleasant young couple and were not planning on going home soon. We wanted to see as much of the country as we could and they gave us directions to go back along the north bank of the Carson River and cross over it to their place and feed the chooks. This meant we could also have a feed of eggs while we were at it. It seemed like a fair deal to us.

The road home was faster than the road out and I think we did it in a bit over two days. I had left a few dog baits on the way up but the only scalp I got was one near New York. He had died in a pool in the creek and was pretty rotten. Armstrong was not impressed with my type of post mortem.

John McMicking, May 2009

The eastern section of the route to Gibb River Station was the responsibility of the Wyndham and East Kimberley authorities who had a very limited operating budget; consequently the standard of the construction and maintenance fell far short of that at the western end of the route.

Sadly, the days of the East Kimberley drovers came to an end in 1974 when Jack Green walked 700 cattle to the Wyndham Meatworks from Mabel Downs.

In 1977 the eastern end of the track was surveyed and built for vehicle use. It was rerouted to take advantage of all the available high ground and sound foundation. Built as a beef road, it no longer went from station to station as in the past.

On leaving the Pentecost Range the present road goes nowhere near any of the old working stock routes; it joins the old stock route for only 16 kilometres. This section extends from the Pentecost River, crossing over the range to Carr's Bottle Tree where the Karunjie track turns south into Menmuirs Paddock from the Gibb River Route.

The upgraded road was extended to connect with the existing eastbound road from Derby, completing the Gibb River Road we know today. In 1996 Main Roads took responsibility for the entire length of this important road and upgraded the standard of the eastern sector to that of the west.

To accommodate the recent increased vehicle usage by road trains and tourists, the road has been widened and the alignment improved. Most of the wet season floodways are concreted and the 'jump ups' on many steep hills have been sealed. Despite these improvements the 647 kilometre Gibb River Road is known as one of Australia's last adventure routes. It is closed to traffic during the wet season and it is not until the rain stops, generally by mid-April, that road maintenance contractors and their graders move in to commence the endless task of maintaining it and preparing it for reopening to the public.

John McMicking. Photo courtesy of Johnny Mac.

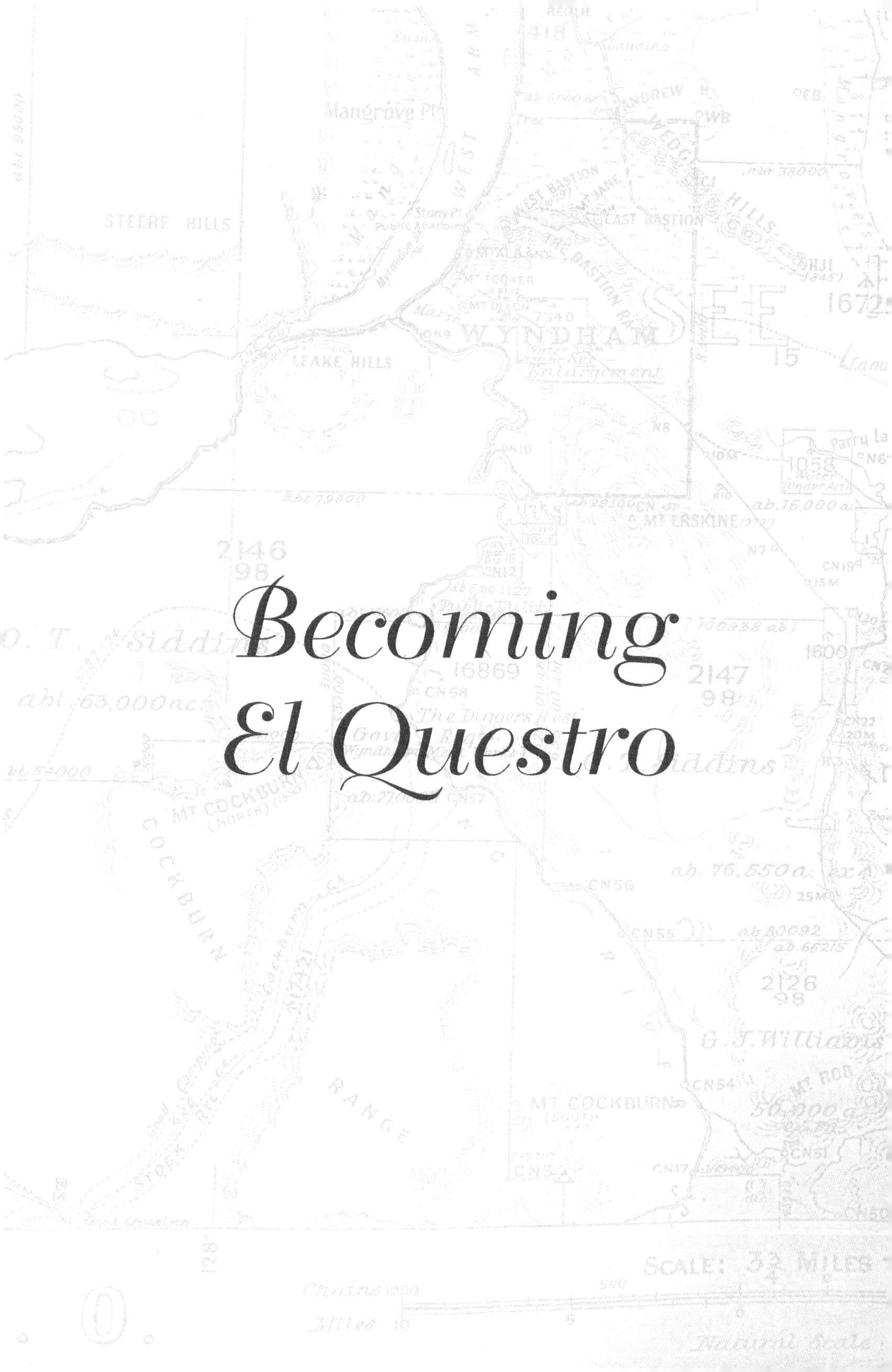

Becoming El Questro

A boab tree at Wild Dog Spring. Photo by Tobie.

Most of the pastoral country in Western Australia is leased from the Crown through the state government. This is the case in the north-west Kimberley, where the country was first successfully opened up to European settlement along the vast flood plains of the Fitzroy River in the early 1880s. Very soon some five million acres had been leased in the West Kimberley.

The first station in the East Kimberley was established on the head waters of the Ord River by William Osmond and Joseph Panton from Victoria. Their 4,000 head of cattle arrived at Ord River Station from Queensland in 1884 in the charge of the legendary drover and bushman, Nat Buchanan. This event was the beginning of some now famous cattle drives across the continent from the eastern states.

In the following year, the Duracks and other pioneering families began arriving and taking up their vast holdings, mostly downstream from Panton and Osmond; their focus was on the alluvial plains associated with the Ord River.

Despite the absence of a reliable market for their produce the pastoral industry developed rapidly and by the end of the 19th Century there were more than 400,000 sheep and cattle in the North West. All of the prime land associated with the Fitzroy and Ord Rivers was now accounted for, and expeditions were pushing into the more central ranges in their search for additional fertile river flats. In the early years of pastoralism in the Kimberley, the boundaries of leases underwent constant changes as they were taken up and released according to perceived opportunities by the leaseholder of the time.

The increasing popularity of owning land in the Kimberley pushed settlers into the less productive country further west and beyond to the high country on the Kimberley Plateau. Many of these rangeland leases had insufficient good grazing areas to justify the cost of purchasing stock, and the only way some of the leaseholders could expect to pay their rent was by mustering the land in the hope of finding sufficient cattle had strayed onto it from larger unfenced neighbouring stations.

Notwithstanding its proximity to the developing town of Wyndham, the leasehold area comprising El Questro Station and Wilderness Park as we know it today was not initially taken up in its entirety. With so much of El Questro acreage being rocky rangeland and quite unsuitable for cattle,

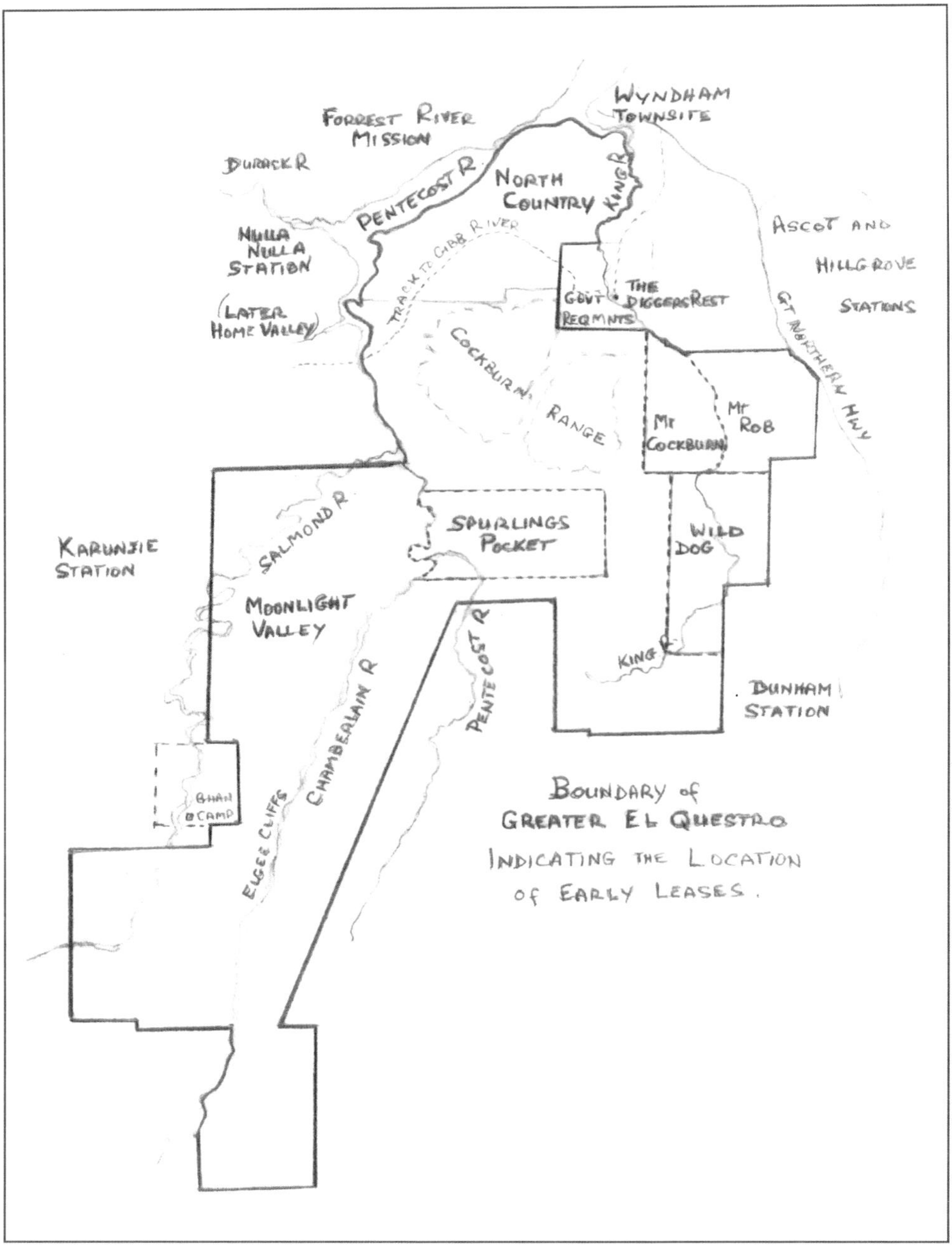

Map of El Questro showing the earliest leases and its maximum area in the 1970s.

most of the country held little attraction for the early pastoralists and their cattle enterprises. Consequently, four of the original pastoral leases on El Questro in the 1880s and 1890s were on the flat country associated with the King River along the eastern margins and in the north of the future million acre station.

The next area of the station to be taken up relatively early in the 20th Century was a lease along the Pentecost River to the east of its confluence with the Chamberlain. This locality was known for many years as Spurlings Pocket. It will be familiar to most visitors today, as the centre of the tourist operation is located within its boundaries.

The present name was not given to the property until 1958 when Torrance MacMicking wrote to the Lands Department naming his leases 'El Questro'. Later his country was described in a Pastoral Inspector's report as 'an extremely rough area with about four-fifths of the lease being steep rugged hill country of little or no value for practical grazing purposes'. In spite of this, recognised names in the pastoral industry such as Kidman and Durack are found amongst the early threads of the colourful El Questro tapestry.

El Questro Station reached its maximum area in 1982 when the combination of leases encompassed some 404,686 hectares, or more than a million acres. However, since 1988 the Station has been diminishing in size as land has been resumed by the Crown or transferred to other parties. Presently the Wilderness Park covers some 274,000 hectares. Details from the early days of its settlement are scant and often amount to little more than a name on a map or a leaseholding recorded in the archives of the Lands Department. Undoubtedly further research would put additional flesh on the Station's historical skeleton.

Let us begin with some known information relating to the early holders of the eastern leases.

The Wild Dog, Mount Rob and Mount Cockburn Leases

The first recorded lease of El Questro country was an area in the east lying to the south of today's Gibb River Road. It encompassed most of the headwaters of the King River and appears to have been leased almost continuously by a series of graziers since 1887 – just three years after the arrival of the first cattle in the East Kimberley. This 50,000-acre holding is comparatively flat and well grassed and today remains amongst the Station's most valuable areas for pasturing cattle. An early map calls the lease 'Wild Dog' and for the purpose of identification, this name will be used when referring to it in future.

Wild Dog country on the upper King River.

The Wild Dog lease on El Questro should not be confused with the Argyle Police Camp located close to the Northern Territory border at Wild Dog Creek. This camp, sometimes known as Wild Dog, was operational between 1896 and 1908. It was manned by three constables and four Aboriginal trackers and was approximately two day's ride from the Argyle and Ord River homesteads. Captured Aborigines were shackled to two large trees at the depot prior to being walked to Wyndham in neck chains. Later a store and sly grog outlet operated at the location catering to the needs of passers-by.

Police camps were set up throughout the East Kimberley district in an attempt to deal with the ongoing conflicts arising from the murder of whites and the appropriation of beef and porcelain by the Aborigines whose traditional lands had been usurped by the early settlers. Some 1,897 beasts are recorded as having been speared in one year alone. The increase in police patrols and the establishment of the camps and pursuit and capture of offenders – together with any Aborigines deemed to have been witnesses – succeeded in at least halving the spearing incidents.

During the first 50 years of European engagement in the North West, hundreds of Aborigines were shot and killed by explorers, pastoralists and other settlers, as well as the miners and police who took the law into their own hands when acting in self defence or seeking retribution.

On El Questro country, two adjoining leases to the north of Wild Dog roughly form a Y arrangement with the King River running down the centre. The 50,000-acre land on the east side of the river has a small monolithic dome called Mount Rob as its principal feature, and to assist with identity we will call this lease 'Mount Rob'. Adjacent to Mount Rob a smaller 25,000 acre lease is sandwiched between the King River and the Cockburn Range, this we will call 'Mount Cockburn'.

The Mount Rob lease.

Further north again, the country lying between the Cockburn Ranges and the Cambridge Gulf will be referred to as the 'North Country'.

William Henry Osmond and **Joseph Anderson Panton** were the first pastoralists to take up land on El Questro country in 1887. Osmond and Panton's brief holding of the Wild Dog lease incorporated country on both sides of the King River and adjoined their 300,000-acre lease that extended east beyond the Dunham River. Both of these leases were given up as unpaid the following year. The pastoralists' principal holding Ord River Station, was located 200 miles further south, stretching to the border and beyond into the Territory. The partnership at its height held some 3,365,000 acres in the North West. Panton's business involvement with Osmond lasted for a decade before he sold out to his partner.

Osmond arrived in Victoria from England during the gold rush in 1850. He started a small smelting plant in Stawell, giving rise to his nickname, 'Billy the Smelter'. Osmond made a fortune in a mining company and travelled abroad for some time. On his return to Australia he stood for parliament and held a seat on the Legislative Council of Victoria until his death in 1901.

In partnership with Joseph Panton, Osmond invested in grazing land in the Northern Territory and the Kimberley District. Joe Panton also arrived in Australia during the early stages of the gold rush and unsuccessfully tried his hand at mining in Central Victoria. He then applied to Lieutenant-Governor Charles La Trobe to become an officer with the gold escort. The Governor, after a visual assessment of Panton, remarked: 'This fellow seems too big for a trooper, too heavy, it would be too severe on the horses. I think he would make a Commissioner.'

Panton took up the position of Commissioner of Police near Bendigo where his sympathetic attitude towards the resented Chinese diggers and merchants earned him a silk scroll of appreciation from the Chinese community. In 1858 Panton left Victoria to study art in Paris. On returning to Victoria he had a series of postings as a Magistrate and became very active in the Victorian Artists Association. Panton was also involved in the wine industry and produced prize-winning wines on his vineyards near Bendigo.

In 1882, 4,000 cattle belonging to the Osmond–Panton partnership left Queensland bound for the Kimberley. They were in the charge of Natalia Buchanan and their arrival in June 1884 heralded the beginning of pastoral settlement in the East Kimberley. Bob Button, who accompanied the cattle on the trek, stayed on to become the first manager of Ord River Station.

Wild Dog is certainly El Questro's most historic land. Although it was released in 1888 it has the distinction of being the first lease to be taken up on the future Wilderness Park. In addition to its association with Ord River Station, this country has variously been linked to Dunham and Hillgrove Stations.

There is no indication of a lease over the Wild Dog area on the next of a series of Public Plans, however Plan No.3 covering the period 1894 to 1901 shows a modified holding in the name of **P.M. Durack**.

Eight of the 21 cousins from two branches of the Durack family were involved in the Kimberley. With a prevalence of Michaels, Jeremiahs, Marys,

Pats and Patricks amongst their Christian names, initials or nicknames were routinely used to avoid confusion. Despite this and the fact there were two family members with the name 'P.M. Durack', I am uncertain which Durack is next represented on the Wild Dog lease and the neighbouring Dunham River country. Given that both P.M.s – Black Pat and young Patsy Durack – add colour to the East Kimberley story, a brief profile of both individuals follows.

Patrick Mantinea 'Black Pat' Durack was raised in country New South Wales and went on to manage Mooraberrie Station on the Diamantina with two of his brothers. It was here in Western Queensland they gained a good reputation as bushmen and drovers. The experience acquired was to prove invaluable later, when in 1883 Black Pat and his cousin Long Michael left the Durack family property,Thylungra in Queensland, with 2250 cattle. They were in charge of one of the four family droving plants bound for the Kimberley. Almost two years later they were at the Roper River with the cattle and only three or four months out from their destination when Black Pat left the group and diverted to Darwin to purchase the provisions required by the cattlemen on their arrival at the Ord River. The supplies were then shipped to the Cambridge Gulf where Pat established a commercial supply depot at View Hill. He later moved the store to the new town of Wyndham when it was gazetted. Later again he took up a small holding on a bend of the Ord River between Ivanhoe and Wyndham. Known as Mantinea – Pat's second name – the property had only a simple shack on it.

Black Pat was in his late forties when he married Susan Downes in Melbourne in 1900. His wife, half his age, was a lively girl, unlike her retiring husband. The couple settled at Mantinea where Susie coped as best she could with the isolation and primitive conditions. Life was tough for women in that remote area and with Pat away mustering and droving for weeks Susie was unable to handle being left on her own at the lonely shack. This prompted Pat to sell his Kimberley property. The couple left the Kimberley in 1901 and took up land in the wheat belt area near Geraldton in the south of the state. At his funeral in 1933, Black Pat was described as a very quiet man with an unobtrusive nature, who believed that actions spoke louder than words.

It is more likely the leaseholder was young **Patsy M. Durack** whose father Jeremiah Durack was known throughout the extensive Durack family as 'Galway Jerry'. He too had been a member of the overland droving team of 1883–85, moving cattle from Queensland to the recently acquired Durack properties in the East Kimberley. Here, in partnership with Tom Kilfoyle and Tom Hayes, Galway Jerry took up and named Rosewood Station on the Behn River, a tributary of the Ord. In addition to Rosewood, Jeremiah took up land around the Dunham River in 1894. At least eight of these leases were in the name of his eldest son Patrick – known as Patsy – aged 12 at the time.

Patsy (P.M.) was barely a teenager when in 1896 the Rosewood partnership dissolved and Galway Jerry moved the family into a mudbrick homestead on Dunham Station approximately 80 miles from Wyndham and only a short distance from Wild Dog. By this time, with only two years of formal education, young Patsy was already acknowledged as an accomplished stockman. The Dunham country was described by his cousin, M.P. Durack, as a 'lonely outpost on the Dunham River, very patchy and cut off – suitable only as an outstation'.

Cousin M.P. was to recount the tragic events that took place at Dunham Station in February 1901 when Patsy, asleep on the homestead verandah, was shot above his left eye and his father killed by a bullet through his head. With a shirt wrapped around his head, 19-year-old Patsy managed to catch a horse and, riding bareback, he covered some 70 miles to Ascot Station where he met up with MP and a party of others. Together they returned to Dunham Station where, after holding an inquest into his death, they buried Galway Jerry. The verdict of their inquest: 'wilful murder at hands of some person or persons unknown'.

A police party from Wyndham followed the tracks of the station natives who had fled after the shooting and took two of them into custody. Fifteen-year-old Banjo was accused of Galway Jerry's murder and Roger, aged 12, was charged with wounding Patsy. Banjo had been a close companion to Patsy and for two years he had been trusted to carry a Winchester rifle. Since it was unlikely the accused would receive a fair hearing in the Kimberley, the ensuing trial was held in Perth where, despite evidence from a native witness to the contrary, both the accused were found not guilty.

The trial over, young Patsy, now the family breadwinner, returned to the Dunham with his widowed mother, his only sister and three young brothers. Patsy's uncle writes of him: 'fortunately he is a wiry, intelligent boy, a good stockman and a devoted son'. By this time the Durack name was gone from the Wild Dog land and Patsy had entered into several partnerships around the Dunham area.

Times were difficult for the pastoralists in the Territory and the Kimberley. Not only were they faced with a limited market for their cattle, but the threat of cattle-tick, *Ixodes bovis,* found amongst some Territory cattle, became a political issue and led to the imposition of quarantine regulations. With no plans for a northern meatworks at that time, live cattle were shipped from the Kimberley to Fremantle. However this was scarcely viable as the cost and animal losses incurred rendered this trade uncompetitive with the southern producers. Overlanding the cattle to the eastern states was an option that was resorted to from time to time. Dunham Station was to struggle on under Patsy, but like many other stations, it failed to make a profit.

With little reason for optimism, Connor, Doherty and Durack were seriously considering an opportunity to sell their properties to Bovril Australian Estates Ltd, when the prospect of developing a market in the Philippines looked like becoming a reality. This prompted C, D & D. to reverse their decision and, instead of selling, they elected to increase their holdings in the Kimberley. In 1910 Patsy and his mother agreed to sell their stock and 307,000-acre Dunham Station to Connor, Doherty and Durack, leaving Patsy to stay on as manager. In 1924 Patsy moved to Argyle, where he remained as manager until his death in 1933.

Concurrent with the P.M. Durack name on Wild Dog we find **Charles Nelson** and **John Mangus Johnson** on the neighbouring 36,000 acre Mount Rob lease on the east side of the King River. El Questro's link with these men dates from 1 December 1897, when the lease for Mount Rob was approved in their names.

The two men known as 'The Danes' arrived in Wyndham on the barque *Edith May* in 1886 and headed directly for the goldfields. They later held the licence for the Six Mile Hotel. Elsewhere Johnson has been described as a drover. In the early 1990s, prior to becoming the first leaseholders on Mount Rob, the partners had taken up two leases, one to the east and the other further north in Parrys Creek Nature Reserve. This adjoining country, totalling 84,000 acres, was called Hillgrove Station. It is also mentioned as 'Dead Horse' station, probably after the creek of this name flowing through it.

In October 1898 a government inspector reporting on the outbreak of pleuro in the area – a contagious disease affecting the lungs of cattle – recorded some 700 bullocks on their run at Hillgrove. With an average mortality rate of around 50 per cent, this infestation was a serious but short lived setback to the pastoralists in the area. Hillgrove is reputed to have been stocked with cattle by Johnson and Nelson throughout the early 1900s.

It appears the partnership of Nelson and Johnson opportunistically took up adjoining land on both sides of the King River. By 1898 their names had replaced P.M. Durack on Wild Dog and by the time of Johnson's death in 1907 the Mount Cockburn lease was held in their name as well. The partners were inconsistent in paying their annual fees throughout their tenure and the property went to auction on 2 October 1899, but it remained unsold.

Monument to John Johnson on Wild Dog.

According to Yvonne and Kevin Coate's book *More Lonely Graves of Western Australia,* John Mangus Johnson died on 25 May 1907 and was buried on Hillgrove Station, witnessed by H. McKinnon, with Charles Nelson and Joseph Wills also present. Johnson was born in Norway and on arrival in Australia spent six years in Victoria, New South Wales and Queensland. He lived in Western Australia for 21 years and married Lily Gardner in Wyndham when he was 35. Johnson is described as a pastoralist who died at his station of natural causes and 'break up of the constitution' aged 48.

Johnson's friends had a cast iron monument and fence made for him in Adelaide. It was transported by rail to the end of the line at Oodnadatta and overland to the Kimberley by camel, where it was erected some two years after his death. Today the monument may be found in the Wild Dog area under a large boab tree that grows amongst the *Petalostigma pubescens,* trees with their bitter quinine-flavoured berries, found in profusion a short distance from the Rock of Gibraltar.

Following the deaths of Johnson and his partner Nelson, about whom little further is known, the Mount Rob holding was to remain vacant for some years. Meanwhile in 1915, the leases of Wild Dog and Mount Cockburn were registered to the partnership of **Connor, Doherty and Durack.**

In 1897 brothers **Michael 'MP'**, **John 'JW'** and **Patrick 'PB' Durack** had joined forces with enterprising fellow Irishmen **Francis Connor** and **Denis Doherty** and formed the company **Connor, Doherty and Durack** (C, D & D) as a cattle and mercantile business. At its height, the estate of Connor, Doherty and Durack totalled almost seven and a half million acres on both sides of the border between Western Australian and Northern Territory, and one-half of the Kimberley cattle belonged to them. The area to the south and east of future El Questro Station was dominated by C, D & D or other Durack family members.

Connor and Doherty had come to the Kimberley from Sydney following the discovery of gold. As partners they established a very successful storekeeping and cattle trading business in Wyndham in 1886, opportunistically selling beef and merchandise to the diggers. They also leased a small selection approximately 20 kilometres from Wyndham where they planned to breed horses as remounts for the Indian Army. This property was called Ascot and, despite the pretentious name, the holding was unfenced and the horses – quick to take advantage of this – sealed the fate of the venture. This selection was later used as a holding ground for C, D & D's cattle, prior to the animals being shipped from Wyndham.

Undaunted by their lack of cattle or stock management experience, Connor and Doherty went on to acquire two pastoral leases near the border in the Northern Territory. These properties, named Newry and Auvergne, adjoined Argyle and Ivanhoe stations held by the Durack brothers.

Following the granting of Responsible Government to Western Australia in 1890, Francis Connor was the second member to represent the East Kimberley district in the state parliament. It was a seat he held in the Legislative Assembly from 1893 to 1904. After the amalgamation of the two Kimberley districts in 1904, he was again elected to the Legislative Assembly, this time unopposed.

The two partners set up coastal shipping trade between Wyndham and Fremantle in 1894 and within two years they had three steamers chartered to carry Kimberley cattle to the southern markets. These ships were capable of carrying around 800 beasts. In 1896 some 8,000 cattle sourced from Durack and other East Kimberley stations are reported to have been shipped to Fremantle. In 1896 Doherty moved to Perth where he established operating headquarters closer to the commercial centre of the colony. From here he conducted an auctioneering, mercantile and shipping business. Connor and Doherty also had cattle and mining interests in the East Kimberley. In 1897 Doherty was elected to the West Australian Legislative Assembly as the Member for North Fremantle.

After the establishment of their partnership with the Duracks in 1897, Connor joined Doherty down south where he concentrated on the land and shipping agency. Back in the Kimberley, MP Durack was appointed general manager of the four stations and was given control of the movement of the cattle. PB was in charge of the stock on the stations and JW managed the mercantile businesses in Wyndham. There was a heavy focus on securing the cattle required to meet the orders for their markets. The firm experienced strenuous competition from their former friends Alexander Forrest and Solomon Emanuel who had formed a similar business partnership in the West Kimberley. This influential alliance, trading as Forrest, Emanuel & Co., had similar objectives and although most of their commercial attention was in the west they were not averse to competing with C, D & D in sourcing cattle from the estimated 58,000 cattle on the East Kimberley stations.

Alexander Forrest also was a member of the state government and represented his electorate in the west from 1890 to 1900. Years later, the rival groups were to come together to lobby the government in support of a freezing works at Wyndham.

Trade with the Philippines commenced in 1914 with C, D & D directing cattle to both Manila and Fremantle. The declaration of the Great War in the same year was the catalyst in the government firming plans for the construction of the meatworks in Wyndham and building commenced in a faltering manner in 1915. This was the year that Francis Connor resigned from C, D & D. The following year the cattle trade with Manila ended, having operated under considerable duress for two years.

MP Durack was encouraged to represent the people of the Kimberley in the 1917 state election and was overwhelmingly voted onto the Legislative Assembly. Durack's political career commenced during the Great War when more men were required in the front line to replace the enormous losses suffered in the conflict. Australia and South Africa were the only participating countries not to have introduced conscription, and this contentious issue dominated the nation as Prime Minister Billy Hughes called for Australians to vote for a second time in a referendum on this emotive subject. The move was once again narrowly opposed.

During C, D & D's tenure on the Wild Dog and Mount Cockburn leases, the future of the meatworks at Wyndham became uncertain under a private developer and, after much argy-bargy, responsibility for the completion of the long-awaited enterprise was passed over to the Public Works Department and the meatworks eventually opened in May 1919. In 1921 the two leases, together with a large holding on the Dunham River, were transferred from Connor, Doherty & Durack Ltd to J.E. Davidson.

During their frequent voyages between Perth and Wyndham, the Durack family made the aquaintance of **James Ebenezer Davidson**. After leaving school Jim had joined the Adelaide Steamship Company and met the Duracks while working as a purser on one of their coastal ships. His intelligence and notable business acumen led to his joining Connor, Doherty and Durack as company accountant and bookkeeper. His agreeable nature and amusing company also attracted the attention of Mary Durack. The couple married in 1900 and settled in Fremantle where C, D & D had its head office. In addition to working in the office, Jim was required to travel to the Kimberley and to Kalgoorlie where the company had a butchery business.

In 1905 Davidson, his wife and three children moved to Wyndham where C, D & D owned an hotel, a store and a butcher shop. These enterprises were in addition to their various cattle stations and the three chartered vessels carrying approximately 20,000 bullocks to their markets each season.

Little more is known of Davidson and his family; however it is interesting to find that some years later their second son, Douglas, was to have a foothold on this same country. In the interim, in 1923 the Wild Dog and Mount Cockburn leases were combined into one 75,000-acre holding, and in 1925 this land was registered in the name of **Edmund Harold Brennan**, a known 'small holder' of the area persistently involved in cattle duffing. The *Sunday Times Perth* in March 1924 described him as 'a station owner of East Kimberley'; apart from this, nothing more is known of Brennan.

The lease was shown as vacant in 1927, bringing us to **Oswald Threkheld Siddons** who took up the Wild Dog–Mount Cockburn lease together with El Questro's 'North Country' land about this time. Like many other pastoralists of the era, Siddons had a scattering of leases across the East Kimberley. In the early 1920s the joint names of O.T. and J.C. Siddons were registered to two external holdings. These amounted to 250,000 acres on the headwaters of the Durack and Wood Rivers, well beyond El Questro's western boundary. Both of these leases were released in 1929 and the country became part of Karunjie Station. 'Threk', as he was known to his friends, also had acreage to the north of Mount Rob and at Nulla Nulla on the lower Durack River. We will learn more of him shortly when reviewing the leaseholders of the North Country area.

The next name on the combined Wild Dog–Mount Cockburn holding was **Philip Collier**. Like Siddons before him, Collier had leases beyond El Questro's future boundaries. These involved several leases totalling 161,609 acres on the Dunham River and it appears that he took over the Nulla Nulla lease from Siddons, who had possibly been in partnership with Overheu there; Collier also was involved on the North Country and we will profile both men later.

The El Questro story took a new direction late in the 1930s when Wild Dog, Mount Cockburn and the North Country were excised from pastoral use classification and designated as **Aboriginal Reserve**. This was an outcome of the Aborigines Act of 1905. Amongst the provisions of the Act was the government's introduction of permits for employers of Aboriginal labour and the establishment of native reserves, setting aside tracts of land across the state for the use and benefit of the Aborigines.

By the end of the 1920s an expanding program of Aboriginal protection and segregation saw a total of 23 million acres under reservation.

In dealing with the North West, the government's policy was largely formulated with pastoral land in mind together with the need to protect the white man's stock. Experience showed the established method of regular mass arrests and imprisonment was not only expensive but was ineffective in deterring the Aborigines from spearing sheep and cattle. To counter this, Aboriginal pastoral stations were set up as government funded feeding depots in anticipation this would reduce the Aborigines' need to take livestock. Accordingly, in 1910, three adjoining pastoral stations were purchased in the Halls Creek area, creating Moola Bulla, a million-acre station run by the

Department of Aborigines and Fisheries. The government hoped Moola Bulla would eventually become a self-supporting institution, training Aborigines in farming methods and educating them in general. For many years the station was home to the largest congregation of Aborigines in the state.

Other reserves were created with the rationale of preserving Aboriginal culture through isolation. A year later the gazetting of the four-million-acre Marndoc Reserve near the Cambridge Gulf exemplified this attitude.

Regrettably, the establishment of feeding depots and reserves for the protection of Aboriginal people was poorly coordinated and consequently tension between the Aborigines and pastoralists over cattle killing persisted, eventually becoming a factor in the Marndoc Reserve massacre of 1926.

Reserve Number 21422, covering some 214,550 acres on both sides of the King River, was created in 1935. This included El Questro's Wild Dog, Mount Cockburn and North Country leases – totalling 138,000 acres. The Reserve was designated Category 1, meaning the land was reserved for the purpose of Aboriginal occupancy and use. This classification was to remain in place until 1956. It was cancelled following a decree in 1948 that reserves 'not being used in the manner originally intended, would be returned to the Crown'.

Mount Rob was not included as part of the Reserve and prior to taking up this lease in 1925, **George James Williams** held a smaller lease on Violet Valley. It was here that he became known as The Mountain Devil because he lived in the hills and pockets of the Osmond Valley in partnership with the brothers Malley and King Gordon.

The Mount Rob holding was known as 'Cockitup' Williams's block; unfortunately there is no record of the origin of this name, which would undoubtedly be an entertaining story. The *Gazette* indicates the lease was cancelled August 1930 and Williams secured the land again in May 1931. Records indicate that 38 cattle were sent to the Wyndham Meatworks from this area in 1938. In the same year, on 12 September the lease underwent a complex transfer process: first from Williams to William Stuart Gordon and then to Doug Davidson.

Douglas Joseph Durack Davidson – the nephew of M.P. Durack – took over the management of the Connor, Doherty & Durack Agency in Wyndham from his father in 1927. He also held the position of postmaster and was the secretary of the East Kimberley Roads Board. In 1936 or a year earlier, he paid £8,000 for all of the Dunham Station properties to the south of and adjoining the Wild Dog country – some 30 years earlier many of these holdings had belonged to Patsy Durack. The station was managed by George Millard until Davidson had a new homestead built and moved into it with his wife, he is recorded as living at Dunham Station in 1956. On the day the Mount Rob land was transferred from Williams via Gordon to Doug Davidson – Davidson immediately transferred it to H.M. King George VI in order to negotiate a new lease for an extended term. It appears that Davidson was an astute businessman, for in 1964 he sold Dunham Station for £90,000 to the Chase Syndicate. This was an American syndicate with Alan Chase and Art Linkletter as principals. Their investments included the disastrous Humpty Doo rice project in the Northern Territory. There were several factors contributing to the failure of this venture, including insufficient drainage, soil that was too saline and an invasion of geese. Some years later Chase and Linkletter successfully established a scheme that opened up vast tracts of agricultural country around Esperance in the south of Western Australia. It is unclear when Davidson released the Mount Rob lease, he possibly kept it until he sold Dunham Station in 1964.

The North Country.

The North Country

The most northerly section of El Questro lies between the King and Pentecost Rivers to the north of the Cockburn Range. This 63,000-acre lease extends north to latitude S15°30′ on the West Arm of the Cambridge Gulf.

Much of the area, being part of the geographic Cambridge Gulf lowlands is inundated by salt water during king tides creating extensive and barren mud flats.

The first lease to be taken up on the North Country was in the name of **Charles Nunn Kidman**. Born in South Australia in 1858, Charles Kidman was the youngest of six boys. Somewhat overshadowed by his older brother (Sir) Sidney Kidman, who came to be recognised as the 'cattle baron' of Australia, it has been difficult to uncover a great deal of information about Charles individually.

The Kidman empire grew from modest beginnings in South Australia with brothers George, Fred, Sackville and Sidney buying, droving and onselling horses, cattle and sheep. They soon took over and expanded mail delivery contracts and coach transport throughout the country. In the 1880s the rapid development of Broken Hill Mining Company brought an influx of people to the mineral field and the Kidman enterprise was well placed to meet their need for transport and meat. Under the direction of Sackville, the Messrs Kidman Bros had large interests in big station properties in South Australia, New South Wales and Queensland where, in addition to sheep and cattle, they bred horses for shipment to India. By the 1890s they had established a chain of stations extending from Northern Queensland, the Gulf of Carpentaria and the Fitzroy River in the Kimberley to South Australia and thence to the lucrative markets in Adelaide and Broken Hill.

Young Charlie joined his brothers in their butchering business at Broken Hill in 1891 and following the discovery of gold in Western Australia the Kidmans moved quickly to provide transport and meat to the goldfields there. Charlie travelled to the West to oversee these activities and establish butcher shops at Boulder, Kalgoorlie and Coolgardie.

Buoyed by his financial success, Charlie ventured into the high life where he enjoyed gambling and a horseracing partnership. He returned to South Australia in 1896 and took up a lease of 5,760 acres in his own name in Wilcannia.

Following the death of Sackville in 1899, Charlie with his extravagant lifestyle was treated warily by his brother Sid who took over the reins of the family enterprise. By the 20th Century, the S. Kidman & Co. Ltd name was scattered throughout the Kimberley where it was at different times associated with Glenroy, Mount House, Yeeda, Fossil Downs and Lissadel Stations.

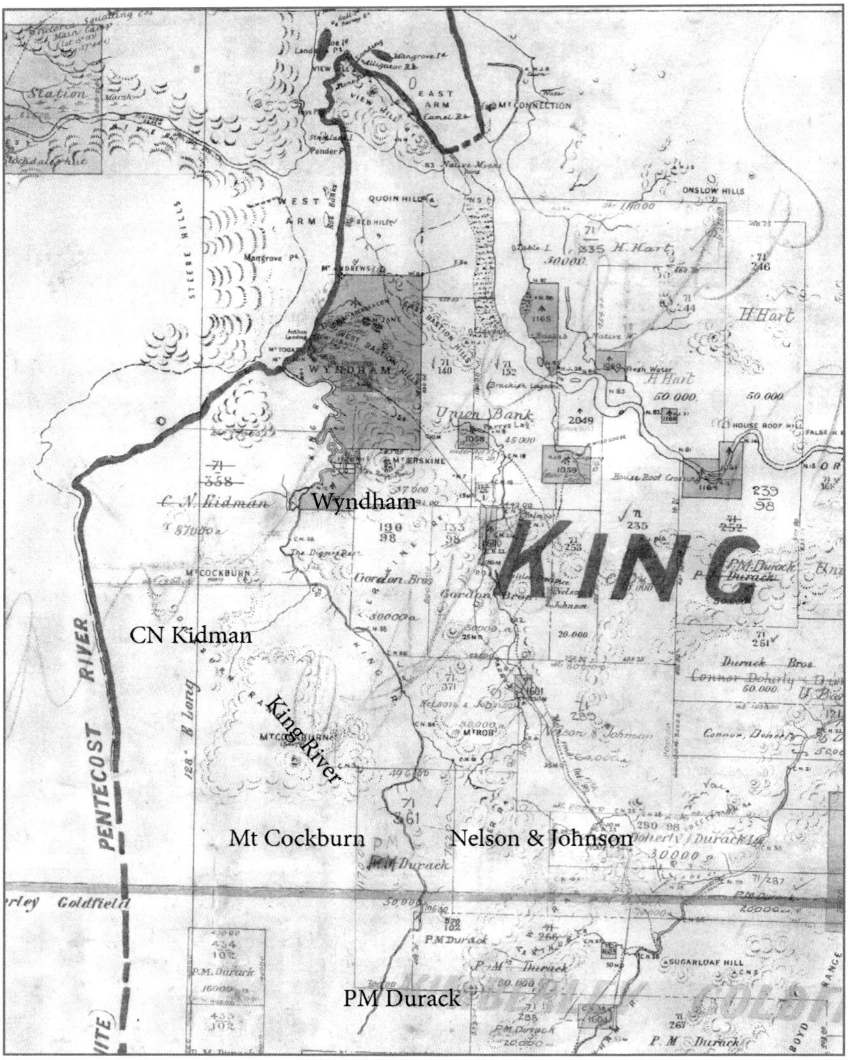

Public Plan Circa 1894 showing the Kidman, Nelson & Johnson and PM Durack leases.

It seems that Charlie also had property in his own name in the Kimberley as some time after 1894, he took up an 87,000-acre lease incorporating the grasslands and mud flats of El Questro's North Country. His lease extended to The Diggers Rest on the King River and beyond to the Erskine Range.

Some years later the government was to gazette a stockroute through this country, giving drovers and their travelling cattle access to Wyndham from stations on the high country to the west. Kidman's tenure would have been concurrent with P.M. Durack at Wild Dog.

There is little known of Charles thereafter except for an interesting headline in *The Advertiser* in Adelaide in 1935. Given the family's background with cattle it is ironic to read: 'Cruelty to Cow' and an account of C.N. Kidman being charged with ill-treating a cow. The Society for the Prevention of Cruelty to Animals claimed that Kidman had turned a cow out of his paddock without providing it with food and water. The cow was reported to have a fractured hip and to be in poor condition. Apparently there was a dispute over the ownership of the cow and when asked by Constable Duthie why he turned the cow out, Kidman replied that he was not going to buy chaff for another man's cow. He was fined £3 with £3 costs. Records show that Kidman died as a result of a shooting accident near his birthplace at Naracoorte in South Australia. He was aged 48.

Following the death of Sir Sidney in 1935, the company S. Kidman & Co remained intact, and is today run by his descendants. Currently the family company has 17 pastoral leases located in the Northern Territory and across three states. The properties cover approximately 110,000 square kilometres.

Shortly before 1920, the lease over the North Country was approved in the name of **Leonard R. Overheu**. Earlier, a 54,000-acre lease incorporating The Diggers Rest on the King River had been taken up by A.G.K. Hunter. On its return to the Crown, 27,000 acres were set aside by the government as a water reserve to meet the future requirements of the planned meatworks. The balance of the holding was returned to the North Country.

Leonard Overheu also leased 200,000 acres on the western bank of the Pentecost River in partnership with Frederick Hay. The partners were returned World War I servicemen who in 1921 applied for a grant of land in the Kimberley under the War Service Land Settlement Scheme.

With some 40,000,000 acres of country already under lease in the region, the government was pressed to find land to accommodate the requirements of the Scheme. Their acreage was excised from the extensive Marndoc Aboriginal Reserve on the Forrest River and subsequently gave birth to

Nulla Nulla Station across the river from Overheu's North Country lease and south of the Aboriginal Mission established on the Durack River. Many of the traditional owners from the reserve were removed and forced to live on the outskirts of Wyndham.

Hay and his friend James Dunnett ran Nulla Nulla Station and in 1923, with encouragement from the government, the two men planted cotton and peanuts and also kept a small herd of cattle. Unfortunately, their agricultural initiative failed and the fledgling cotton industry was abandoned in Western Australia. During this time Overheu worked in Wyndham as a bookkeeper providing cash flow to the business.

Although subsequent events did not take place on El Questro country, the name of Overheu remains associated with one of Australia's most notorious and controversial massacres of Aboriginal people. Details of the Forrest River or Oombulgurri Massacres are too long and convoluted to be included here at any length. Dozens of compelling entries relating to this appalling event may be found on the internet and conflicting accounts have been recorded in books and documentary films. Briefly, Reverend Ernest Gribble recorded in his Forrest River Mission diary reports of Hay attacking and harming Aborigines. Later the Reverend was obliged to assign guards to prevent Hay from molesting the women whenever he visited the Mission. Issues with the Aborigines continued: Overheu complained of station cattle being speared and the Aborigines reported cases of wilful injury and the abduction and rape of their people. The conflicts persisted until Sergeant Buckland eventually refused to renew Nulla Nulla Station's permit to employ Aborigines.

On 23 May 1926 Hay was speared while riding the station boundary. In a memoir, the Reverend Gribble gives the following account of his murder: Lumbia, an Aboriginal man, and his two child-wives were resting at a billabong north of Nulla Nulla when Hay rode up and demanded sex with one of the wives. Hay stripped to his boots and raped her in front of Lumbia and indicated he intended to take her back to the Nulla Nulla homestead with him. Lumbia objected and Hay attacked him with his stockwhip and then broke his spears. Still naked, Hay grabbed his clothes and mounted his horse, but Lumbia stabbed him in the back with a broken spear. At a preliminary hearing at the Dorriman Creek Court, the two girls confirmed Lumbia's story and claimed that Hay had also shot at Lumbia during the argument.

The death of Fred Hay sparked a series of European atrocities. A police patrol of 14 men including Overheu left Wyndham at the beginning of June. All were armed with .44 Winchester rifles, some with side-arms and a total of 850 rounds of ammunition. A later investigation revealed there were at least three massacre sites involving killings and deliberate attempts to conceal the evidence. Seven empty ammunition boxes were found at one of the police camps.

No-one in the white community wanted it known that Hay had raped a child and the prosecutor presented the situation to the court as a settler murdered while protecting his stock from a cattle killer. Details of some of the occurrences filtered through to an outraged public down south, and on the recommendation of the Police Commissioner, George T. Wood was appointed to head a government inquiry into the events. During an evidence-gathering mission and as part of a Royal Commission, many witnesses retracted statements, refused to testify or simply disappeared. Several key Aboriginal witnesses to the killings 'went missing' or 'escaped' from custody at Wyndham before they could give evidence to the Commission. None of the Aborigines named to the Commission, who had witnessed the massacres or who had relatives killed, were called to testify. As a result Gribble was the only witness for the massacres. Material also came to light revealing Overheu's hatred of Aborigines and details of his vindictive sentiments expressed in a letter to his father before he joined the search for his partner's killer became public knowledge. A witness stated that it was Overheu who continually urged the police to kill the prisoners they had taken. The number of deaths will never be known.

Commissioner Wood submitted his report on 21 May 1927, concluding that the police patrol killed 11 Aborigines at three sites and reported there was a conspiracy of silence in the Kimberley. In the same year, Forrest River Aborigines specified that the massacres had taken place at five different sites. Lumbia, having confessed to the spearing of Hay, was tried and found guilty. After it was successfully argued that Hay had provoked the attack, the initial death sentence imposed on him was commuted to life imprisonment. The case attracted widespread international attention and because of the Mission's involvement it was followed in England by the Archbishop of Canterbury. The committal hearing that followed Wood's report found that no evidence of any murders could be established beyond reasonable doubt and that much of the case was built by Gribble on unfounded Aboriginal rumours. Following the closure of the case, pressure continued to be brought to bear on Gribble and questions were asked about his mental stability and he was eventually dismissed from the Mission.

In recent years historians and writers have put forward compelling arguments for and against the existence of a massacre at Forrest River. Regardless of where the truth lies, there is no doubting that the names of Overheu and the police constables, St Jack and Regan, remain inextricably linked to claims of one of the last great massacres of black Australians.

It appears that Overheu did not hold his North Country land for long and 'Sid', **Oswald Threkeld Siddons**, took up the lease in 1927 or possibly prior to 1924. Siddons was a former Lighthorseman and it seems he was also a fortune-hunter in search of pastoral land. The *Brisbane Courier* reports in June 1921 an exploring expedition setting out from Derby in the North West, led by W.R. Easton. After experiencing difficulty in crossing swollen rivers and precipitous ranges, their camp was burnt by hostile Aborigines. The fire destroyed their clothes, blankets, boots, saddles and ammunition and Siddons received severe wounds from exploding cartridges. Short of food and clothing, the party managed to reach Port George mission station where they replenished supplies and continued on to Swift Bay, having seen some good country on their travels.

In the same year, Siddons turned his attention to the East Kimberley and took up Bindoola Station located along Bindoola Creek on the western side of the Pentecost River. The station had a common boundary with Nulla Nulla to the north.

Over the years the Reverend Gribble at Forrest River Mission made a series of accusations against pastoralists and the police in the North West, claiming neglect of duty, grievous bodily harm, sexual exploitation and murder. These attacks eventually culminated in his accusations of the mass killings in the Forrest River Reserve in 1926. During Siddons' time on Bindoola, the Reverend Gribble accused him of murdering an Aborigine named Nunjune at the Mission. Gribble claimed a report had been brought to the Mission that Siddons had shot Nunjune. The story continued, claiming the Reverend held a meeting attended by 200 Aborigines including Nunjune's wife. Apparently they were adamant that a murder had been committed. Constable Regan was called to conduct an investigation into the claim, but some time later Nunjune turned up alive and well after having 'bin longtime walkabout'. Constable Regan's findings were reported up the line to Sergeant Buckland in Wyndham who wrote: 'I may state that I know Siddons personally and considering the interests he has in the district I do not think he would risk the consequences of shooting a native unless under great provocation, then from what I know of him, I think he would report the matter himself.'

Siddons later sold Bindoola Station to Harold McNamara and the lease is today known as Home Valley Station.

Concurrent with the 63,000-acre North Country lease, Siddons held a second lease on the eastern side of the King River, which incorporated part of the Erskine Range and extended eastward to Parry's Lagoon. Although it was never part of El Questro, this 76,000-acre lease shared its southern boundary with Doug Williams's Mount Rob country.

Siddons is also reputed to have entered into a partnership with Leopold Overheu on the adjacent Nulla Nulla Station south of the Forrest River. Presumably this would have been some time after the death of Frederick Hay. This assertion is supported by an article he wrote for the *Sydney Morning Herald* in 1929. The article gives details of his participation in the search for Charles Kingsford Smith following the failure of his aircraft *Southern Cross* to arrive at Wyndham. Siddons describes himself as 'a bushman of Nulla Nulla Station'.

Channel country in the north.

In another article in relation to the *Southern Cross* incident, Mr J.W. Durack is quoted in the press as saying 'there probably was no man better than Siddons, whose Wanduria Station was some miles east of Wyndham, to be taken as an observer and guide for pilot Woods in the aerial search. He was an excellent bushman and had traversed most of the country in the north of Australia.'

From 1930 **Sir James Mitchell** is shown as the leaseholder on the North Country. Born in 1866 near Bunbury in Western Australia, James Mitchell had a rural upbringing and having started work as a banker, he soon became a manager at Northam where he was very supportive of enterprising farmers. In 1892 he engaged in farming and was soon to gain a good reputation locally. Mitchell was a keen horseman and was alleged to have the best collection of hacks in Western Australia. He was a member of the Nationalist Party and stood as a candidate for Northam in the 1905 state election, when he won a seat in the Legislative Assembly. This was the beginning of a lengthy political and public life.

In his biographic notes, C.G. Bolton describes Mitchell as:

> 'Handsome in the heavy-moustached style of his day, though already somewhat portly, Mitchell was a presentable and popular figure, soon marked out for advancement. No great public speaker, he earnestly advocated agricultural settlement and deplored Western Australia's dependence on imported produce, seeking to place families on the land, particularly as the goldfields declined and miners looked elsewhere.'

It was James Mitchell who, in his capacity as Minister for Agriculture, promised sufficient Government funding for positive planning for the erection of the freezing works in Wyndham. In 1919 he became Western Australia's thirteenth Premier. Mitchell also held the position of Colonial Treasurer and Minister for Lands and Repatriation. A Ministry for the North West was created during Mitchell's first term as Premier and following the opening of the meatworks at Wyndham, a resident Commissioner for the North West was appointed in 1921 with a view to encouraging cotton growing and other tropical agriculture. Unfortunately, none of these initiatives prospered at that time.

Mitchell was defeated by the Labor Party at the 1924 state election, but was returned again in 1930 and remained as Premier for three years. Ousted again by the Labor Party during the height of the Great Depression, he then moved to Government House and served for 15 years as the Lieutenant-Governor of Western Australia without salary, until in 1948 he became the first Australian-born Governor of Western Australia. Mitchell remains today as the only person to have served as both Premier and Governor. On his death in 1951 he was given a state funeral and later the Mitchell Freeway was named in his honour. A National Park and general park also carry his name. Today Sir James Mitchell remains amongst the best loved of Western Australia's father figures.

The next name registered against this lease in 1938 was also a state politician. It is ironic that Mitchell should have been followed onto the land by the same man who, over the years as both friend and rival, ousted him as Premier on two occasions.

Philip Collier MLA was born in Victoria in 1874 and commenced a mining career in the eastern states before moving to Boulder in Western Australia in 1904 where he worked with Perseverance Gold Mining Company. Collier was a strong supporter of the labour movement and joined the Labor Party. In 1905, in a natural political progression from his involvement with a number of labour councils and associations, he was elected to represent Boulder in the Legislative Assembly.

In 1911 he accepted the Mines and Railways portfolio in the Scaddan government. The issue of conscription in World War I divided the Labor Party, eventually leading to defeat of the government. Collier, who was strongly opposed to conscription, was elected to replace Scaddan as Leader of the Opposition in 1917. In 1924 he led the Party to victory over his friend Mitchell's Nationalist government and held the office of Premier for two terms, serving also as Treasurer and Minister for Forests and Industries. In its emphasis on rural development, the Ministry differed little from its predecessor. The wheat and dairy industries flourished and a migrant scheme was established which saw more than 4,000 British migrants assisted annually from 1925 to 1928.

After losing government in 1930, the Labor Party was returned in 1933 with Collier as Premier. A referendum held simultaneously with the election resulted in an overwhelming vote by the Western Australian electors in favour of secession from the Commonwealth of Australia. The Labor Party's opposition to the proposal contributed to the British Government's refusal to act upon the request.

Mitchell and Collier are credited with achieving an unusual degree of friendship and cooperation between parties during the 1920s and 1930s, which was most clearly demonstrated by Collier recommending Mitchell's appointment as Lieutenant-Governor.

Collier died at Mount Lawley in 1948 after almost 43 years of continuous parliamentary service which was recognised with a state funeral. Unfortunately nothing is known of his interest in pastoral activities in the Kimberley.

Following Collier's tenure, the North Country lease was integrated into the **Aboriginal Reserve 21422** and remained unavailable for pastoral use until the mid-1950s.

The Leases at Spurlings Pocket and Moonlight Valley

The Durack Range to the south of El Questro Station is the birthplace of the Pentecost River. Over millennia this river has incised its way through the range, creating a spectacular gorge system and depositing the resulting sediments in the open country beyond. In recent times this fertile country located along the Pentecost River was for decades known as Spurlings Pocket, 'pocket' being the term used for an area of flat land sheltered by hills or ranges. Enriched over time by the alluvial deposits from the Pentecost River in flood, the merits of the pocket with its constant supply of fresh river water made it eminently suitable for a homestead site. In 1963 a family residence was built and later the headquarters of the tourist operation was established at the same location.

Spurlings Pocket.

The first known lease associated with this country was in the name of **Favell & Co**. However, before setting his sights on this isolated area on the western side of the future El Questro Station, William Favell is known to have been managing Hillgrove Station for Charles Nelson and John Johnson. He appears to have led a colourful life as his name is liberally scattered throughout the police records in the Kimberley and he featured from time to time in the media in both the Territory and Western Australia. Drawing on newspapers from that time and research of police records by historian Dr Darrell Lewis, the following excerpts give a frustratingly brief glimpse into his character and activities:

3.11.1883	The Northern Territory Times & Gazette: William Favell at the Police Court in Port Darwin was fined 10 shillings and the cost of one witness, for creating a disturbance.

The same newspaper in 1887 mentions that Favell entered in 150-yard and 300-yard foot races at Adelaide River. (He would have been aged about 30 then).

11.11.1892	The Derby Police Station records a letter regarding Favell and others being horse thieves.
15.5.1899	W.E. Favell, Manager of Hillgrove Station, reports blacks robbing his place and threatening his life, etc.
26.5.1899	Wyndham. Police Constable Farley warns W. Favell to appear for prosecution of Aboriginal offender.
27.5.1899	Sergeant Evans to Sub Inspector Brophy: P.C. Farley reported that 9 year old Aboriginal girl Linda told his tracker that W. Favell tried to have 'connection' with her but failed – no witnesses, so her word against his – no action but took girl as witness in another case.
30.5.1899	Sergeant Evans to Commissioner of Police: In response to allegation by W. Favell that Evans had underage Aboriginal girl, Evans replied that it was a fabrication, that the girl was an orphan, that she complained that Favell tried to 'carnally know' her, and Evans had placed her with the Goaler's wife. He said Favell had been suspected of such behaviour before.

In fact the Wyndham police investigating an attack on an isolated hut in May 1898 had found the complainant named Favell had two captive females in his hut, one about nine years old. It appears that the alleged attack was an attempt by the women's family to rescue the girls.

7.12.1900	The Northern Territory Times & Gazette reports that Messrs W. Favell and A. Gardiner, two well known

> West Australian identities, left Port Darwin in the *S.S. Koonookarra* for Wyndham whither they are returning after a few months spell in Palmerston.

In June 1901 at the Wyndham Race Meeting, Favell's horse Hector ran second in the District Plate and again in the Wyndham Cup while carrying a 10 lb handicap. The horse was unplaced in the Bracelet with 11.8 lbs on board.

In November 1903, William Favell applied for 25,000 acres and in the following month was granted a 50,000-acre lease on Spurlings Pocket area in the name of Favell & Co. The annual rent was set at £25 and his land extended eastward from the Chamberlain River along the Pentecost River where the Station Centre is today. He called his land Limerick Park Station. Finding his name given to a creek and permanent waterhole near the then uncharted Salmond River, indicates the likelihood that his activities extended south along the Salmond River to this point on the eastern side of Mount Throssell. Records show the station was stocked in 1903 and 1904, signifying the owner had stock somewhere in the Kimberley district but not necessarily on the same land. Despite his brief tenure, Favell was to have yet another brush with the police when Constable Clements, during a patrol of Limerick Park Station in mid-1905, recorded 'arresting William Favell the part owner of Limerick Park Station on charge of horse stealing'.

1906 Limerick Park. Favell's engraved boab tree. Photograph by Tobie.

A year later Favell's case was reported in the *Sunday Times* giving an example of the regional attitude of established pastoralists towards their lesser neighbours. The headline read:

> 'The extraordinary case of W.E. Favell. Sentenced to 12 months – on the flimsiest of evidence – for a crime he never committed – appeal dismissed by the convicting Magistrate – startling allegations against the beak and police – how the small man is dealt with in the North.'

In a complex newspaper article we read about W.E. Favell aged 49, being committed in Wyndham to 12 months imprisonment for 'secreting horses'. The presiding magistrate refused to allow the accused to call evidence and informed him there would be no appeal against his sentence. Favell's account of how the Carlton Hill horses belonging to Forrest, Emanuel and Co. came to be on his property and details of the hearing followed. The intervention of a Perth barrister eventually assisted with the reduction of Favell's sentence to six months and the guilty man was to bring the irregularities of his plausible case to the attention of the *Sunday Times*. The following sympathetic comments by the newspaper give some idea of the perception of the justice system in the far north at that time: 'The case is abhorrent to all principles of justice: it is an indictment of the civilisation existing in the North, also: 'It may be only a coincidence that the victim was a small man, that he was charged with hiding horses belonging to a firm of cattle kings, but it is a coincidence worth noting in view of the current idea that the small pastoralist is not wanted in the Black North.'

With the possibility of imprisonment hanging over him, it appears that Favell gave up thoughts of continuing as a leaseholder and on 29 March 1906 the lease of Limerick Park was transferred to John Spurling and Joseph Wills and the area became known as Spurlings Pocket thereafter.

There is however one more police record of William Favell's activities on El Questro, but due to its brevity we are left wondering how the incident unfolded:

> Item 1908/5815. Derby. Journal of Constable Fanning, at Wyndham. Whilst searching King River for Aboriginal Native accidentally shot by W.Favell on 27.9.08.

Like Favell before them, **John Spurling** and **Joseph Wills**'s tenure was only for three years. Not a great deal is known about these partners. They purchased a town lot near Anthon Landing in Wyndham in joint names and in the second half of 1909 they allowed the lease at Spurlings Pocket to lapse and revert to vacant Crown Land. In the same year Spurling took up an area closer to Wyndham and worked as a stock inspector at Goose Hill, one of the last staging posts for Wyndham bound cattle. Nearby a store and hotel known as Three Ways catered to the drovers and other travellers. Spurling appears to have also become a horse dealer and between 1906 and 1909 his name frequently appeared on the shipping arrivals into Darwin. Horses were always in short supply on the stations and Victoria River Downs Station provided a ready market. Spurling is recorded as selling 80 horses to the station and later trading another 100 in 1909. The Australian Stock Horse is recognised throughout the world for its intelligence, stamina and courage and, as a result of these and other qualities, many were shipped to India in the 19th and 20th Centuries for military use. The horses also served with the Australian Lighthorse regiments in World War I.

The 1910 Western Australian Legislative Council Roll for the North Electoral Province records John Spurling as a civil servant and householder residing in Wyndham. Later in the year an amalgamated electoral roll for the Kimberley District listed him as a labourer and his partner, Joseph Wills, as a miner, also resident in Wyndham. Wills's attendance at the burial of John Johnson in 1907 is amongst the last of Joseph Wills's known activities. There is an interesting reference to John Spurling amongst the personal files held in the State Records Office. This relates to 'Aboriginal Matters', but public access to the file is restricted until 2026.

Joseph Wills of 20-Mile, Wyndham, died intestate five years later. The value of his estate was shown as £10/10/- when it was placed under the charge of the State Curator in March 1912.

Richard George Chartier Prior took up the 50,000-acre lease on Spurlings Pocket in 1925. Apart from his death in 1986, the only information relating to 'Chart' Prior is a Public notice in *The West Australian* in 1947. This advises the dissolution of his partnership with Charles Farquhar Fisher who was retiring from their Avon Trading Company. The notice describes Prior as an agent from Beverley.

Mention has been made of a man named **Jack Follock** having a paddock at Spurlings Pocket in 1929 however this reference remains unsubstantiated.

The ruins of the first known dwelling on El Questro can be found on high ground above the eastern side of the Salmond River. This was **Mohammed Sahanna**'s homestead on Moonlight Valley. Today this country containing the stone ruins and other archaeological material is part of neighbouring Kachana Station. For years, Sahanna lived here in isolation with a small herd of cattle. He was not an Australian citizen and was therefore unable to hold the station lease in his own name; instead it was held by Dick McKenna on Sahanna's behalf. Despite his affection for the animals, Sahanna walked some of them into the Wyndham Meatworks each year and topped the works for weight and grade. His route to Wyndham was out along Maitland Creek and then through Menmuirs Paddock. After crossing the Pentecost River he pushed his cattle between the North and South Cockburn Ranges where his name is immortalised at Sahanna's Jump-up. His body was found drowned at Koolamon Creek near the station some time prior to February 1944.

On 30 January 1940 **Frederick Edgar Bahr** took up 141,500 acres to the south of the Cockburn Range. The lease covered the country between Wild Dog and the confluence of the Chamberlain and Pentecost Rivers.

Although little is known of Bahr it should be remembered that throughout his tenure World War II was underway. In 1942–43 the Japanese dropped more bombs on Darwin than on Pearl Harbour. The enemy made several air raids on the Kimberley's coastal towns from Wyndham to Port Hedland and opportunistically attacked church missions and other targets. On 3 March 1942 the East Kimberley experienced the first of five air raids targetting Wyndham airfield and the meatworks, closing the latter. The meatworks remained closed for the duration of the conflict and all white women and children from Broome, Derby and Wyndham were sent south.

During one of these attacks the coastal vessel *M.V. Koolama* was sunk at the Wyndham jetty. Some two weeks earlier the ship had been attacked at sea close to the Kimberley's most northerly point and the passengers on the stricken vessel were put ashore. The ship's distress calls were heard at Kalumburu Mission 100 kilometres away and Father Sanz and four Aboriginal trackers eventually found the group. They accompanied the men back to the mission through rivers and inhospitable country while the women and the injured passengers were transported on the mission barge.

M.V. Koolama was built in Glasgow as a freighter and passenger ship for the State Shipping Service of Western Australia. She had served the northern coastal towns well during her previous 47 voyages. *Koolama* was a diesel engine vessel specifically designed to handle the 11-metre tidal variance in the state's northern waters and had a reinforced keel enabling her to rest on the bottom at low tide. The 4,133-tonne ship carried 90 crew members and provided luxurious accommodation for up to 200 passengers. She had a freezer hold for perishable cargo and capacity for 500 live cattle in the other holds.

Ten days after the first Japanese attack the damaged ship limped into Wyndham requiring constant pumping to keep her afloat. During the air raid on Wyndham the pumps were abandoned and after taking water *Koolama* keeled over and went to the bottom. Her sinking obstructed other large vessels from using the jetty and effectively closed the Port of Wyndham until the meatworks was reopened in 1946.

Food and clothes were rationed, identity cards and permits to travel were required by station people and the few remaining residents had to travel more than 1,000 kilometres over rough tracks to Broome for supplies. As a security precaution pedal transmitters on stations were initially banned and later restricted to use on a short wave length only. Station personnel were censored from mentioning weather and road conditions, military activity or any movement of supplies. Horses and mules were commandeered for the army. It was during this period that many remote airfields were constructed throughout the region in defence of our northern shores.

During Bahr's tenure D.J.D. Davidson held the lease on Mount Rob and had extensive acreage to the south and along the Dunham River. The North Country, Mount Cockburn and Wild Dog leases were still designated as Aboriginal Land. Bahr's tenure on Spurlings Pocket was cancelled in October 1945.

In 1948 **Lancelot Henri Hughes** took up the Spurlings Pocket holding stretching west to the Chamberlain River from Wild Dog which was still held as Aboriginal Reserve. There was an adjustment to this lease in 1954 when 6,651 acres were removed to provide for government exclusions in Spurlings Pocket. Hughes held this lease on the future El Questro country until January 1955. Farther afield Hughes's name features on a large 740,600-acre lease some 100 kilometres to the west of Spurlings Pocket. Much of this holding located between the Gibb and Durack Rivers, is known today as Ellenbrae Station.

Finding the name **P.J.S. Plant** on a 75,000-acre lease on the Salmond River, adds weight to Jack Plant being a name associated with El Questro. Plant was the policeman and butcher in Wyndham and in 1956–57, using his short wheelbase Blitz and tripod, he accessed his block on the south side of Mount Throssell to kill and butcher cattle. He would have been the last leaseholder on Moonlight Valley before Torrance MacMicking's tenure.

El Questro Station

Charles Torrance MacMicking 1958–1966

Charles Torrance MacMicking was born at Mount Magnet in the Murchison area of Western Australia in 1928. Thirty years later Torrance was to name El Questro and become the first in the continuous line of owners of the collective leases.

The MacMicking family tree registers many spelling variations of their name from the year 1200 to the present time. Torry's father raised sheep and cattle on Cashmere Downs while his son started his working life in the muster camps on neighbouring stations and spent several years on properties in the Sandstone area. He was only 19 when he took over management of Depot Springs in 1947. But in 1949, ready for a change, Torry sold his stockhorse, Warrigal, and with the proceeds from this, his only asset, he bought a plane ticket to Wyndham.

MacMicking first worked as head stockman on Bow River Station and afterwards ran a droving plant for Jimmy Klein who had a contract with the Peel River Company for the Connor, Doherty and Durack properties of Argyle, Newry, Auvergne and Ivanhoe Stations. He spent most of his early working life on horseback and reckoned he covered some 58,000 kilometres during his 12 years of droving in the Kimberley. It was during these years he acquired the name Mulaga, an Aboriginal word meaning 'boss man'. Working as the boss drover for the Peel River Company in the 1950s, Torry yearned to have his own station.

Early in 1951 Torry's younger brother John, who elected to spell his name McMicking, joined him and they worked together droving cattle from the Peel River stations to the Wyndham Meatworks. Their first delivery from Argyle Downs opened the meatworks for 1951. They were to make five more deliveries during the season and both men met their future wives at the works in the process. The contract price for delivery was eight shillings per beast with Torry and Klein sharing equally in the profit. The brothers are reputed to have been good singers and with their good looks, they were jokingly known as 'Clark Gable' and 'Errol Flynn'.

Torry first saw El Questro country in 1956 when he was mustering along the Salmond River on Moonlight Valley for Dick McKenna. This country lay to the west of the Chamberlain River and had previously belonged to Mohammed Sahanna.

In Wyndham on 28 August 1957, in pursuit of his dream of having his own land, Torry applied for leases over Spurlings Pocket and the vacant block to the south between the Pentecost and King Rivers. The area of Spurlings Pocket was estimated to be 105,000 acres and the second holding – which adjoined D.J. Davidson's land and Speewa Station – was approximately 50,000 acres.

On 30 July 1958 MacMicking wrote to the Lands Department in Perth naming the country between the Pentecost and King Rivers 'El Questro' and he requested their final notice on his pastoral leases so he could register his brand and earmark. The application was finally approved by the Minister for Lands on 22 August 1958 and MacMicking was recorded as being the leaseholder of 159,300 acres. The record does not indicate when or if he took up the lease over Moonlight Valley although he is recorded as mustering this area in 1961. A lease document shows Moonlight Valley as part of El Questro in 1968, but by then Torry had left the property. These were among the last few pastoral leases available in the East Kimberley and almost the most useless. The annual rent calculated at 5/- per 1,000 acres, was £40. The document recording the application and subsequent approval indicates his occupation changes from 'Master Drover' to 'Pastoralist'.

We will never know for certain what lay behind the name that has become so universally associated with the rugged beauty of Torry's country. El Questro has no Spanish translation and, despite subsequent assertions to the contrary, there was no Spanish speaking employee or friend who

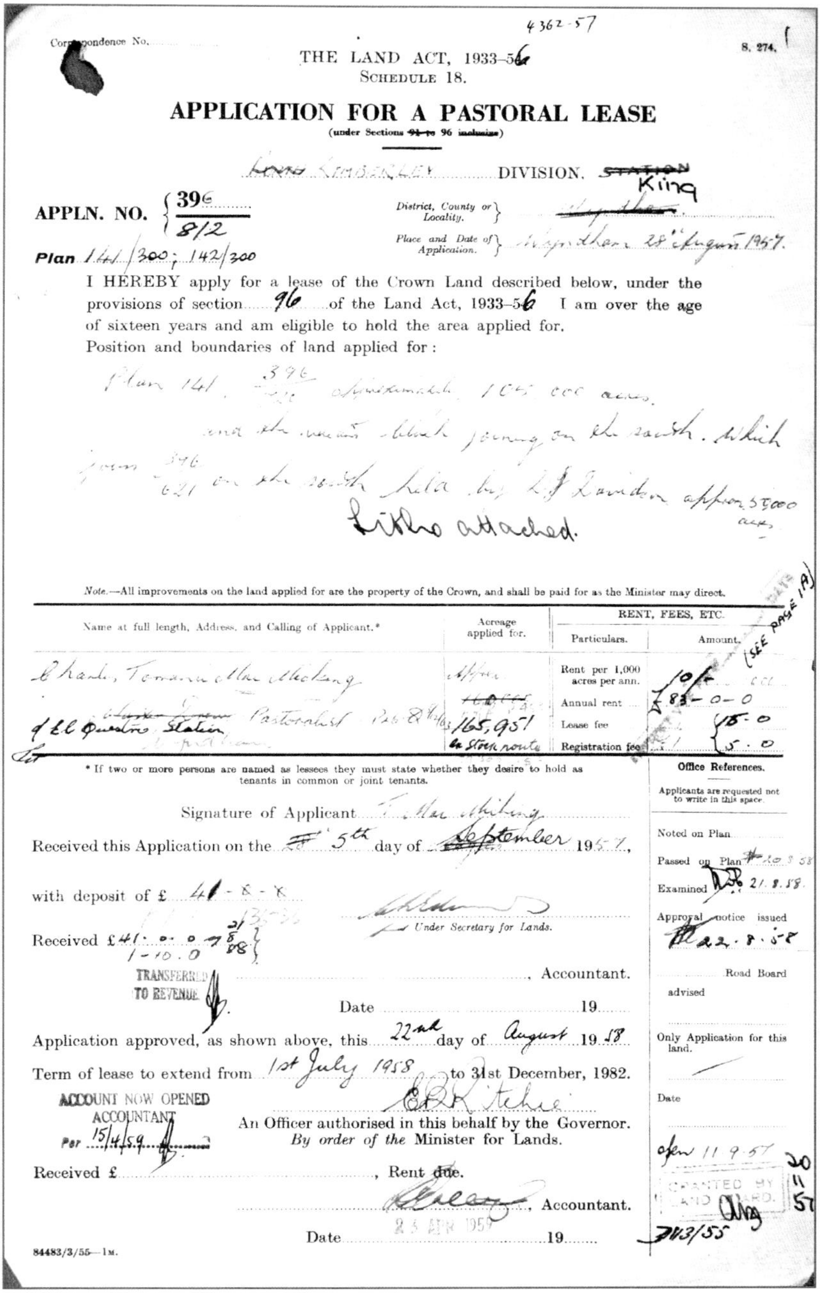

4362-57

Correspondence No. ......

THE LAND ACT, 1933–56
SCHEDULE 18.

S. 274.

APPLICATION FOR A PASTORAL LEASE

(under Sections ~~94 to~~ 96 ~~inclusive~~)

~~East~~ KIMBERLEY DIVISION. ~~STATION~~

APPLN. NO. 396 / 8/2

District, County or Locality. King ~~Wyndham~~

Place and Date of Application. Wyndham 28th August 1957.

Plan 141/300; 142/300

I HEREBY apply for a lease of the Crown Land described below, under the provisions of section 96 of the Land Act, 1933–56 I am over the age of sixteen years and am eligible to hold the area applied for.

Position and boundaries of land applied for:

Plan 141, 396/?? approximately 105 000 acres, and the vacant block joining on the south, which ... 396/621 on the south held by L J Lawdon approx 55000 acres

Litho attached.

Note.—All improvements on the land applied for are the property of the Crown, and shall be paid for as the Minister may direct.

Name at full length, Address, and Calling of Applicant.*	Acreage applied for.	Rent, Fees, etc. — Particulars.	Amount.
Charles Tomasina Allen MacMicking	Approx ~~105 000~~	Rent per 1,000 acres per ann.	10/-
~~[illegible]~~ Pastoralist P.O. B??	165,951	Annual rent	£83-0-0
of El Questro Station ~~Wyndham~~	to Stock route	Lease fee	15.0
		Registration fee	5.0

(SEE PAGE 1A)

* If two or more persons are named as lessees they must state whether they desire to hold as tenants in common or joint tenants.

Signature of Applicant T. Allen MacMicking

Received this Application on the 5th day of September 1957,

with deposit of £ 41-8-8

[signature] Under Secretary for Lands.

Received £41-0-0 / 1-10-0

TRANSFERRED TO REVENUE

......, Accountant.

Date ...... 19......

Application approved, as shown above, this 22nd day of August 1958

Term of lease to extend from 1st July 1958 to 31st December, 1982.

ACCOUNT NOW OPENED ACCOUNTANT Per 15/4/59

[signature]

An Officer authorised in this behalf by the Governor.
By order of the Minister for Lands.

Received £ ......, Rent ~~due~~.

[signature], Accountant.

Date 23 APR 1959 19......

84483/3/55—1M.

Office References.

Applicants are requested not to write in this space.

Noted on Plan

Passed on Plan 20.8.58

Examined 21.8.58.

Approval notice issued 22.8.58

Road Board advised

Only Application for this land.

Date

open 11.9.57

GRANTED BY LAND BOARD. 20/11/57

343/55

MacMicking's application for three adjoining leases. Courtesy of the State Records Office of Western Australia.

influenced the naming of the Station. Torry told his brother the name meant ‘the hills’: the hills he had been looking at for ten years. It meant a place where a man could put his tarpaulin over a ridge pole and call it home, a place where he could go mustering in the hope of putting enough scrub cattle together to start a herd of his own. El Questro was the realisation of Torrance MacMicking’s dream.

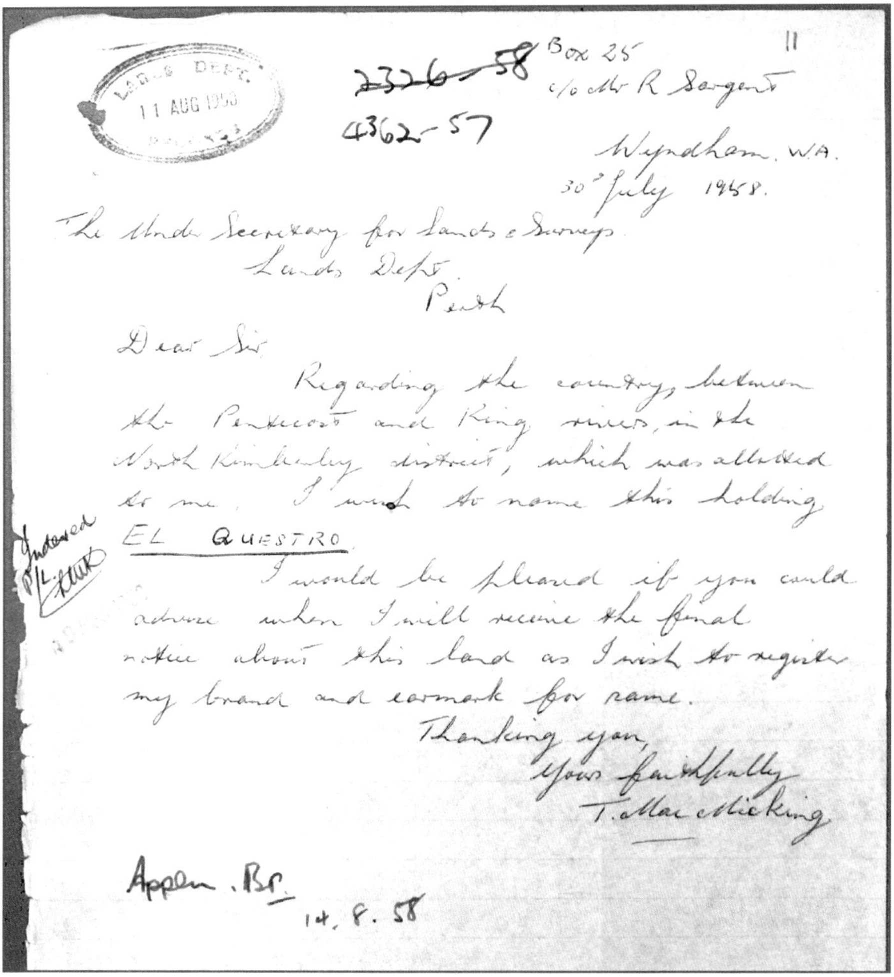

LANDS DEPT. 11 AUG 1958

~~2326-58~~ 4362-57

11

Box 25
c/o Mr R Sargent

Wyndham. W.A.
30th July 1958.

The Under Secretary for Lands & Surveys.
Lands Dept.
Perth

Dear Sir

Regarding the country between the Pentecost and King rivers, in the North Kimberley district, which was allotted to me, I wish to name this holding EL QUESTRO.

I would be pleased if you could advise when I will receive the final notice about this land as I wish to register my brand and earmark for same.

Thanking you,
Yours faithfully
T. MacMicking

Indexed PL

Appen. Br. 14. 8. 58

MacMicking’s letter to the Lands Department naming his country El Questro. Courtesy of the State Records Office of Western Australia.

Torry was known to enjoy reading the best-selling novels by Zane Grey who loved the colours and grandeur of the American West. Grey wrote convincingly of its characters and landscape and commonly used Spanish terms like *mesas* and *cuestas.* It is possible this inspired the name he gave to his station.

The pastoral lease was without official stock, however leaseholders could keep any unbranded cattle found on their property by paying a levy to the government for beasts over 12 months old. Younger stock were exempt from the levy. All cattle on El Questro were thus acquired; none were purchased during MacMicking's tenure.

With funds in short supply following his purchase of a 4-wheel drive Ford truck, Torrance postponed his plan to build yards and muster his land at El Questro in favour of managing Lissadell Station for John Naughton. At that time he had a droving plant of less than 40 horses and mules and he arranged for Doug 'Kiwi' Harrison, a mate from New Zealand, to take the plant to Victoria River Downs with a mob of cows from Rosewood Station.

Since his first brief visit to the Kimberley, John McMicking had married and been living and working down south. In 1961 John and his family rejoined Torry at Lissadell Station.

One evening in the 1960s their mother was watching television in Perth when the rugged good looks of a stockman in the Ascot cigarette advertisement seemed familiar. 'I think I know that man!' she exclaimed. 'You ought to,' said her sister Madge, 'he's your eldest son!' The advertisement, filmed behind the Wyndham Hotel, earned Torrance 100 quid and a book of bush poetry. Back on 22 July 1928 Aunt Madge had delivered the infant Torry at home at Mount Magnet while his father and the family doctor were preoccupied in the local hotel.

In late 1961 MacMicking and Kiwi Harrison managed to complete a brief ten day muster of El Questro around Spurlings Pocket and the Moonlight Valley areas. But this was a largely fruitless effort and they returned to Wyndham with only five bullocks for the local butcher. The effort was to some extent compensated for by the very good price paid by butcher Warnock.

Tom Orley bought adjoining Karunjie Station from Dave Rust and Scotty Salmond in 1960. Orly was not a cattleman and took little notice of brands or boundaries. In 1963, he went mustering and branding through the

Moonlight Valley part of El Questro, over the top end of the Durack Range and on into the Pentecost valley where he encountered Torry at his camp. Orley had a small mob of about 60 head bound for Wyndham. After giving Tom and his men damper and tea, Torry saddled his horse and checked Tom's mob where he found 25 had the El Questro brand 8XM and the rest were freshly branded with Karunjie's O5K. Had Orley taken the cattle to Wyndham he would have done El Questro a favour because payment by the meatworks was according to the brand on each beast.

Torrance MacMicking on Soverign circa1958. Photo courtesy Brad MacMicking.

Orley was a big rowdy bloke from the Argentine. He was intent on following the success of his brother back home who was seen as a cattle king. According to 'Johnny Mac' McMicking, on one occasion Orley came to town in a jeep and, rigged out with a sombrero and .45 revolver holstered low on a belt full of cartridges, he made his way to the bar of the Wyndham Hotel. Sgt Gilchrist or one of his fellow cops took the gun from him and, in an attempt to avoid looking foolish, Orley went across the road to Bessie Wiley's and bought a toy gun to fill his holster. Being new to the country it didn't take him long to get the blackfellas to hate his guts. One night they took to him with rocks and did a lot of damage to his head, from which the poor man never fully recovered.

John Naughton, with financial interests in Lissadell, Texas, Mabel and Alice Downs, was convinced the struggling Home Valley and El Questro Stations were stocking from his places and had Sgt Gilchrist set up a police muster using boys and horses from Dunham Station. The police party spent several weeks looking for stock with brands or earmarks that did not belong to El Questro or Home Valley Stations. It might have been a coincidence but Torry and his neighbour Harold MacNamara, the owner of Home Valley Station, were away running brumbies on the Underwood family's Inverway Station in the Territory at the time. Fortunately for them their mate Ivan Jackson was in the area and possibly influenced the outcome of the exercise, which ultimately netted a couple of frustrated policemen, several amused blackfellas and two relieved battlers, with no charges being laid.

When MacMicking's contract at Lissadell Station was terminated in 1962, Torrance, his brother John and wife returned to Wyndham and set up camp at Seven Mile. Shortly after settling in, the MacMicking parties found themselves catching up with friends and enjoying the general Kimberley gossip at the annual racing festivities.

Annual race meetings continue to be a popular event on the social calendar of all outback towns and the people of the Kimberley always look forward to the races and the opportunity they provide to enjoy the company of friends visiting from remote stations and further afield. Similarly the local rodeos and agricultural shows are a community highlight for the same reasons.

In August 1962 race week in Wyndham was no exception. The town's population exploded as station folk and their horses came in from outstations hundreds of miles away and set up temporary camps of stables and makeshift bough shelters around the racecourse. The newly arrived MacMicking party found themselves camped alongside the Marshall family who were in Wyndham visiting friends. This proved to be a significant encounter that was to result in a leasehold partnership at El Questro.

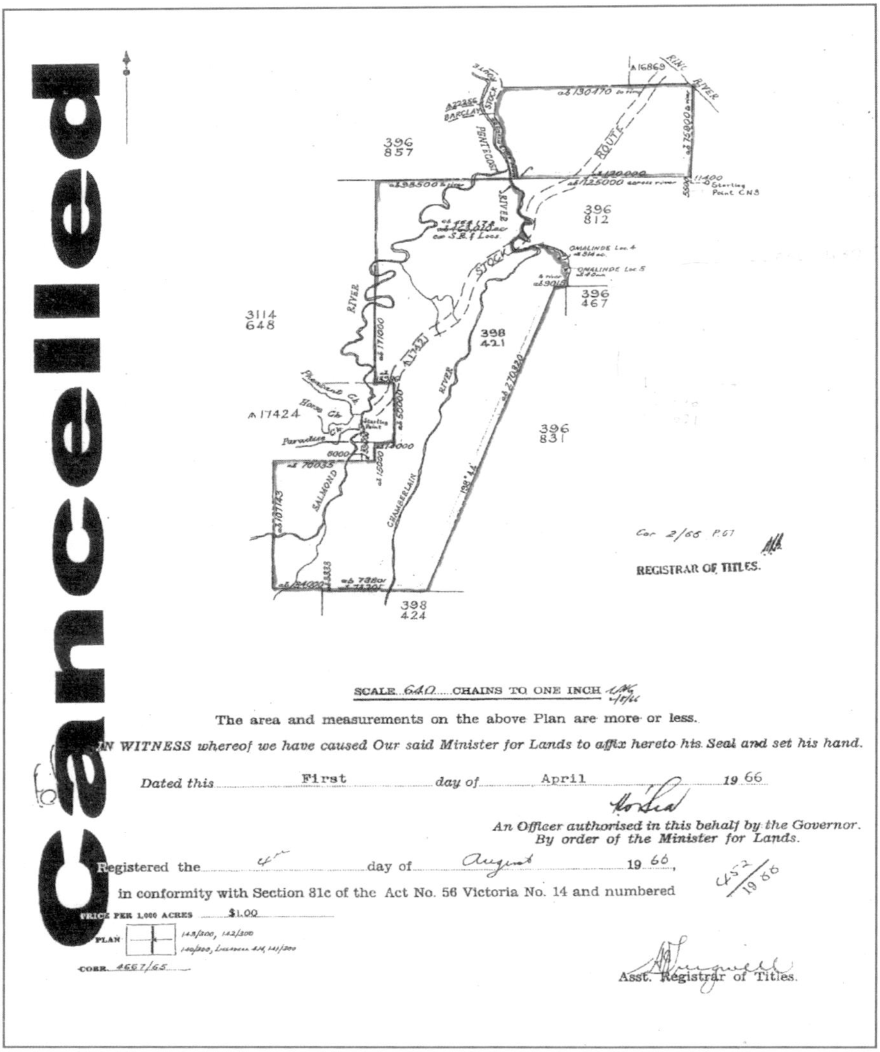
Cancelled

Cor 2/66 P.67

REGISTRAR OF TITLES.

SCALE 640 CHAINS TO ONE INCH

The area and measurements on the above Plan are more or less.

IN WITNESS whereof we have caused Our said Minister for Lands to affix hereto his Seal and set his hand.

Dated this First day of April 1966

An Officer authorised in this behalf by the Governor.
By order of the Minister for Lands.

Registered the 4th day of August 1966, in conformity with Section 81c of the Act No. 56 Victoria No. 14 and numbered 452/1966

PRICE PER 1,000 ACRES $1.00

CORR. 4667/65

Asst. Registrar of Titles.

The Spurlings Pocket and Moonlight Valley leases. Courtesy of the records held at Landgate.

The MacMicking–Marshall partnership 1962–1966

Morris Leslie Marshall, having sold his two farms at Katanning in the south of the state where he had grown grain and fattened sheep and cattle, set off to travel around Australia with his wife Pam and their young daughters, Lee and baby Kelly. The sale had been very successful in financial terms and the family, travelling in their Willys Jeep with a 30-foot caravan in tow, allowed themselves two years to complete their journey. They took their nanny Pat Watson with them to help with the girls. Their two sons Michael and Chris remained at a boarding school near Perth and flew to join their parents for the summer holidays. With only 11 months' difference in age, the boys were inseparable.

After almost two years on the road the Marshalls found themselves enjoying a brief stay amongst old friends in Wyndham while Morris explored opportunities to invest in an irrigation venture in the area. One hundred kilometres upstream on the Ord River, Australia's latest project was underway and the first step in the ambitious Ord River Irrigation Area (ORIA) scheme was almost completed, offering unlimited opportunity for employment and new businesses. When Marshall met Torry MacMicking at the races and learned of his financial difficulties, he perceived irrigation possibilities and was keen to inspect El Questro with a view to joining forces with Torry.

Morris Marshall in 2000.

Chris Marshall recalls flying into Wyndham with Michael early in 1962 at a time when Wyndham provided the only aerial access to the East Kimberley. From there they were driven the 100 kilometres to the fledgling town of Kununurra where the Marshall family lived briefly in a rental house close to the headquarters for the Ord River scheme. It is interesting that on completion of the project the headquarter buildings became part of the Country Club Hotel.

Morris Marshall worked first at the government funded Kimberley Research Station where exploratory work was being conducted on developing agriculture suitable to the area. He drove a cement truck for the ORIA construction development and, once the cotton industry received the go-ahead, he assisted with building a cotton gin on one of the farms. His son Chris, then aged six or seven, ran the flags to guide the crop dusting plane as it spread chemicals over the fields.

Unusually early storms and heavy rain in October thwarted Marshall's hopes of getting to El Questro before the wet set in. The early rains also brought pressure to bear at the construction site of the almost completed Diversion Dam at Kununurra where it would have been a disaster had the level of the Ord River risen before the work was finished.

Fortunately the rain abated in November, allowing Marshall and MacMicking's friend Doug 'Kiwi' Harrison access to El Questro in two vehicles. The track to Wild Dog on the eastern side of the King River was generally plainly visible, but beyond that the vehicles had to make their own way. With no evidence of any track to the present Station Centre at Spurlings Pocket, Kiwi gained the impression that theirs were the first vehicles to make their way over the 60 kilometres of rough country from the main Halls Creek Road. However, there was only one way to get to Spurlings Pocket and vehicles had been using it for years. It took the two men four days and all of their spare tyres to get in and back out again, leaving no time for Kiwi to start building the yards that Torry had planned.

In his next letter home to his family in New Zealand, Kiwi wrote:

> Following the visit, Morrie took me back to the Ivanhoe Research Farm where he is working and I got on to Mac on the radio. Anyway the upshot of it all was that Mac sold him a half share in the block, and they are going to borrow a lot of money and go in for fattening cattle in a big way.

Subsequently an unofficial working partnership was formed between MacMicking and Marshall although it was not formalised until 1964.

With plans to irrigate the flat land along the Pentecost River and fatten cattle, one of the **MacMicking–Marshall** partnership's first tasks was to apply for a loan from the Federal Development Bank. This bank had been established by the government expressly to finance projects they felt would help develop and populate Australia's remote northern regions.

During the wet season Morris Marshall and his family travelled south. Michael, the apple of his parents' eye, had developed leukaemia as a small boy and his desperate battle with the illness took its toll on the family. Christmas in 1962 was spent in Perth in order that seven-year-old Michael could have medical treatment. The family returned to Wyndham on one of the State Shipping Line vessels. Air travel was extremely costly in those days and without good road transport into the area, most folk and supplies travelled by ship.

In January 1963 MacMicking went to Perth to register the new company and to raise the finance required to get their project underway in the coming season. The partners were optimistic about raising the £16,000 required from the bank. A bank official travelled up from Sydney and spent three weeks assessing the property. With no infrastructure at all on El Questro, there was an endless list of tasks to accomplish in order to make the station operational; yard building and fencing were at the top of the list. Word came through from the bank in March approving only two-thirds of the minimum funding required for a good start. This was insufficient to allow them to begin full scale operations that year.

MacMicking and his droving plant continued to work on Lissadell Station while Kiwi and his offsider George Thompson went out to El Questro in May to build as many yards and fences as possible. It was intended this task should be completed prior to MacMicking and the horses finishing their droving commitments and joining them on the station, in time to muster and brand as many cleanskins as they were able before the onslaught of the next wet season.

Early in the partnership Marshall had a route surveyed to Spurlings Pocket and shortly afterwards a Main Roads Department grader cut a new road into the Station.

A small sawmill was set up to cut timber for fences and to build sheds to house the gear and other equipment. The yards were constructed of ironwood, an exceedingly heavy and durable local timber. Today the remnants of the Cattle Creek bronco yards, the first to be built by Kiwi Harrison, may still be seen beside the driveway at the turning to Jackaroos Waterhole.

The plan to irrigate El Questro had captured the imagination of many people, and the partners were offered a lot of free advice and assistance with soil and level surveys.

A bulldozer came out to the station to form a stone causeway across the Pentecost River, providing access to the fertile flats at Spurlings Pocket where the homestead was to be constructed. Among other tasks, the dozer driver moved a huge boulder out of one of the creek crossings on the driveway and having done so, remarked to Marshall, 'This rock is my tombstone.' Four months later the driver met his death and Chris remembers his father placing a pair of horns on the rock and calling the creek Tombstone Creek. Marshall told me the bulldozer driver was taken by a croc while fishing on the King River, however Johnny Mac denies this incident.

With plans to grow Townsville Lucerne and other tropical grasses under spray irrigation, a second Cat D9 bulldozer was brought to El Questro on a low loader, and dragging a heavy chain between them, the two dozers cleared some 16 hectares of land on the river flat, close to the future homestead. Some of this was to be sold as hay and the rest used to fatten cattle. The cleared area incorporated most of what is now Black Cockatoo campground and extended close to the Workshop and equipment stores.

With the road graded and the use of a Ford Blitz truck, a Jeep, a lot of hard work and some assistance from the Shire, Marshall managed to get a Ferguson tractor, the caravan, an old Thames truck, plus a lot of gear out to El Questro before the wet set in. Their route from Wyndham took them south along the original Halls Creek Road and then west to the King River, passing between Mount Rob and the Tier Range as the Gibb River Road does today. Once over the King River it took them eight hours to reach the station, travelling down to Canteen Hole and west below the Nimberline Range to the track that today is the driveway.

In mid-June Kiwi reported to his family in New Zealand:

> I have all the holes dug and nearly all the timber cut and carted to the yard. I also have over two miles of fencing pegged and 100 fence posts cut. However the timber I'm cutting is not called ironwood for nothing and it sure is hard on gear. Most people won't cut it with an axe as it takes the face out of all but the very best steel. I lose a tooth a day off the chainsaw and these take time to replace, eventually I ran out of spares, necessitating a trip to town for parts and repairs. Everything is going very nearly on schedule and the future looks quite rosy. My offsider and I are in the best of health. My new address is c/o El Questro Irrigation & Grazing. Box 53. Wyndham.

It appears the graded track to El Questro was still very rough as Kiwi writes:

> It took 2 hours 40 minutes to get into town the other day and 25 miles of that was on good bitumen.

Two weeks later the yards were completed and Kiwi and the men had moved camp down to the river flat at Spurlings Pocket to commence fencing the area where the house was to be built. Plans and measurements for a Colonial Homestead were forwarded to Bunnings in Perth, who were to supply the building materials and other station requirements and deliver them to the State Shipping Line. Shipping space was at a premium due to the quantity of material being transported to Wyndham for the Ord River Project.

The shipping proved to be a frustratingly protracted affair; it appears the 60 tons of space that Morris had booked through Elder Smith & Co. was insufficient to accommodate all of the building requirements for the house, plus two miles of fencing and irrigation materials and the rations, stores, machines and tools needed by the station.

Once landed in Wyndham the bundles of material were trucked in two loads to Spurlings Pocket by Bob Wainwright of East Kimberley Transport using his eight-ton Leyland truck, with each trip taking a full day each way. Bob recalls having great difficulty transporting the lengths of jarrah timber, sheets of asbestos, masonite and other items along the rough track to the home site.

Wainwright subsequently sold East Kimberley Transport and bought into the Turkey Creek Roadhouse on the Great Northern Highway. During his time there he led a television documentary film crew into the nearby Bungle Bungle Range. Prior to 1983 this geographic feature with its extraordinary beehive shaped dome formations was unknown to all but the local Aborigines and cattlemen in the region.

Operating under the name of Turkey Creek Bush Safaris, the Wainwright family opened 'the Bungles' to tourism. Under the banner of East Kimberley Tours, they won many tourism awards and were responsible for bringing this unique attraction from obscurity to the international recognition it enjoys today. A remarkable scenic and geological phenomenon, it was opened as a National Park in 1987 and the name was changed to Purnululu, meaning 'sandstone' in the local Kija language.

In 2003 the natural beauty of the area was internationally recognised when Purnululu was given World Heritage listing. Inspection of the outstanding cone karst formations from ground level reveals the intimate details of the texture and composition of the massif, with its orange and grey banding of stratified lichen and silica; however, to fully comprehend the size and nature of the unique beehive shaped towers, visitors are well advised to participate in an aerial tour as well.

Having spent almost six months solidly fencing and building yards, first at Lissadell Station and then constructing the Cattle Creek and Cockburn Yards at El Questro, Kiwi Harrison was looking forward to mustering cattle with Torry. In preparation for the muster he burnt all the long grass in the country. Anticipating the resulting green growth would attract a number of cattle there was a reasonable expectation of putting a good mob together. Burning off also gave a galloping horse and other stock clearer view of the ground and minimised the chances of a fall.

In August Kiwi writes home again. This time he is in Wyndham attending the annual race week and enjoying the chance to break out after the extended period of heavy work. He writes:

> The muster went off quite well – though no records were broken. We put about 95 branders in the paddock & left another 40 scattered about for technical reasons. The horses still have quite a bit of work left in them and we might treble those figures by the end of the year. The homestead is in the process of erection by very good men & the fencing is progressing well but slowly. I have some very good men with me, which has certainly allowed me to get through a lot more work at a higher standard than I had anticipated.

In his letter, Kiwi also mentions experiencing mechanical breakdowns at El Questro, priority being given to establishing a workshop at the station and the irrigation equipment still awaiting shipping from Perth.

He closes:

> Well the last two days have been a bit lively for letter writing. I didn't win any fortunes from the bookies so I guess I'll have to go back to work tomorrow.

Even though the Lilly and the Quilty families were regarded as having the top horses in the area, the Marshalls boasted the best bough shed at the racecourse. It was constructed from bush timber and roofed with palm fronds providing shelter for the the family and their visitors for the duration of the event. Friends and relatives from Perth and other southern centres found it an opportune time to visit Western Australia's most northern town and enjoy the two days of horse races, parties, dances, sports events and barbeques.

Every station competed in the races. A year or two later, Marshall bought a brown mare named Debonair in Darwin and with a professional jockey on board was expecting it to do well. Unfortunately, the jockey was unable to ride on the day and the children's governess Val Bristow who tipped the scales at the appropriate weight, was the substitute jockey. She rode Debonair into second place in the Stockman's Purse – a consolation race for horses that had not had a win at the meeting. It was a requirement that competitors rode this race in stock saddles instead of the regular lightweight racing saddle.

Naturally it was a time to be seen at one's best and, with no local fashion alternative, mail order shopping came to the rescue of people living in remote areas. Each year the large stores in Perth and Brisbane forwarded their illustrated catalogues to eager prospective clients in the Kimberley. Some catalogues even had fabric samples glued alongside the illustrated dresses. The transportation process to and fro was accomplished by sea mail and the greatly anticipated transaction took months to be completed. Unlike today, there was no stigma attached to finding oneself in the company of an identical outfit at the same event, it was quite usual. Men's requirements were catered for locally by three resident Chinese tailors in Wyndham. Full dress for men was the tropical standard – all white.

Following race week at Wyndham, MacMicking went to Mabel Downs and Lissadell stations to pick up his horses and move them onto El Questro.

Kiwi's next major task was to dig out the roots of the bauhinia trees that had broken off close to the ground when the dozers cleared the land in preparation for irrigation. This arduous work required that the roots be grubbed out manually and then cut up and stacked for firewood. The residue was burnt and the area thoroughly tidied up prior to the installation of the irrigation equipment.

The Marshall family and their governess moved onto the property and established themselves on the Pentecost River in their caravan and tents. They were accompanied by stockmen and their families, totalling around 21. All of the stockmen on El Questro with the exception of Kiwi were Aborigines. The permanent Aboriginal camp was erected on the nearby river flat. It consisted of canvas army type tents accommodating up to six, with the boys together in one tent. Bathing was done in the river and there is no record of any toilet facilities in those early days.

The workers were paid an agreed wage of £2 per week plus their keep. This payment was for the hours worked and it was given in cash, prior to the employees going to town, where they spent it all and gave away the clothes the station had provided. By arrangement Morris would drive into Wyndham a couple of days later to collect them all and bring them back to the station.

The full blood Aborigines included the Clarke and Toby families. Conrad Clarke, with his wife Susan and their children was the station's handyman and carried out most of station's repairs and maintenance. John Toby and his mother Mary, who did the baking at El Questro, came from Lissadel Station.

Jimmy and Margaret Smith and their two daughters were of mixed blood as were Sandy and Noreen Morton and their two children; Tony and Johnny Ah-Won were half-Chinese – Tony was a stockman who worked whenever he felt like it.

Despite the diversity of tribe and tongue, the families on El Questro lived harmoniously together using English as their common language. Aboriginal people from outside hardly ever visited El Questro and were not encouraged to do so by the owners, thereby averting the provision of alcohol to the residents. The employees themselves generally moved any visitors on after only a short stay.

The women cooked their meals over an open fire or in a camp oven in a large hayshed. Sometimes the beef was cooked in a big hole in the ground. Occasionally they would join the Marshall family for a barbecue.

The Aborigines used hand lines for fishing. They did not use traditional methods or eat bush tucker, nor did they participate in any cultural or spiritual rituals; they were aware of some cultural sites on El Questro but did not pay any attention to them. They knew about the painting on the 'snake wall'. The mythical 'big snake' is reputed to have been approximately 40 yards long with its head at Python Pool and its tail at the King River Crossing.

The Brown family also lived on El Questro Station. Mrs Brown was the cook and other members of her family worked randomly on the station. Aboriginal brothers Tom, Patrick and Peter Birch lived and worked on the station at various times during the MacMicking and Marshall tenure. Young Peter was part Aborigine and part Afghan and came to El Questro from Forrest River in 1965. At 14 or 15 he was considered too young for stock work and instead attended to the garden. When his older brother Tom moved from El Questro to Carlton Hill Station, Jimmy Smith took his place as leading hand and head stockman. Jimmy's name can be seen carved into several boab trees; one of these is only a short distance from the Chamberlain Gorge car park. In 1993, after working around the Kimberley in various capacities, Peter returned to El Questro and worked for a decade on the grader, maintaining the roads and tracks throughout the station during its development as a tourist destination.

With MacMicking unemployed and the partnership badly in need of further funding to meet their plans, Marshall continued chasing the banks and the government for support. Several authorities came out to El Questro and appeared suitably impressed. While not declining to lend the funds, the institutions kept the partners dangling and despite adding the Cockburn country to the leased area to help substantiate the loan, little financial assistance was forthcoming.

To ease the situation, Marshall approached Eddie Warnock, the local butcher, inviting him to come out to El Questro and kill bullocks on the property. As Wyndham's only butcher, he operated out of a cool room in the basement of the huge meatworks complex. On average, he killed 10 beasts weekly, initially selling the meat to the local market from the back of his truck. During the off season between September and May, he was obliged to source his meat from nearby stations taking only quality cattle, mostly from Auvergne Station. Warnock later moved to Three Mile where he had the first commercial building and took his brother Geoff into the business. Their old butcher shop has now been incorporated into a supermarket complex.

Warnock recalls travelling out to El Questro in his refrigerated 3-ton Bedford truck and killing bullocks there at various locations. The cattle were generally mustered and held in yards to await their fate. There was a set of yards called Dogwood Yards near the homestead and another on Donkey Yard Flats known as the Cockburn Yards. The remains of the latter may be found beside the Gibb River Road opposite Caroline Valley where a slaughter yard and gantry were constructed to comply with Health Department requirements but rarely used. Instead, a portable tripod was utilised to butcher the carcass wherever the beast was killed. Cattle were also mustered and held at Canteen Hole although no permanent yards were ever constructed there. A further large set of horse and cattle yards called the Homestead Yards were built near the pool close to the Station Homestead.

No El Questro cattle were sold to the abattoirs during these years. Warnock estimates he would have taken a maximum of 50–60 beasts from El Questro annually. Years later Marshall reported that El Questro ran approximately 1,000 cattle on the 70,000-hectare unfenced northern section of the property.

Kiwi's letter dated 22 September 1963 reads:

> The house is finished, painted and occupied. Considering that five months ago there wasn't even a road out here this is a pretty good effort in my opinion. All the Marshall's four kids are here and the two boys start on their correspondence lessons tomorrow with the aid of 'the school of the air' over the Flying Doctor radio network. We have no electricity yet—the plant is in Wyndham I think. Everything (water & power) will be worked from

> the same engine and the set-up has been designed so that the unit can be rigged up in a reasonable space.

The homestead consisted of a large kitchen, dining room, lounge, three bedrooms and an all-round verandah. It was built on a concrete floor with asbestos and a steel frame lined with plasterboard. Shortly afterwards a 72-horsepower Lister generator and pump combination was installed, capable of producing 15 KVA at 240 volts and pumping 136,000 litres per hour for irrigation. The diesel unit was set up to provide power and light to both the house and workshops when the latter were built. The plan was for the 10-centimetre centrifugal pump to deliver water to 42 acres under sprinkler irrigation.

Initially, Val Bristow taught the Marshall and Clarke children; Lee Marshall recalls having three governesses during the three years the family lived at El Questro. Schooling for the Marshalls and up to 12 Aboriginal children was conducted in the enclosed verandah at the rear of the colonial-style house. It was the Marshall children's first experience of the School of the Air programs broadcast over the Royal Flying Doctor Services radio. Con Clarke was the guardian of Patrick and Peter Birch. Both boys were in their mid-teens and they too attended some lessons as well as doing stock work.

On completion of their morning lessons Chris and Michael Marshall, now aged seven and eight respectively, were permitted to roam at will and would run off beyond the sound of the bell as it rang for afternoon lessons. As is the case with most country children, there were many adventurous outdoor activities to enjoy and formal education was not among them. Even at their tender years, the boys had a cut down .22 rifle and hunting and shooting crocodiles was a favourite activity. Among the victims to fall foul of this weapon was a 4-metre long python snake containing the bumpy remains of 14 recently consumed chickens. The resultant corpse was too heavy and unwieldy for the boys to carry home.

In mid-October 1963 there was great excitement when the sprinkler irrigation system was turned on over the first six acres. Only four and a half weeks later this area cut just over a ton of sorghum to the acre and by then Kiwi had almost cleared a total of ten acres for irrigation. The intention was to irrigate the whole valley but little more than ten acres were ever covered. Marshall claimed that El Questro produced some of the best hay in the Kimberley; it was known as 'feisty bean mix' and cut about four ton to the acre. Lucerne also grew very well under irrigation and other crops were tried with mixed success.

In 2000, in a sworn statement relating to land claims, Marshall declared the Agriculture Department stopped the irrigation project in 1962 because El Questro did not have the correct tenure. In order to continue the project, the partners were later allocated 1,000 acres as freehold near the homestead in the Pentecost Valley extending to the Chamberlain River.

In 2003 when R.J. Benetti, a licensed surveyor, visited El Questro as a tourist he mentioned he had been commissioned by Marshall to work around the old homestead on the Pentecost River. He surveyed two allotments, but did not know the reason for this work. Apparently it was to be the 1,000 freehold acres Marshall proposed, however there is no record of it ever being approved.

An Englishman named Charlie Grice came to El Questro during the 1963/64 wet season. Charlie had been a gardener for many years and while working in the nursery industry had become competent in Latin in order to understand the botanical names and terminology. He was also an accomplished musician having played trumpet in a part-time orchestra and later took up classic guitar. Utilising three-quarters of an acre of irrigated land, Charlie produced cabbages, lettuces, broccoli, cauliflower and a variety of melons and fruit required on El Questro. Any surplus was sold in Wyndham and to 'native welfare'.

Recognising the natural beauty of the Pentecost River, Marshall had both banks fenced near the homestead to protect them from damage by cattle and horses. Lucerne hay, corn and vegetables were grown on the adjacent flat land, irrigated by the water pumped from the river.

The Aboriginal women worked in and around the newly completed house, baking bread and doing laundry, housework and gardening. Mary Toby is remembered with affection, and for being especially good at her work. She told Marshall the Pentecost River was taboo to Aboriginal people because of an incident in the 1920s when a 'half-caste' Aboriginal policeman from Queensland shot all the original people from the area. Mary said she saw the Aboriginal spirits from time to time.

On the large unfenced cattle stations of the Kimberley mustering was an ongoing activity during the dry months. Heavy horse losses from liver poisoning meant each station needed to keep a large number of horses. At the beginning of the wet season all the Aborigines walked off the station, generally returning three months later.

The wet season provided time to repair saddlery and attend to general maintenance of equipment and plant. Before the start of the muster season the horses were rounded up and brought into the home paddocks. The young ones needed branding and handling, all of them were shod, and the new ones broken in and 'mouthed' prior to handing them over to the stockmen who would start them on light work while they were 'green'.

The men assisted with the fencing and stock work. Approximately 64 kilometres of fencing were erected using steel pickets with post strainers and four-strand barbed wire. Chris Marshall remembers Johnny Ah-won as an excellent stockman and bronco rider, he was the only one who could ride a temperamental grey horse called Bluemare.

Towards the end of 1963 and with the wet season threatening, Marshall went to Perth chasing much needed funding. Back at the station all hands were cutting and selling hay as fast as it was baled and frantically building sheds in an attempt to get people and gear under cover before the rain started.

In March, Kiwi Harrison and the other stockmen went out mustering with Torrance MacMicking. They were dealing with some particularly wild cattle and were putting a number of bullocks together for Warnock. Towards the end of the day one broke from the mob and Kiwi set off in pursuit. Galloping alongside the beast, he leaned over and slipped from his horse as he grabbed it by its tail. Normally a man performing this manoeuvre would simultaneously unbalance the beast and throw it to the ground, but on this occasion Kiwi failed to throw the bull and was horned in the lower abdomen. By the time he staggered back to camp it was too late to ride the 14 kilometres back to the homestead. After an uncomfortable night he set off on one of the mules accompanied by another stockman, and eventually reached home.

Since there was no airstrip on which an aircraft could land, instructions for Kiwi's treatment had to be relayed by radio from the remarkable Royal

Flying Doctor Service (RFDS), using items numbered for easy identification in the station's medicine chest, which had been issued and stocked by the RFDS network to cover a wide variety of complaints.

Making low passes over the irrigation paddock near the homestead, the RFDS aircraft dropped the antibiotic and tetanus needles required for Kiwi's treatment. Using parachutes the size of a handkerchief, individual phials were dropped at each pass and the children were paid two shillings for each phial they found and brought in from the sorghum crop. It was the first time that Pam had injected anyone, but she rose to the occasion and the outcome was a total success, leaving Kiwi with only a neat scar to remind him of the incident.

Kiwi subsequently recovered sufficiently to dig four wells on the salt flats to the north of the Cockburn Range in search of much needed fresh water to support the grasslands in the area. The exercise was unsuccessful, but Kiwi recalls that the King River provided water all year round, and in other places the feral donkeys with their superior intellect dug for drinking water at soaks beneath the surface.

With the partners short of cash and the continuing uncertainty about funding, Kiwi, who was one of the few on the payroll, fell victim to the partners' financial crisis and moved on from El Questro in March 1964.

In August the same year after two years of bargaining, MacMicking and Marshall's application for joint ownership of the property was approved and they were officially registered as tenants in common in equal shares. Later they acquired pastoral lease – P/L 398/421 adding another 463,010 acres. This area was recalculated in September 1966 bringing it to 464,172 acres. Both leases were then surrendered in accordance with the Land Act and redesignated as P/L 3114/921 containing 623,172 acres.

They were a progressive team, responsible for experimenting with new pasture.

In late 1964 Chris Griffith, a journalist with *The West Australian* newspaper, spent two days in the saddle inspecting the property. In an article written for the paper, he describes the diesel powered irrigation plant pumping 113,500 litres of water per hour from the Pentecost River and distributing it to the area where it was expected to fatten four steers per acre during the annual six month conditioning period. Griffith outlined the partners' scheme to fatten these station cattle on irrigated pasture for about three months – sufficient time to produce tender young beef to sell to a Wyndham butcher for the local market. On other stations Kimberley cattle were being turned off straight from the pastoral country and sent directly to the meatworks. The resulting ground beef was sent to the United States for the hamburger trade. Marshall informed Griffith that they planned to cut two tons of hay per acre on the same area. However their ambitious plan required more pastoral land in order to run the 6,000 cattle needed to make it a profitable fat-beef scheme. Marshall said: 'We would put about half the cattle for turnoff on to the irrigated pasture at about 18 months of age. The rest would go straight off to market from the station country as four-year-olds during the wet, like a normal station.'

In response to the partners' request for additional land, pastoral inspector B.K. McWhinney from the Department of Lands and Surveys visited the property. His report dated 1 June 1964 was less than enthusiastic. He describes the country as 'an extremely rough area situated on the south side of the Cockburn Range'. Being steep rugged hill country, 80 per cent of El Questro was considered of little or no value for grazing purposes. The remaining 20 per cent was river flats and pockets. Vegetation was bloodwood, cabbage gums, ironwood and nutwood, grassed with some grasses and poorer types of annuals on the sandy acacia flats, of little value except when green. Pastoral Inspector McWhinney went on to describe the homestead as:

> ... a new building of 3 bedrooms, with sleepout, wide verandas, living room, modern kitchen and bathroom, situated on a 40 acre river flat on the south side of the Pentecost River. The area under irrigation produced good cuts of hay, sorghum and phasey bean for topping up cattle prior to sale to a Wyndham butcher for £44 per head. Englishman Charlie Grice leased ¾ acre and grew vegetables. Sales of cucumber, melons, tomatoes and pumpkins were recorded, with Wyndham and the construction workers on the Ord River irrigation scheme providing a ready market for the fresh produce.
>
> ... should this attempt to farm the land by irrigation succeed, it would be of great value to the district. There is ample land and water available but at present El Questro is not an economic unit.

Marshall Grave and memorial at El Questro. 2005.

Tragically, Michael lost his battle with leukaemia on 23 October 1964; born on 9 July 1955, he was barely nine years old. Special permission was granted to have his remains buried beneath a boab tree on the station close to the driveway where the grave may be seen today. The plaque on the tree at the graveside has the year of Michael's death incorrectly recorded as 1963. In later years the tree gained additional significance when in 2006 Morris

Marshall's ashes were ceremonially scattered over and buried beside his son's grave. Close by is a plaque installed in remembrance of Peter Birch, one of Michael's playmates and a long term and much loved employee at El Questro in subsequent years when he was known to all as 'Black Pete'.

Marshall spoke of carving Michael's initials alongside the Durack 'D' on a boab tree located somewhere close to the homestead. At the time of writing, this tree has not been located.

Around November 1965, Marshall and a couple of Aboriginal stockmen were on their way to collect a mob of horses from Mongrel Downs for Chuck Denning from Dunham River. On their way to the station Marshall met up with Tom Birch and invited him to help with the horses. On completion of the project Tom stayed on at El Questro for the 1966 season. He recalls his work was generally within a day's ride of the homestead and consisted of mustering, branding and marking the Shorthorn herd.

Almost all the work involved mustering the wild cattle and herding them into the yards with a mob of tamer cattle known as 'coachers'. Tommy was the 'tailer' and spent his time following the mob and keeping them together. Morris remembers him as a good stockman.

In 1965 following a dalliance between Torrance and one of the governesses, harmony at Spurlings Pocket was at an all time low and MacMicking set up camp at a spring in the vicinity of Emma Gorge or Caroline Valley; the latter was called Cockburn Gorge at that time. The spring became known as Mulaga Springs after the name given to MacMicking by his stock boys. His other blackfella name was Bundunjie, given him by the Warman Aborigines.

There was insufficient work to support both Marshall and MacMicking and the latter found work elsewhere on the agreement that he would channel funds into El Questro. About this time the Aboriginal Welfare Department visited El Questro to inspect the conditions of the employees. Their review ordered septic tanks be provided. This was deemed an expense that could not be borne by the struggling station and many of the Aborigines had to leave the property.

With the partnership in disarray and experiencing ongoing financial difficulty, the time had come to seriously consider selling the station and on 29 August 1966, after establishing El Questro as a working station, the partners sold the property to Helen and Gordon Ohrt. Many more of the Aborigines departed with the Marshalls. At the end of the partners' tenure the station had the following buildings on it: a garage and saddle shop made of galvanised iron; the homestead and native quarters already mentioned; a workshop, chicken house and cow shed. According to Marshall, there were no airstrips or man-made watering points on the station.

Years later, Marshall's second wife Marjory recounted an incident when, in an effort to drum up some cash, Morris and a couple of blackfellas travelled to Balgo some 200 kilometres south of Halls Creek to collect horses for on-selling to the Americans. The deal was to nett him $40,000 but the sale fell through. Apparently they nearly died in the process and on his return to El Questro he found Pam packed and ready to leave with the rest of the family. Chris, now ten years old, stayed on with his father until the sale was completed and the station was handed over to the Ohrts.

Patrick Birch recalls that following the sale MacMicking was paid out and, after being in a loss situation, Marshall came out square following settlement. Pam took the girls to Perth for their education and Marshall and Chris spent some time on the Mitchell Plateau caretaking for a mining company at Camp Creek. They then moved to Newman where Morris impulsively purchased Sylvania Station in the desert. Having had enough of country life, Pam separated from Morris and returned to the Perth metropolis where she ran a boarding house.

In 1974 Chris Marshall was amongst 33 young men to be accepted into Western Australia's first police cadet scheme. One of his duties was to transcribe the records from old police station diaries into replica books for public viewing. The old diaries were kept in the Commissioner's office and in the course of the work Chris uncovered records of an incident which he came to believe might have accounted for the naming of 'Spurlings Pocket' on El Questro. Quite coincidentally, Chris was given the log books from the Wyndham Police Station to work with and he was naturally intrigued to read the old entries from around 1929 that he remembers as having been written by Sgt Sperling. He recalls the entries went something like this:

> Received a complaint about Aborigines spearing cattle.
>
> Sent a runner out to a location some 60 miles from Wyndham to investigate and to instruct them to tie their dogs up.

Later, on returning from his rounds and having investigated the complaint. Sperling recorded:

> Shot all the dogs. There will be no further trouble with the Aborigines.

As a child Chris had always wondered why the Aboriginal stockmen would not do night watch near a pocket of country close to the cattleyards. On reading this police report, he recalled the reservations Mary Toby had expressed to his father about Spurlings Pocket. In a sworn statement before his death, Morris Marshall stated that he understood Aboriginal people did not like El Questro because it was taboo. He went on say that in the 1920s, Sperling – a half-caste Aboriginal policeman from Queensland – had shot all of the Aborigines. He believed this was how the area came to be known as Spurlings *[sic]* Pocket. This claim is unsubstantiated and research indicates the name Spurlings Pocket almost certainly referred to Jack Spurling, the co-owner from 1906 to 1909.

Torrance MacMicking, his second wife Des, whom he married in 1970, and their two daughters Lisa and Allison moved to Halls Creek where he bought a block of land and built his own house. The money made from nine years of successful contract mustering on Moola Bulla enabled him to build a butcher shop and a small slaughterhouse; it was the first in the East Kimberley. Torrance served as a Shire Councillor and a Justice of the Peace in Halls Creek where he died on 20 June 1995.

Gordon and Helen Ohrt 1966–1968

On 29 August 1966, transfer of El Questro Station was registered to David Millard Pty Ltd, a company belonging to Gordon and Helen Ohrt. The purchase was initially financed through Marshall who was paid out in July of the following year.

The Ohrts, with property and business interests in southern Western Australia, had decided to move north with their children to experience the Australian outback lifestyle. The children would attend schools in Perth, taking advantage of prevailing government policy that assisted with airfares for school children from remote areas.

When they took on the lease of El Questro, the Ohrts were aware it was a marginal operation and they did not have unrealistic expectations of its earning potential. Nevertheless it appears they did not make an inspection prior to accepting the property, as they claim that cattle numbers and some of the infrastructure fell far short of the levels they had anticipated.

Apart from the yards, there was only one small paddock around the irrigation area and some block fences to make a paddock of Spurlings Pocket. At the time of the sale the plant consisted of a Thames truck which served as a platform to put fertilizer on, a Ford Blitz truck, a Ferguson tractor, a diesel engine with a pump to supply water from the river for irrigation and domestic use, a saddle shed made from secondhand corrugated iron and bush timber and the small house with a light plant.

During his three years at El Questro, Gordon Ohrt modified the homestead, installed a three-phase power plant, constructed a large workshop and shed, and installed a large refrigerator/freezer for storing a bullock carcass. The house and vegetable gardens enjoyed pristine water drawn from the adjacent Pentecost River by the refurbished pump. New horse yards were built close to the homestead and fences erected across the valley to contain domestic stock nearby. The stockyards, fences and gates, erected during the previous tenure, were repaired.

Gordon, a machinery enthusiast, took possession of a bulldozer and formed and maintained a 3000–3500 foot airstrip enabling friends to fly in to visit. This strip is now part of the Chamberlain River road some 500 metres beyond the present airstrip. He cleared the area between the old homestead and the Pentecost crossing, possibly removing the previously mentioned boab tree with the Durack and Marshall engravings. The bulldozer was also utilised for contract work, levelling the plains on nearby Dunham Station.

Now a Stock Inspector, MacMicking's brother John reports drenching 27 horses on El Questro and shooting and performing a post-mortem on one with the deadly crotalaria poisoning shortly before Christmas. By April the following year only 12 horses remained, the balance having been lost to crotalaria. Ohrt purchased 70 more horses from Billaluna Station.

From the outset of European settlement the consumption of an unknown plant led to the death of up to 50 per cent of horses in the north-west of Australia. The cause of the deaths was not known until 1952 when it was attributed to the leguminous *Crotalaria* plant, known variously as Rattlepod, or Kimberley Horse Poison or Walkabout weed. The Crotalaria is a member of the large pea family Fabaceae, and its flower spikes develop into pods containing seeds that rattle on maturity.

When pasture is scarce horses eat the weed and over time the cumulative effect of the alkaloid poison in the plant causes cirrhosis of the liver. Loss of weight, twitching and aimless walking are visible symptoms of the disease. John McMicking performed post mortems on dozens of horses that died from this cause. He states the liver becomes dark in colour and twice as hard as normal. He believes it to be the most painful malady a horse can suffer – even worse than tetanus or grain poisoning. The agonised horse continues to walk around until it dies. With no cure, early euthanasia is the kindest way of dealing with the horse once the illness has been diagnosed. While most crotalaria species are to some extent toxic, *Crotalaria crispata* is considered the most deadly of the many rattlepod species on El Questro and has been responsible for the loss of hundreds of horses over the years.

The showy yellow spikes of the crotalaria flowers may be seen growing in colonies close to roads and tracks in the Spurlings Pocket area throughout most of the dry season. Despite supplementary feeding, horses continue to die from consuming it. During my first weeks at El Questro all staff rose at daybreak to weed the eight hectares of the horse paddock. About 20 of us spread out in a line some metres apart and moved across the paddock, clearing it of all crotalaria before breakfast.

Equal pay for black and white stockmen had been legislated throughout Australia in 1966, but there was strong resistance to it in the Kimberley where the basic wage was not generally implemented until late in 1968. In place of increased wages the Ohrts looked after their employees well. Former employees who stayed on with the new owners included the Clarke family, Johnny Ah-Won and Patrick Birch, and Jimmy Smith remained as head stockman. Johnny Ah-Won and the Clarke family were all good workers.

Donkeys were shot by the thousand and Patrick Birch recalls only 30 to 40 cattle being sent to the meatworks during one year of the Ohrt's tenure.

The Ohrts enjoyed good times with friends in Wyndham and Kununurra. Although there was no social life on the station when the men were out working, Helen and the Aboriginal women spent their days fishing and enjoying each other's company. The fishing was good along the Pentecost River close to the homestead as well as along the Chamberlain and King

Rivers and the results were delicious. Helen found El Questro a lovely place to live and she derived great satisfaction from producing quantities of fruit, vegetables and flowers, all afforded by access to unlimited fresh water. In the wet season the wild flowers and beautiful birds appeared as if from nowhere.

Helen recounted air freighting a consignment of young chickens up from Perth and her horror at finding a large python in their pen with a series of swellings down its body from devouring many of the precious chicks.

Prior to the Ohrt tenure, the Department of Agriculture commenced an Australia-wide campaign to eradicate pleuropneumonia in the cattle industry and stock inspectors were subsequently located in Halls Creek and Wyndham. From 1964 all calves and as many grown cattle as possible were required to be vaccinated at branding. Throughout the nation the movement of all cattle had to be recorded and the stock were required to be blood tested prior to any relocation. Record keeping continued in the Kimberley until 1972 when 'pleuro' was successfully eradicated.

John McMicking took on the Wyndham-based Stock Inspector job in 1966 and held the position until 1988. The pleuro campaign provided an insight into the Ohrt years in the following details recorded in McMicking's note book:

1967	
19 Jul	Camp mustering & on way to Wyndham with bulls & bullocks. (maybe 80).
26 Oct	26 horses. All poor & on supplementary feed. 170 cattle branded for the season. No vaccination.
1968	38 inches rain
8 May	Shot & p.m. horse with walkabout.
26 Jul	Mustering between Mount Rob & King River. Don Tate contracting. 80 in hand (mainly belonging to Dunham River)
25 Nov	Branding & Vaccination negligible. 3 inches rain recently. Station now for sale.
1969 June	Gordon Ohrt sold out to NSW buyers George Lansell, Edgar Pickles, and Geoff Gregory.

Cattle numbers on El Questro were minimal and Ohrt reported only 200 head in 1968. McMicking's records indicate that 1,200 calves were branded on El Questro during the eight years between 1964 and 1972, when record keeping ceased.

The Speewah and adjoining Wild Dog leases were then held by Doug Davidson as part of Dunham Station. The latter was transferred to El Questro about 1970 or soon after.

Equal pay for the Aboriginal workers had become a reality throughout the Kimberley by the time Helen and Gordon Ohrt sold the lease in 1969 and the situation with the Aborigines had entered a new phase.

Late in 1956 the Grayden Report into Aboriginal welfare was tabled in the Western Australian Parliament and it became the catalyst for a national movement for Aboriginal Rights in Australia. Activists and the newly formed Federal Council for Aboriginal Advancement petitioned the federal government to change discriminatory clauses in sections of the Constitution and continued their activism until a national referendum was held in May 1967. The same year saw the establishment of the first national organisation controlled by Aborigines. The voice of black Australia was becoming louder and falling on more sympathetic ears.

At the referendum more than 90 per cent of the Australian electorate voted 'yes' to the two proposals presented. The vote gave recognition to Aborigines as citizens of the country they had occupied for at least 40,000 years and determined they should be included in the census. They were also entitled to vote at elections and were eligible for the same social service benefits as white citizens.

Once full award wages were introduced, the Aborigines, who over the decades had become the backbone of the pastoral industry, were dispensed with and replaced by white wage earners. Jobs became increasingly scarce for Aboriginal workers. The fencing of stations and the increased use of motor vehicles and helicopters reduced the need for manual stock work, and to worsen the situation for station employment there was a decline in world beef prices.

By the late 1960s most Aboriginal families had been turned off the stations and had drifted to the outskirts of the Kimberley's few towns. Some were dumped at Warmun where a community was established by the government in the early 1970's. Humpies were exchanged for angle iron houses with communal ablution blocks, and families began a life of government medical and social welfare handouts, pensions and child endowment. The move to the towns separated people from the land to which they had deep spiritual and psychological attachments. Their few remaining ancient laws became diluted or forgotten.

Many of these displaced people had their first experiences with alcohol after moving to the towns. Amongst urban Aborigines the rate of crime increased alarmingly, principally drunkenness, violence and burglary. Those caught in this urban situation found themselves subject to both the Australian white man's law as well as to their tribal laws that had evolved over millennia. Passed down the generations orally or through ceremony, the tribal laws, now diminishing in significance, had been the framework supporting Aboriginal society, providing complex rules of behaviour, interaction, kinship and punishment.

The 1970s saw the struggle for Aboriginal rights intensify. In 1972 the Tent Embassy was established on the lawns of Federal Parliament House in Canberra drawing national and international attention to the plight of the Aborigines. The colours of the new Aboriginal flag began to gain recognition: black for the people, red for the earth and yellow for the sun and the hope of a new day.

El Questro's neighbour, Doon Doon or Dunham Station as it was then called, was the first property in the East Kimberley to be purchased by the Federal Aboriginal Land Fund Commission in the mid-1970s. Dunham and other properties were purchased as an attempt by the government to give the displaced traditional owners and other Aboriginal people somewhere to live and hopefully develop an economic base.

El Questro Pty Ltd 1969–1985

Interest in ownership of land in the remote north-west of Australia was a romantic concept for many would-be white pastoralists in the 1960s and in 1969 the lease of El Questro was transferred from the Ohrts to a syndicate registered as El Questro Pty Ltd.

Tom Connor was an engineer and farm machinery manufacturer in Victoria who specialised in tillage and seeding. His company Connor-Shea Farm Equipment had business as far afield as Katherine in the Northern Territory.

Connor and his brother-in-law, Des Lougoon, had been planning to purchase a cattle station in the Kimberley for their children when Des's son Charles saw El Questro Station advertised for sale in the *Weekly Times*. The asking price of around $80,000 covered little more than the value of the plant and equipment on the station and the annual lease rental previously $312.50 was increased to $982.80.

Lougoon and a former air force mate, Edgar Pickles, flew to the Kimberley in Connor's plane to inspect the property where they found the marginal operations of El Questro did not suggest it was the way to make a great fortune, however it did provide an inexpensive way of fulfilling one's dreams. Pickles also believed El Questro had potential as a recreational and holiday destination as well as an operating cattle station.

In 1969 George Lansell, a sheep farmer from the Riverina and a former air force pilot acquaintance of Pickles, was likewise considering acquiring property in the Kimberley. He and a couple of mates chartered an aircraft to fly around Australia and when the party reached Kununurra, Lansell made some enquiries that led him to Gordon Ohrt at El Questro.

The upshot of these visits was for Pickles, Lougoon, Connor and Lancell to combine their resources and form El Questro Pty Ltd in order to purchase the station from the Ohrts.

They found the homestead was in good, habitable condition. It had a water cooling system on the roof and the double doors opening onto the front and back verandahs provided a refreshing breezeway through each room.

The plant left by Gordon Ohrt consisted of the bulldozer, three Willys utilities and two old tractors, one of which had a grader blade and front-end loader. The syndicate also inherited a 4WD Blitz truck capable of carrying 4 bulls. The new owners bought a David Brown tractor and a Connor off-set disc and disc-seeder along with a 1970 model conventional Toyota truck, which although it was unable to go 'off road' was capable of transporting up to 12 bullocks to Wyndham.

At the beginning of each wet season the truck returned to Victoria towing a dog trailer carrying machinery and other gear from the station requiring repairs. At the end of the southern summer it was driven back to the station loaded with the repaired or new equipment, chaff for the horses, seed and any necessary supplies.

Connor's plane was a Cessna 172, which he left at El Questro, enabling most of the station to be explored from the air. His 17-year-old nephew, Charles, had the use of the aircraft.

Charles worked on El Questro for a couple of years after the syndicate purchased the station. One of his first tasks was to bulldoze a new airstrip in its present position closer to the homestead. He also formed a crossing of the Chamberlain River below the Big Hole at the Durack Tree. From there he reopened the track along the valley floor and up to Branko's Lookout and beyond to the plateau where, unsurprisingly, no cattle were found. This track across the plateau almost to the Salmond River is said to have been cut in 1960 by Hugo Austla for a mining company.

In the early days of the syndicate, the road to El Questro from the Great Northern Highway only went to the top of the driveway leading to the homestead at Spurlings Pocket. Later, in the 1970s Charles Lougoon assisted the Shire to extend this road to the Pentecost River crossing, thus completing the last section of the now famous Gibb River Road and consigning the Kurunjie Track to history.

Throughout the 15 years the syndicate held the lease, the station was engaged in beef production with a series of managers at the helm. In the early years of their tenure from the late 1960s to around 1973, the station barely paid its way. There was no money made from the property and the partners soon discovered the few cattle on El Questro were predominantly barren cows and scrub bulls. Thus, as additional funding was required over the years, more than a dozen names bought into the leasehold on the property.

Prior to the flooding of Argyle Downs and the creation of the huge lake for the irrigation scheme, the former Durack property was mustered by helicopter and a thousand horses were submitted for auction in Kununurra where the syndicate partners purchased 50 or more. Shortly afterwards they bought more horses and a few mules from Bullo River Station, but during their transportation to El Questro a skirmish between the horses and mules led to the latter being off loaded.

The syndicate appointed the first station manager, Bill Amos, in 1969. About a dozen Aboriginal stockmen were employed to assist with mustering at the end of the wet season and throughout the cooler months. They brought their families with them to the station, where they camped on the Pentecost River near the homestead. The stockmen worked continuously out of the various stock camps for six weeks and were then taken to Kununurra or Wyndham for a week off, where several gave away their work clothes and required a fresh set when they returned to the station. Jim Russell kept the station's books and Margaret Molyneaux, a solicitor in Kununurra, was responsible for ensuring everyone was paid correctly.

The King River catchment area provided good grazing country and was a focal point for mustering. There were two airstrips and wire yards located at the headwaters of the river close to the boundary with Dunham Station and to the east at Wild Dog. Airstrips and yards were also constructed on the south side of today's Gibb River Road within a few kilometres of the Pentecost Crossing to the south west of the Cockburn Range. A wire trap yard was also erected to capture cattle when they came to drink at a waterhole near the top of the station drive.

Some of the cattle mustered from the King River area were walked through the Nimberline Valley to the bronco yards that Kiwi Harrison built at Cattle Creek – a distance that could be covered in a day.

During the mustering the bulldozer was used to push tracks through to the temporary stock camps where portable yards were assembled at a muster point in preparation for working with the cattle. Amos and the next manager, Trevor Kells, both used quiet coacher cattle to assist with the mustering process. These cattle would be moved to a selected location and held together by mounted stockmen while pilots like Charles Lougoon – flying a fixed wing aircraft and using radio communication – made low overhead passes to flush out the wild cattle and move them close enough to merge with the coacher herd. The collective herd was then walked to the waiting yards where the calves were inoculated, marked and branded and the steers drafted out and trucked to the meatworks by semi-trailer. It is reported that 209 cattle were branded and turned off in 1970, averaging $45 a head.

By the time the second stage of the muster commenced it was much later in the season and the daily temperature had increased significantly. Nutritional grazing had diminished, causing the condition of the remaining cattle to fall away. This muster concentrated on reducing the number of wild bulls on the property. Generally these 'mickey' bulls lived a solitary existence sheltering from the heat of the day among the shadows in the scrubby country.

Amos and his partner had a pack of 12 feisty bull terrier dogs, a breed known for their fearlessness and ferocity. When young Charles Lougoon located a bull from the air the dogs were released. They would bail up the beast and seize it by the muzzle, thereby distracting and enraging it sufficiently to allow the stockmen to move in and throw it in order to remove the tips of its horns in preparation for transportation to the meatworks in the Toyota truck.

Stock Inspector John McMicking's record book gives details of the following managers:

1969	Bill Amos from NSW was the first manager for approximately 2 years.
1970	Trevor Kells from N.T. at the start of the season with 60 horses and 6 boys.
May 1971-1972	Craig Lorimer from Queensland.
1974	Ian Smith
1975-1978	Digger Flohr. Cattle prices recovered in 1975 and when they fell again in 1978 Flohr moved on.
1979-1983 Des	Lougoon was a part owner/manager.
1984	Dennis Wells, mustered bulls and was a good worker.

The bottom fell out of the cattle market in 1973 and many Kimberley Stations were placed on the market. No cattle from El Questro were sent to any works between 1972 and 1975. McMicking's records indicate El Questro's best bull catching years were between 1976 and 1983 with Timmy Farrell catching 626 during this period.

During World War II countless airstrips were built across the Kimberley for use in the defence of the country and there are unconfirmed reports of the remains of two Spitfire aircraft on El Questro. There have been many other airstrips on El Questro at various times for unknown reasons. Des Lougoon reports there were three strips close to the headwaters of the King River near Dunham Station and Dennis Wells also mentions seeing several in that vicinity.

Des was questioned about the number of airstrips on the station by authorities who suspected they were being used for the importation of marijuana and the export of native birds.

In later years some of the more remote strips in the Kimberley were indeed utilised for the lucrative but illegal export of wild birds. The many species of colourful finches found in the North West were especially popular and their great numbers gave rise to the Kimberley being regarded as the 'finch capital' of Australia.

Some biographies of Kimberley residents record childhood memories of legally trapping birds in the early half of last century. Anne Marie Ingham's book *Pioneers of the Kimberley* recounts young Maggie Lilly's activities during the short annual bird catching season. Maggie set her nets amongst the boab trees in the valleys south of Wyndham where the name of a valley and a creek bear testimony to her youthful enterprise. She also drove her old Ford into Spurlings Pocket in pursuit of birds.

Each year a dealer travelled from Perth to purchase the captive birds. Trappers were paid about seven shillings and sixpence per dozen birds. The dealer returned to Perth and travelled on to London with hundreds of birds where the beautiful creatures were sold and kept captive far from their native grasslands.

Joe Long was a serious bird catcher in the 1940s and 1950s and he would make his way into Spurlings Pocket late in the dry season when the waters were drying up elsewhere. He kept his birds in cages in a shed at Anthon's Landing and continued catching until the rains came, he then transferred all his cages onto a ship and travelled to Perth where he sold them. Today the dozens of bird cages found on the west side of the highway at Six Mile are remnants of this now illegal trade.

For a brief period young cockatoos were traded among the seamen visiting Wyndham. Juvenile birds are more easily taught to talk than older birds, and in the days when there were few other entertainments, teaching the birds to talk was a popular pastime.

In Western Australia a £2 bounty was paid for a dingo scalp and for some time there was a bounty of two shillings and sixpence paid for the head of an eagle. The latter were responsible for preying on lambs in the sheep grazing areas in the south, while further north and in the Kimberley young goats were their victims.

Trevor Kells bought another 20 horses from a wild horse muster on Dunham River. Once they were broken in, they were added to El Questro's mob, replacing those lost to the crotalaria and bringing the total to around 120. Mustering was strenuous work and hard on the horses; generally each man was allocated four animals for the six-week work period, enabling him to change mounts throughout the day. Thus half of the horses were worked at a time, allowing the balance to be spelled for up to seven weeks.

At Spurlings Pocket the flat land adjacent to the Bronco Yards was cleared and approximately 100 acres sown to Townsville Lucerne. Nearer to the homestead, the area on both sides of the drive between the Pentecost River and the Telecom Hill range was also cleared, irrigated, and sown to peas, beans and pasture in an attempt to supplement the horses' diet and reduce their loss to crotalaria. Kells purchased pigs and ducks from the service station owner at Timber Creek and they joined the chickens on the domestic scene. The pig numbers increased greatly and many went wild although thankfully none are found on El Questro today.

In an attempt to increase the profitability of the station John Montague was brought into the syndicate as Managing Director late in 1970. With cattle interests in Queensland and a property near Khancoban in New South Wales, Montague was interested in following the popular trend of owning land in the Kimberley.

A stock agent from Elder Smith & Co. in Queensland introduced Montague to Craig Lorimer. Lorimer was a stock inspector at Newcastle Waters and had a good reputation for mustering scrub bulls. He was employed as manager at El Questro in 1971 and 1972.

By the time Craig and his wife Estelle came to El Questro, Kununurra was established and growing at a spectacular rate. The damming of the Ord River at the Bandicoot Bar had been completed in 1963 and the irrigated farms had been allocated and were already operational. Work was almost complete on the Argyle barrage, creating the vast Ord River Dam, or Lake Argyle as it became known.

El Questro had access to both Kununurra and Wyndham by way of the present Gibb River Road and Great Northern Highway, and the King River track offered an alternate route to Wyndham. This rough track on the eastern side of the Cockburn Range ran northwards and parallel to the river bearing its name.

The 1964 Homestead. Photographed by Craig Lorimer in 1972.

Lorimer recalls the heavy horse losses and the need to purchase replacements and break in the colts at the beginning of each year. He was assisted by 'stockmen' who came from the Aboriginal reserve or the welfare offices in town and were brought out to the station after the wet season. Using stock and pack horses, Lorimer sucessfully mustered the Chamberlain Valley as far south as Bedford Downs where they found branded cattle from other stations. The unbranded scrub bulls and bush cattle were walked north along the valley and across the river to the Home Paddock. By the time they reached the Bronco Yards the cattle were fairly quiet and relatively easy to handle, but unfortunately none of them were in suitable condition for slaughter at the meatworks.

Alternative arrangements were made to transport a consignment of 800 cattle almost 2,500 kilometres to Queensland for an auction at Richmond. In May 1971 Kevin Dickenson from Dubbo brought his double-decker semi-trailer to the area. It is believed this was the first multi-level mode of transport in the Kimberley. Of the consignment, 215 of the cows and steers were from El Questro and the balance was made up with cattle from neighbouring Home Valley and farther afield.

Five months later another 134 mixed cattle followed. Although this strategy raised some desperately needed funds for the impoverished station it reduced the breeding herd and had a detrimental effect on future calving numbers.

Tom Cannon, a contract bull catcher, mustered the King River area in 1971 on a percentage basis which Craig believes was a 50 per cent split, and apparently Wattle Stewart did the same in 1972. Craig recalls seeing a couple of grave sites in the King River area which he believes date back to the gold rush days.

Buoyed by the success of the Queensland sales, John Montague embarked on an ambitious repeat enterprise. In 1972 he approached John Naughton and offered to match the meatworks price for their cattle and save them the expense of getting the animals to Wyndham. The deal was accepted and 4,000 cattle were trucked to Queensland. Cattle tick was found among the animals on arrival, necessitating quarantining. Despite this extra cost the enterprise was financially successful.

Saddling the horses and mules.

Stockwork. Photos by Craign Lorimer.

At El Questro the stockmen spent most days mustering wild cattle using the coacher herd. Generally the solitary bulls had to be run down and captured individually and then held over until a sufficient number had been yarded to make up a load for transportation to Wyndham in the Toyota truck. The Wyndham Meatworks was still operating seasonally, accepting El Questro bulls between Easter and the end of October. Although it was generally necessary to make a booking some two months in advance nominating the date and estimated number of beasts to be killed, El Questro was able to slip the odd truckload into the system without making a booking. A decent sized bullock brought $100–$150. The meat was sold by the meatworks to the United States as grinding beef for their burgeoning burger trade.

Craig remembers these days as good fun for a young bloke in his mid-twenties. He would drive to Wyndham to pick up stores or visit the rapidly developing town of Kununurra for a variety of social activities.

Working in the stockyards. Photo by Craig Lorimer.

Approximately 20 Aborigines lived harmoniously in family groups in five iron sheds. These were located on the high ground beyond the workshop where the stone bungalows are today. There was no alcohol. Only the men worked and they were paid out prior to the wet season when they left the station with their families. Ziggy, an itinerant German, lived around the homestead and grew fruit and vegetables along the riverbank for sale in Wyndham.

Telephones were non-existent and the only method of communication was a telegram service provided by the Royal Flying Doctor Service radio. El Questro's radio call sign was 8WQL and the call sign for the RFDS at Wyndham was VKF. The first daily session time for telegrams was 7.00–8.00am, followed by medical calls with the doctor, each up to 30 minutes duration. The next telegram session was at 11.00am and again at 4.00pm. Three times each day telegrams were taken to the Post Office for transmission and the responses collected by the RFDS were relayed back to the outlying stations.

The syndicate's funding arrangements for the station appear to have been unstructured and totally unreliable. Any income from cattle sales was irregular and the cash flow frequently proved insufficient to pay El Questro's accounts. On one occasion Craig resorted to barter to cover the station's dues. He mustered some 90 head of cattle into the Cockburn Yards and walked them 90 kilometres to Kununurra to settle an account with Oliver's Kimberstock for pumps and other related hardware. This exercise involved closing the Victoria Highway at the Diversion Dam to allow the cattle to cross the Ord River at that point.

While Craig was away on this mission, Ziggy was left in charge of the daily chores around the house. In the course of discharging this duty he discovered John Montague's stash of home-brew. On his return to the station Craig found Ziggy out cold, the generator out of fuel and the putrid contents of the refrigerator leaking all over the floor. Eventually Ziggy came around and on realising the extent of his misdemeanour he took off. Craig managed to catch up with him at Six Mile and return his belongings to him.

The same year a potential buyer from America offered to pay $180,000 for El Questro. Lansell and Montague were happy to accept the offer but other syndicate members rejected it and after due negotiation, Edgar Pickles, Des Lougoon and Tom Connor bought George Lansell and John Montague out. The two vendors went on to purchase Oomagooma Station in the West Kimberley.

At the end of his contract Craig and his wife worked for a while at Tableland Station before moving back to Queensland and working for many years in the cattle industry as a stock agent. During his travels he came across the following lines painted on an old tank on Murrungie Station:

> *The old grey mare will do no more kicking,*
> *She was ridden to death by Torrance MacMicking*

Quite co-incidentally Craig found himself back on El Questro 30 years later to oversee the muster and handover of the cattle following a change of proprietor.

In 1973 or 1974, the syndicate took up the lease of the North Country which appears to have remained vacant since its cancellation as an Aboriginal Reserve in the 1950s. This area with a fringe of grassland skirting the picturesque Cockburn Range, incorporated the Barclay Stock Route. It was considered useful but, as the early drovers discovered, there was little fresh water available during the dry season. Windmills were brought in to provide water to the area, but only one was assembled and it had mechanical problems, so the exercise was not a success.

According to Edgar Pickles, there was a plan to acquire Tableland Station on the south west boundary of El Questro and to use the Yarrabar area to rest the Tableland bullocks on their way to the meatworks. However this idea was dropped when late in 1973 the effect of the oil crisis on the American market reduced beef prices by up to 75 per cent causing the Kimberley to fall into recession between 1974 and 1978.

Although the search for oil and minerals had been going on for decades, the 1970s was a period of serious mineral exploration in the Kimberley, and El Questro saw its share of activity by exploratory drilling companies and geologists in helicopters. Drums of jet fuel abandoned by a mining company on the Pentecost River provided evidence of this.

During this decade Planet Mining Co. from Sydney made exploratory surveys for uranium along the Chamberlain River. They constructed an airstrip and some 85 miles of track from the river crossing downstream from where the Homestead is today. Apparently for many years the remains of one of their abandoned trucks could be seen along the Chamberlain River somewhere to the south.

Longyear Australia Exploration Drilling Company is reported to have had drilling camps every two to three miles on El Questro between 1975 and 1978. One of their geologists based at Turkey Creek at that time has spoken of seeing large numbers of cattle, horses, donkeys and emus in the exploration area. One might expect that emu numbers would be quite prolific in the Kimberley and old-timers claim they were around but sadly nowadays they are rarely seen.

The search for diamonds began in earnest in 1972 with the occasional stone and other indicators found at a variety of sites during the following three years. It was not until 1979 that CRA Exploration with their camp based near El Questro at Kingston Rest Station, found a diamond pipe in the Ragged Ranges close to Lake Argyle. At the time of their discovery a uranium seeking company held a temporary reserve over the Ragged Range and Smoke Creek location, requiring CRA to maintain tight secrecy and take steps to divert attention from their find which eventually developed into the world's largest diamond mine.

Charles Lougoon recalls assisting a Bell Resources truck laden with drilling rigs when it became bogged on the King River shortly after turning off the Gibb River Road heading towards Speewah. He now wonders if it was part of a CRA diversion ploy. Charles also flew some mining personnel to an exploratory base near the Elgee Cliffs just south of El Questro.

The Kimberley continues to provide a focus for mining activities and in 2002 geologists from AngloGold Ashanti were briefly based at El Questro whilst looking for gold in the region. There were reports of fluoride on neighbouring Doon Doon Station and, more recently the commencement of iron ore mining on the station.

Digger Flohr, noted as a hard worker, took on the management of El Questro in January 1975, just after Cyclone Tracy devastated Darwin on Christmas Day. During his three year term his children attended school in Kununurra as weekly boarders. The station initially ran some 800 to 1,000 head of Shorthorn cattle. Another 800 quality breeding cows and 300 calves were purchased from Moola Bulla in September for $25 and $7 respectively. Digger took delivery of the cattle and walked them as far as Bow River Station where the country had recently been burnt. Because of the resulting shortage of grass and water it was necessary to truck the cattle the remainder of the journey to El Questro. They were unloaded on the western side of a three or four-strand wire block fence running across the Gibb River Road between the Nimberline Range and the South Cockburn, not far from Mulaga Spring. A wire 'cocky' gate across the road allowed travellers to pass through. Yards and a portable dip located near the top of the Station drive were used to spray the cattle against the blood-sucking parasitic tick prevalent at the time.

The syndicate purchased a wartime surplus 6x6 American Studebaker truck. It was equipped with a Perkins diesel engine and fitted out for use as a cattle truck with a stock crate, ramp and winch. The 6-wheel drive truck was driven up from Melbourne in 1974 and remained in active service at El Questro until after the turn of the century.

Cut-down jeeps known as 'bull-catchers' were used to chase and run the wild 'mickey' bulls to a standstill. A stockman would deftly grab the beast by the tail and throw it off balance, bringing it to the ground, where it would remain with its legs strapped together until it was winched onto the Studebaker.

The 1974 6WD Studebaker truck in 2005.

A typical bull-catcher.

Continuing the practice started a decade earlier, most cattle were killed and butchered on the property by Eddie Warnock. During Digger's years on El Questro only 40–50 cattle were trucked to the meatworks – he cannot recall the number of cattle sent to Queensland. The Station killed their own beef for domestic consumption and turned some of it into beef jerky for use on muster camps.

To cover the ongoing loss of horses, Digger purchased an additional 30 horses from Torrance MacMicking who was on Moola Bulla Station at the time. Heavy rains caused a flood shortly after they arrived at El Questro and all the horses took off back to Speewah.

Jim Rankin was a young man in his early twenties when in 1976 he and his mate Robert Baxter decided to drive to the Kimberley to work on El Questro Station for a few months. Jim had heard talk of life at El Questro from a relative of one of the syndicate owners.

The two young men arrived at El Questro in June after an adventurous drive from Victoria through the Red Centre and Tanami Desert. Digger and his wife Anne were the only Europeans on the place. There were several Aboriginal families camped on the river flat and Jim recalls Rosie and Saturday Button. Saturday, the lead rider during mustering, had missing front teeth and tribal scars on his chest indicating a traditional initiation. Churchill was another good stockman who had worked with Digger during his time at Tableland Station, and there was Jack Rider the camp cook and his son Peter. Jack's specialty was steak and unpeeled potato chips.

In the 1970s bird catching was still a popular activity around Wyndham and young Roderick Woodland would join the El Questro musters in order to check out the location of birds. He was especially interested in the Gouldian Finch. In later years Roderick established an 1,800-acre dude ranch style holding on the King River and called it Diggers Rest. Today his property is involved in tourism and horseback safaris.

Mustering was in progress almost continually and Jim recalls working cattle at Yarrabar and at Wild Dog Spring where Digger had erected yards with a spear gate trap – an effective one-way funnel arrangement allowing animals to enter but not exit. When mustering cattle beyond the permanent yards on the property, the beasts were corralled at night using a temporary wire yard. This was constructed by running a strand of barbed wire waist high between trees in a small circle. The contents of two cartons of toilet paper were strung along the wire and a floodlight erected in a tree in the centre of the yard with a small Honda generator on the ground below to power it.

The light and hum of the generator prevented the cattle from 'spooking' and eliminated the need for an overnight watch.

Some of the cattle targeted for mustering were wild and dangerous and Digger brought another mob of quiet coachers to assist with the mustering. On one occasion young Peter moved too close to the cattle and a charging 'scrubber' got its horns under his horse, opening its belly. During the ensuing scuffle that took place under a boab tree Peter lunged for but missed an overhanging branch and landed on the ground. He ran around the bulbous tree trunk and, to the horror of the onlooking stockmen, met the bull coming the other way. Fortunately, at this point quick thinking Digger managed to save the situation by distracting the bull. Back at camp and badly shaken by the incident, Peter kept muttering to himself and anyone within earshot: 'A man could-a get killed, a man could-a get killed' – a quote that endured in Jim Rankin's memory.

Jim remembers a white 'authority' on Aboriginal matters telling him the origin of the Wandjina cult came from white sailors being shipwrecked on the west coast and showing the Aborigines, who had possibly never seen Europeans before, a picture of Christ crowned by a halo. This offered a feasible explanation at the time, but recent research indicates the Wandjina cult has been in existence longer than Christianity.

I have long been fascinated by reports of the bizarre Australian outback phenomenon known as the Min Min lights. These mysterious lights are generally associated with western Queensland, around Boulia in the Channel Country, but they have also been reported in the Kimberley and other open outback country regions. The ghostly lights are mentioned in country folklore and pre-European Aboriginal mythology. Over the years they have been observed by drovers, stockmen, miners, truck drivers and bushwalkers, and their existence is accepted as fact. However, scientists researching the phenomenon of the Min Min have yet to come up with an agreed explanation for them.

Jim might not have seen the mysterious Min Min but he does recall a surreal experience one night when he was camped by the side of the Gibb River Road. He awoke to the sound of an approaching vehicle and watched in astonishment as a truck roared past. In the moonlight he could clearly see the cabin had been flattened and the driver was sitting proud of the machine. Thinking he had been hallucinating, Jim was relieved to learn later that a truck belonging to one of the Aboriginal stations to the west had rolled over and, despite having a flattened cabin, was still drivable.

Digger estimates there were about ten members of the syndicate during his time on El Questro. Neil Larson and Terry Fogarty of Fogarty's Flying Club were early owners. Fogarty had ideas of flying tourists to El Questro but he died before getting the scheme into the air.

In response to the need for additional funding Neil and Fred McNabb were brought in. The property was used as a holiday destination and the owners and their friends travelled up and camped on the station while the manager and his family lived permanently in the house.

According to the station's labour requirements, approximately half a dozen Aboriginal workers came and went during Digger's time. The station had practically no income and, as in the past, Digger's difficulty in obtaining funds from the syndicate earned the station a poor reputation amongst its suppliers.

During recent decades the prevalence of fires throughout the Kimberley in the dry season – between July and December – has become of increasing concern as it accounts for the indiscriminate burning of large areas of pastoral and crown land each year. Fires have become a major challenge to pastoralists as well as to those responsible for the National Parks and crown land throughout the Kimberley. Most of the ground-storey vegetation is readily flammable and during the hotter months damage to the flora is severe and recovery slow. Digger burned patches of spinifex at the beginning of the wet season.

In 1982 the syndicate made a successful application to take over approximately 50,586 hectares held as a Native Reserve along the upper King River. The area was not in use at the time and the acquisition of this land brought the El Questro Station holding to more than a million acres – 404,686 hectares.

The value of El Questro's rugged beauty was not lost on its owners or those residing on the property. Edgar Pickles had a dream of building affordable cabins along the Pentecost River and offering fishing and a long-term seasonal escape to retirees wishing to avoid the southern winters.

Adventurous campers travelling along the challenging Gibb River Road were made welcome by several of the syndicate managers.

Dennis Wells came to manage El Questro in response to an advertisement in the *Queensland Country Life* newspaper. He was interviewed in Townsville and employed by Edgar Pickles and Des Lougoon. Wells, with his wife Coleen and four children aged from three to eight years arrived in the Kimberley from Queensland early in 1983 shortly after the wet season.

However the Gibb River Road, normally capable of carrying road trains, was in poor condition and the station driveway was horrendous. Both reflected the annual ravages of the wet season with the runoff from the seasonally heavy rains badly scouring the roads and leaving debris and rocks obstructing all of the floodway crossings. Driving their four-ton truck with a 30-foot caravan in tow, the Wells's cavalcade became bogged twice on the 16-kilometre-long, two-wheel rutted driveway and it took about ten frustrating hours to reach the station homestead from the highway.

The homestead pocket seemed to have been vacant for years with the sheds on the bank of the Pentecost River derelict and the garden and grounds around the house overgrown from the preceding humid wet season. Before starting on the cattle work, Dennis employed three members of his family and Billy Hally, a local Aborigine, to clear the jungle around the house and orchard areas and dispose of the rubbish and old chemicals from the sheds. Some remnants of this rubbish may be found above the airstrip today. The large bougainvillea in front of the house was pulled out using a vehicle and chain.

It took over a month to clean up the place and get the old bull-catcher and Studebaker 6x6 vehicles going again. The back end of the tractor had seized up and had to be dealt with. Dennis's next job was to build a set of horse yards close to the house using posts cut from trees along the creeks and tea tree for the straight rails. Today the stone and cement water trough near the Station Store is all that remains of this work.

Wells wisely insisted on having full control of the station bank account and a committed budget to work with. The syndicate accordingly flew a bank manager up from Victoria and organised a bank loan for $50,000 prior to his arrival.

In the general clean up process, two government helicopters working between the jump-up on the driveway and the Chamberlain River, shot approximately 960 donkeys in an afternoon on their first run through the station. Afterwards two men drove around in the bull-catcher to dispatch any wounded animals but very few were found. Twenty-four dingoes were poisoned in the same area.

The Wells children were taught by School of the Air and supervised by a governess whenever one could be found.

Several of the syndicate owners had served in the RAAF during the war so naturally the use of light aircraft was the order of the day. For this reason, as well as providing for emergency evacuation in the event of an accident, the maintenance of the airstrip was another of Dennis's responsibilities. This was accomplished by using the truck to drag lengths of railway iron across the surface of the runway.

On one occasion, while flying over the Cockburn Range with Edgar Pickles at the controls, the engine stopped. Dennis feared the worst as the nose dipped towards the ground and the horizon disappeared from view, until Pickles casually pumped fuel from the full tank and fired the engine back to life. Apparently Pickles, a Squadron Leader in the Air Force, whose war service was recognised with the Distinguished Flying Cross and Bar, was quirky about emptying one tank completely before switching over to the other.

The ongoing problem of the crotalaria had taken its toll and there were no horses to be found when Dennis arrived at the station. He purchased 16 from a sale in Katherine and later bought another 42 unbroken and ageing horses from Dick Northcott on Moola Bulla near Halls Creek. One of the many horses to be lost to crotalaria during the next wet season was the children's pony which, in its dying stages, found its way into the homestead kitchen where Dennis had to shoot it and drag it outside.

As in the past, most of the work focussed on bull-catching and in the 1984 season some 500 bulls averaging $160 were sold to the meatworks in Wyndham. A new bull-catcher vehicle purchased for $8,400 was one of his first major expenses and this together with the invincible Studebaker with its stock crate capable of carrying six beasts provided the ground support for the Slingsby muster helicopter. Most of the mustering along the King River and in the Spurlings Pocket area was done using helicopters.

Dennis recalls the old Ghan's stone ruins on the west side of the Elgee Cliffs and he remembers sitting in the spring at Wild Dog, now Matteo Springs, and finding old saddle trees and mustering equipment in the sand under a nearby boab tree.

During the wet season he was maddened to find the butchered remains of 16 cattle along the King River. Some weeks later, after being tipped off by a local who had seen an unfamiliar truck driving away from Fish Hole, Dennis went to investigate. He followed the vehicle tracks past Home Valley and came across the responsible party in a deep creek bed, cooking a freshly killed shoulder of beef on hot coals. Leaving his offsider in the bull-catcher, he grabbed the single barrel shotgun which was always kept in the vehicle and went to confront the mob, telling them if they desperately wanted beef they should call in and ask rather than shoot a beast and take only the shoulders, leaving the rest of the carcass to rot. A month later police informed Dennis that civil charges had been laid against him and that his case represented a challenge to his right to defend his property. The outcome of the incident was a hearing where he had to answer to charges of threatening the men with firearms. Fortunately, the magistrate dismissed all charges, declaring that Dennis had a right to protect his property.

During Dennis's time on El Questro someone from Perth came to the station claiming to be a traditional owner of the country and asking him to mark any known cultural sites on a map. Dennis, whose main focus was on mustering cattle, was often in remote areas where sites were likely to be found, but he did not go out of his way to look for them and he dismissed the request, telling the Aboriginal man that if he had a valid claim to the country he should know where the sites were.

The start of tourism on El Questro appears to have come about by accident. Dennis was out bull-catching early one morning and almost ran his vehicle through the campsite of sleeping tourists who appeared to have no idea how close they had come to being killed. The incident proved to be a catalyst in changing the control of access to the property by travellers. The Wells family decided to provide amenities for visitors and to charge a fee. A large red sign was duly erected on the Gibb River Road advertising the availability of camping near the homestead.

The fee was $5 per car for a night and, instead of putting people off, it had the opposite effect, bringing Amez and Kings tour buses and other visitors to camp. Coleen claims she sometimes made more money from tourism than her husband received in salary. They could not have imagined the magnitude of the tourism development that was to follow.

El Questro proved popular with local residents as well and it soon became necessary to employ a man on a full-time basis to dispose of rubbish, cut up firewood and maintain the driveway using the tractor and blade to give better access to visitors. The use of recreational 4-wheel drive vehicles was still a decade away so most visitors drove conventional cars. Pit toilets were dug, barbeques built and camping spots cleared along the river bank.

Coleen painted a map on the door of a refrigerator located on the verandah of the house; it highlighted points of interest and the camping areas. Coleen and Dennis sometimes put on beef and barramundi barbeques for visitors and occasionally took them on the exciting bull-catching activity.

During Easter 1984 the RFDS fishing competition was held on the property. Arthur Vagg from Wyndham donated a pallet of beer, which was sold to raise funds and at the end of the day approximately $500 was collected for this worthy cause.

Dennis's father came for an extended visit, which sadly ended in tragedy. The two men were travelling in convoy along the driveway, when the axle and a set of dual wheels came out of the housing on the Studebaker at the creek crossing just north of Tombstone Creek.

With no brakes, Dennis ran the bull-catcher he was driving into the bank in order to avoid his father, who had left the troubled Studebaker to alert Dennis to the situation. The incident caused his father to have a heart attack and Dennis had no alternative but to make his father as comfortable as possible on the roadside in the shade of the Studebaker, and go home for help in the bull-catcher.

The RFDS base in Wyndham was the only communication the homestead had with the outside world, and the El Questro airstrip was unregistered for use by the RFDS. Peter Reed from Ord Air Charters was contacted and he picked up the patient in his six-seater single engine plane for transport to hospital, where he died a little later.

The Wells family left towards the end of 1984 after two dry seasons on El Questro. Dennis returned to El Questro in 2006 and revisited some of the areas he had mustered more than 20 years earlier. He was astonished by the growth of scrub and trees that due to fire had colonised areas he remembered as open country. He was also shocked by the number of tracks and roads crisscrossing the property. Today his initials and those of his brother Roy can be found carved into several boab trees; one of these is on Moonshine Creek behind the Grave Tree, another at the Dump area and among the family of boabs at Wild Dog. The Wild Dog locality abounds in quinine trees and Dennis frequently persuaded new employees into having a bite of the small orange fruit, leaving a bitter, dry taste in their mouths for hours.

Dennis declined an opportunity to purchase the station from the syndicate for $350,000 and it was later sold to the Salerno family for $450,000.

According to a company report dated 31.12.1982, the following were shareholders of El Questro Pty Ltd at that time:

Connor T.J.B & M.M.

Northvale (Connor)

Estate of T.H. Fogarty

Lougoon family

A.C. McDonald & co

Fred McNabb

Neil McNabb

E.L. Pickles

D.J. Russell Pty Ltd

N.W. Larson No.1 & No. 2

Larson family

R.H Ingram

Selleck Trust

F. Steedman

The total equity in the company was $274,000.

The Salerno family syndicate 1985–1991

El Questro Station had been on the market for a long time when James Salerno and members of his family syndicate, trading under the name Centaninti Pty Ltd, saw it advertised in an old newspaper and phoned to enquire about it. The despairing agent, keen to make a sale, suggested alternative stations that were more viable – and more saleable. But James could not be dissuaded; El Questro had captured his imagination and his decision was reinforced by a visit he made to a clairvoyant while living in Adelaide, who predicted he would purchase a property with water in Northern Australia.

James and his brother Ben travelled to Kununurra to inspect the station and in late 1984 the lease of El Questro passed from the syndicate to Centaninti Pty Ltd. All family members were involved in James's social research into seeking peaceful mediation of conflicts and his lifelong quest to develop the Ideal Human Environment.

When the Salernos first viewed El Questro the original intention was to run cattle, but James was so attracted by the beauty of the land and its many geological features that he purchased the station with a view to expanding into tourism.

His belief in the benefits of the outback country experience for young children prompted James to invite his first wife, Margaret, and their two children, Emma and Christian, to join him and his wife Kerrian and their extended family group living at El Questro. The families remained in residence for almost five years and during this time the children, like most others in the outback, were educated over the airwaves by the School of the Air.

One of the greatest boons to outback living conditions was the introduction of generated electricity, and by the 1980s its use was widespread throughout the Kimberley. The days of kerosene refrigerators and hurricane lanterns were at an end and air-conditioning was beginning to make a favourable impact on the humidity of the wet season.

The station was in excess of a million acres at that time. In response to an outbreak of tuberculosis in cattle, the entire station excluding the area to the west of the Chamberlain River was mustered in 1985/86 so that cattle could be tested for the disease by John Curran, the local veterinarian. The task was accomplished in the Yarrabar area using horses and a helicopter, elsewhere a helicopter and portable yards were used. During the testing process the cattle were kept yarded for three days until they were found to be disease free. Forty-four gallon drums were used to water the cattle during their time in the yards.

Once the station was declared clear of tuberculosis, stock rationalising took place; the poor quality cattle were culled and the surplus bulls sold. With a view to improving the quality of the cattle, six Brahman bulls and 35 cows in calf were purchased from Katherine. The consignment was trucked to El Questro and kept in the Home Paddock for a month, grazing with the horses during the day and yarded at night to quieten them prior to their release into the existing herds in the Spurlings Pocket and King River area.

Bull-catching was an ongoing activity that utilised the old Studebaker truck and portable yards. The cattle were mustered by the family during the dry season at Yarrabar and along the King and Chamberlain Rivers where yards were erected in the form of a trap using bales of hay to lure the cattle into them. Getting the wild beasts onto the truck was challenging and many times the workers would be seen atop a vehicle with an enraged bull bellowing below. Later, outside contractors were employed for bull-catching and the family continued with the general mustering.

El Questro's North Country extended to within a few kilometres of Wyndham and over the years cattle grazing on these grasslands have presented a temptation to local poachers. Determined to put an end to the shooting and rustling of his cattle, James soon realised his chances were poor when the police investigating a fresh kill found the evidence led them to the home of a prominent citizen and rather than press charges the matter was settled by a compensatory payment. In another incident Roderick Woodland, El Questro's neighbour at Diggers Rest Station, noticed a couple of men cutting up a beast on the verandah of their house in Wyndham and went to investigate. The animal's head, still attached to the carcass, carried an El Questro ear tag. The men concerned ended up in court where it was discovered that James, believing he was helping them with obtaining a gun licence, had given them permission to shoot donkeys on El Questro. Needless to say he was disillusioned by their ungrateful response. In another instance, despite his disability, a shady character by the name of One Arm Harry Layton was to spend time behind bars after being found guilty of stealing El Questro cattle.

As Donkey numbers built up throughout the Kimberley the Agricultural Protection Board used helicopters to conduct random donkey shoots on El Questro. The Salernos also shot donkeys and brumbies and butchered the carcasses for dog food.

On his holding at Diggers Rest, Woodland had for years allowed his cattle free range over the surrounding El Questro country. A joint muster of Diggers Rest and El Questro cattle was conducted and the cleanskins were divided between the two parties.

In 1985 Chris Henggeler approached the Salernos and expressed an interest in purchasing acreage on El Questro. Initially reluctant, the family eventually agreed to sell an allotment of 77,500 hectares of their lease. This was the most southerly section of El Questro, extending over areas of rarely utilised country along and between the Chamberlain and Salmond Rivers. It took in Sahanna's ruins on Moonlight Valley and a little of the Bedford Stock route.

The sale to Henggeler was completed in 1986. Henggeler and his partner Danny Waser were attracted to this inaccessible and remote country because of its central location, the constant water supply and their belief it could be self-sufficient. Today the country is known as Kachana Pastoral Company and Henggeler, an exponent of the Holistic Management Movement, uses it to showcase his sustainable development strategies whereby much of the erosion on the property has been arrested and, through controlled grazing, the valleys are permanently densely grassed.

After the purchase, Danny Waser and Albert Gobius, following the old mining exploration route, pushed a track through to Kachana along the western side of the Elgee Cliff line, but it was never used as access.

Within 12 months of Salerno's purchase and after years of fluctuating cattle prices and industrial disputes, the meatworks, with its average annual kill of 47,400, closed down. The loss was a major setback to the economy of Wyndham as well as to the Salernos and other pastoralists.

With rapid development continuing around Kununurra, citizens, government and other infrastructure began to relocate from Wyndham to the new centre, accelerating the decline of the struggling historic town and demoralising the old timers and others who elected to stay on. The population of this old town had, by the end of the 1980s, fallen to barely 1,000 and the white representation to a mere 25 per cent.

Prior to the closure of the meatworks, Margaret Salerno was preparing to attend a meeting there when she was seconded to assist James's wife Kerrian with the birth of their third child. Margaret's daughter, Emma, was looking forward to witnessing the birth of a half brother or sister and as the critical time approached Emma, who was attending School of the Air, excused herself over the airwaves explaining that she was going to watch a baby being born. After the delivery Emma returned to her lessons and the teacher, thinking that it must have been a pet or station animal that had given birth, asked 'What colour is it?' 'Pink of course!' came the reply from the perplexed Emma.

After the meatworks closed the Salernos sent semi-trailer loads of cattle to Broome and Adelaide, but generally they trucked half a dozen bulls at a time to Mistake Creek Station near Katherine where there was a small abattoir.

Accommodation at the station was in the three bedroom house and two caravans. Margaret attended an auction of plant and material from the defunct meatworks operation where she purchased the Social Shed in which the employees had spent their recreational time. The iron and timber from the shed was recycled to build a small dwelling on the riverbank that now forms part of the Steakhouse Restaurant at El Questro.

A small derelict shed adjacent to the Steakhouse had been the saddle shed in former days. Picturesquely covered in bougainvillea, this shed later became part of an outdoor art gallery. A short distance away stone stables were constructed, they were linked to the horse yards and trough previously built by Dennis Wells. The stables became the Bar and Store in the early years of the following Burrell tenure and today they are the stone annexe attached to the Station Store.

The RFDS radio was the only form of communication when James and Margaret's five-year-old son Christian was run over by a bull-catcher vehicle. The accident happened outside the operational radio hours of the RFDS. In a panic, Margaret screamed and shouted over the airwaves until she was miraculously overheard by Kerry Slingsby in Kununurra, who arranged for an ambulance to meet them on their way into town. Christian was flown to Darwin Hospital where he fully recovered.

Using a motorbike or bull-catcher, James spent a great deal of time exploring the unique landscape. He found and named many geological features after members of his family. Thus the spring located close to the Rock of Gibraltar at Wild Dog became Matteo Springs after his son. Caroline Valley and Amalia Gorge are the names of his nieces. The thermal springs were named after his brother Ben. Moonshine Gorge was then known as John Rat Gorge after James's nephew who was born in the Chinese Year of the Rat. The Salernos named the rock outcrop opposite Mount Rob on the eastern end of the Gibb River Road, Waltja Rock, 'waltja' meaning 'play' in the Pitjantjatjara language. It is now called Gningling Rock.

By the 1980s the remote and generally little known Kimberley area was gaining recognition throughout the nation. Many of the rough bush tracks and perilous river crossings had been replaced by sealed roads and cement causeways or bridges. The year 1988 marked 200 years of European settlement in Australia and amongst the many commemorative initiatives was a government funded project to bitumenise the last section of the Great Northern Highway near Halls Creek, thus completing a 14,500 kilometre sealed highway around the circumference of the Australian continent.

Despite the road improvement, tourism to the East Kimberley was still in its infancy with only the most adventurous tourists travelling through El Questro and beyond to Derby via the challenging 670-kilometre Gibb River Road.

Following his early exploration of the spectacular gorge near the south-east corner of the Cockburn Range, James Salerno graded a track to its entrance and constructed stone gate posts where the track left the Gibb River Road. Picnic shelters, a toilet and a couple of caravans were installed at the entrance to the gorge and the lovely attraction was opened as a campground. Some years earlier the Main Roads Department had opened a bore hole at this location to provide the water required for construction of the eastern end of the Gibb River Road.

The gorge with its spring-fed creek was named Emma Gorge after James and Margaret's first child. On his first exploratory venture up the gorge, James was mystified to discover abandoned clothing on the west side of the creek near the Turquoise Pool. He did not know that he had come across a likely clue to the mysterious disappearance of a man reported missing in Sydney in 1983 and thought nothing more of it.

In 1998 bushwalker Chris Jackson was searching for rock paintings along the base of the escarpment in Emma Gorge when he came across an abandoned campsite only a short distance from the falls and pool where the clothes had been found. It was set discreetly amongst a stand of *Pandanus spiralis* on an elevated and secluded stony ledge with commanding views down the gorge. Rocks had been arranged to make a fireplace and close by a flat table had been formed. Chris found tins of beef and condensed milk, a large battery and a pair of shoes cached in a crevice in the rocks, empty tins and other debris were tucked away in the hollow trunk of a nearby tree. Further examination of the site revealed a plastic bag containing personal letters, photographs and documents concealed in a recess in the rock face. Amongst these was a Czechoslovakian Passport and a bank savings book divulging the identity of the owner as Teodor Mastihuba.

Police were notified and initially it was speculated that some material found in the campfire may have been human bone. Needless to say, the media ran riot with headlines such as 'Mystery body found in bush', and 'Grisly find in Kimberley'.

Mastihuba arrived in Australia in 1968 and settled in Sydney where he established a photography business in the northern suburbs. Fifteen years later in 1982, he was reported missing in Sydney by his flatmate who had not seen him since he left home with his briefcase.

Nothing is known of him since. The last recorded banking activity was at the time of his disappearance. A photograph featuring a woman and children eating at a dining table accompanied a letter from the mother of the children; it was handwritten in Czechoslovakian. The letter claimed Mastihuba was not paying his dues for the children's upkeep and threatened that if he did not meet his commitment she would 'tell his friends what he had done'. We will probably never know what he had done; perhaps the mysterious deed was the reason for his emigration from his homeland. Apparently Mastihuba had not been in contact with his wife or any family member since leaving Czechoslovakia in 1968. Forensic testing of the suspected 'human bone' showed the assumption to be incorrect and police some years after the discovery mentioned that local

Aborigines reported seeing a deranged and half naked white man in the area and it was thought the Czech would have perished.

The 25-year-old mystery received media attention again in January 2009 when police acting on behalf of the coroner sought assistance from the public to close their Missing Persons file on this case. This time the focus of creative journalists changed and hysterical headlines in the press read 'WA croc probably took long-lost Sydney man' and 'Croc death mystery' accompanied by inaccurate reports that Emma Gorge was infested with crocodiles. The mysterious case remains unsolved.

During the Salerno years camping continued to be available on the Pentecost River flat at Spurlings Pocket with campers using the stockman's shower and toilet located close to the old saddle shed. The House Waterhole was used for swimming. Tracks were put into eight secluded riverside locations downstream on the Pentecost River. These camp sites were named after birds found in the area – a practice expanded on by the next owner and continuing today. One such site is named Osprey after an osprey's nest in a tree at that location.

Despite the road conditions being substantially rougher than they are today, there were still few recreational 4-wheel drive vehicles; occasionally visitors travelled by tour bus but most arrived at El Questro in conventional cars. Margaret sometimes took tourists to Ben's Springs and very occasionally to the beautiful but ecologically fragile El Questro Gorge nearby. In Salerno's time the sensitivity of these rainforest attractions was acknowledged and great care was taken to minimise human impact.

James recalls crossing the Pentecost River on the driveway during the wet season when the river level was over the bonnet of his vehicle, and how thrilled the children travelling with him were when a crocodile was swept onto the windscreen of the vehicle.

In order to have all-weather access to El Questro there was a plan to build a modest wet season dwelling in the Wild Dog area on the eastern side of the King River. It was to be located partly underground near Matteo Springs. Some second-hand building materials from the meatworks were taken to the site, but the dwelling was never completed. Instead the family merely camped there, and during the installation of the first telephone line to the homestead at Spurlings Pocket a branch line was run out to Wild Dog and a telephone installed in a small tin shed, enabling James to manage his business affairs from afar. The Telstra tower and line to this remote site have since been removed, and the area with its interesting rock formation, Aboriginal art sites and old monument for John Mangus Johnson's grave has become a tourist attraction known as Matteo Springs.

The freshwater spring and unusual formation of the nearby Rock of Gibraltar was once significant to the Aborigines who frequented the area. There are several art sites around the rock and a grinding hollow with stones that have since been 'souvenired' by tourists. Two large bailer shells, used by traditional Aborigines to carry water, were found by the Salernos and given to the Western Australian Museum in Perth.

The Salernos were not immune from the devastating effect of the crotalaria and many of the Appaloosa mares they brought from Adelaide were lost. Margaret remembers with horror the night James's favourite mare died after walking blindly around in a shed, crashing again and again into the walls.

The Futurity Cup.

With a view to promoting the station and attracting visitors, a 45-kilometre endurance horse ride and 25-kilometre marathon footrace were introduced in 1986; these were conducted annually until 1989 when James took his family south. The marathon with its $1,000 purse was designed to be a test of the mind and all senses, as well as testing the physical stamina required to complete the challenging course. Attracting international and interstate contestants, the event was run on the first Saturday in September when the temperature was constantly above 30 degrees. It was featured in the media on Channel 9's *World of Sport* television program and the following year it was covered by a Darwin television station. It took up to three weeks to set up and mark out the courses with thousands of small white plastic bags attached at eye level to bushes and trees along the route. On two occasions members of the Australian Army Reserve's Norforce regiment manned the check-point stations along the course of the footrace and coordinated the progress of the race using their two-way radios.

Chris Henggeler from Kachana competed in two footraces and recalls the route began at today's Station Township. It followed a trail towards El Questro Gorge, over the jump-up near Moonshine leading to Doon Doon Station and then back along the Pentecost River to a steep climb up Good Luck Hill to the old Telecom station overlooking Spurlings Pocket. From there it continued to the Chamberlain River and back to the homestead via the Pentecost River. Today visitors walking along the Pentecost River on the first section of the trail to Champagne Springs can see *'halfway–good luck'* painted on the rocks of a low cliff overlooking the river. This is the point where the marathon track ascended the 300-metre incline from river level to the now redundant remains of the Telecom station.

A way-point along the rugged marathon course.

In 1988, the 57-year-old Canadian runner John Richardson learned of 'the world's hardest endurance run' and came to Australia to compete in the Sydney and Adelaide marathons in preparation for his run in the Kimberley. After completing the El Questro run in just over six hours, he said he could never have conceived of any course being as rugged as it proved to be. That year the gruelling marathon attracted 31 contestants, both men and women, and all but four finished the course.

El Questro Station
Endurance Run

This is to certify that
Vernon Crewe

Completed Australia's Most Rugged
Course in a time of
2 hours 42 minutes

Position 1st

The winner's certificate for the Endurance Run.1987.
Courtesy Margaret Hudson.

Names of winners inscribed on the futurity cup for this event are: 1986 and 1987 local athlete Vernon Crewe from Kununurra who completed the course in 3 hours 4 minutes, and 2 hours 42 minutes respectively; 1988 Alexander Guthrie from New Zealand in 2 hours 49 minutes, and in 1989, the last year of the race, Mr T. Kleiner from Queensland took 3 hours 10 minutes.

The horse race was run later at the end of the mustering season and attracted a great deal of outside interest. Many competitors and their families came to El Questro for the event and camped on the river flats near the homestead. The horses and riders set off from the home paddock at Spurlings Pocket, crossed the Pentecost River and travelled through the hills emerging at the driveway near the stone gate posts close to the Zebedee Springs turning, then along the base of the range and over the jump-up into the neighbouring Doon Doon valley, around Moonshine Gorge area crossing the creek at Jackaroo's Waterhole and then heading across to the Chamberlain River. The airstrip was the finishing stretch. A check point was set up at the stockyards near Jackaroo's Waterhole and at the finishing post on the airstrip, enabling John McMicking to conduct fitness inspections of all competing horses. On one year the atmosphere of the race day was marred by the death of a competing horse. The unfortunate animal was a former racehorse and appears to have died from a heart attack while cooling off in a watercourse.

In June 1987 two Kimberley residents, Marcus Bullen and his son Lance, were killed by a mystery gunman whilst fishing in the Northern Territory near Timber Creek. A week later Kimberley police were advised that a young couple from Kununurra and their friend from Derby had failed to return from their fishing weekend on the Pentecost River. When the alarm was raised, the earlier Timber Creek incident prompted the police to contact Ian and Sue Sinnamon from neighbouring Home Valley Station and ask them to investigate along the riverbank.

The Sinnamons drove the short distance to the Pentecost River crossing and turned down the Karunjie Track where they found the remains of a burnt out car still smouldering and realised something was seriously wrong. They returned to the nearby riverbank where they found the campsite and discovered the naked body of Julie Warren. The bodies of her husband Phillip Walkemeyer and their friend Terry Bolt had been carried away by the tide and were not found until the following day; the first was located in shallow water about three kilometres downstream and the other four kilometres further down again. All three had been shot in the back and their clothes and possessions placed in their vehicle and set on fire. It was believed the killer had shot them near their camp close to the Gibb River Road and dragged their bodies into the river anticipating the evidence would be consumed by crocodiles.

Investigations indicated the killer had turned his vehicle off the road at a view point before it descends to the river crossing. He had approached the victims from the high ground overlooking the river, concealing himself in the low ground of the breakaway that ran parallel to the road. Julie was shot from behind while she was sitting reading in a camp chair on the river bank. The two men were shot as they fished in the Pentecost River.

Margaret Salerno had been working on the fences at nearby Yarrabar when the police drove up and warned her of a killer at large in the area. For almost a week fear prevailed throughout the region as Western Australia's largest manhunt and logistical nightmare continued. The nation held its breath awaiting daily media reports, everyone wondering where the gunman would strike next.

Shortly after the shooting a Toyota Hilux answering the description of the suspect's vehicle pulled into the homestead at El Questro where the driver was warily met by Ben Salerno and Albert Gobius armed with .303 rifles. It was not until he had been thoroughly frisked against a tree and a comprehensive search of his vehicle was completed that the nervous traveller was offered the refuge he sought in the company of others.

Several days later a helicopter pilot mustering horses on Jubilee Downs Station close to Fitzroy Crossing sighted a camouflaged vehicle. The police were alerted and the gunman was ambushed and killed in a shootout. The registration of the hired vehicle revealed a German tourist named Gustav Schwab as the killer of the five West Australians. Schwab, aged 26, arrived in Brisbane from West Germany in mid-April 1987 and hired a 4-wheel drive Toyota from Avis at the airport. His last contact with his family was a postcard from Darwin on 21 May.

Following their investigation in Germany the media reported that Schwab had a very quiet childhood near Munich. He later worked for three years and then travelled to Australia where he was employed for 18 months at a joinery in the Adelaide area before returning to Germany to do national service. In his mother country he led a lonely life, preoccupied with his dream of returning to Australia and the freedom it offered him.

The tidal stretch of the Pentecost River where the tragedy took place is renowned for good fishing and today one of these popular locations close to where one of the bodies was found is known as The Killing Tree.

In 1969, some 15 years prior to the Salernos' time in the Kimberley, another incident in Western Australia attracted nationwide attention when a confrontation arose between the state government and Leonard George Casley of Hutt River Station near Geraldton. Casley was a farmer who staked his livelihood on wheat production and the sale of his produce through the government's national representative. Each year he sowed between 7,000 and 14,000 acres to wheat. In November of 1969, with thousands of acres of crop ready for harvest, the Wheat Quota Board reduced his quota to the equivalent of a 100-acre crop in a last minute attempt to avoid a national glut through overproduction.

Faced with financial ruin brought about by this untenable situation, Casley confronted the government and, after a period of threats and discord, eventually found legal recourse in seceding from Australia in 1970. Any reader interested in exploring the history of Australia's first micro-nation and the remarkable story of one man's extraordinary tenacity in the face of adversity should consult the home site of the Principality of Hutt River on the internet. Unsurprisingly, the legal loophole Casley found which enabled him to become an independent nation has since been firmly closed. Today the economy of this province, located mid-way between Geraldton and Kalbarri, is based on tourism and related activities in addition to agriculture.

The somewhat tenuous connection between Hutt River Province and El Questro came about when James Salerno made the acquaintance of the self-appointed Prince Leonard of Hutt and, finding a man with shared values, Salerno accepted the role of Ambassador to the 75-square-kilometre Principality.

Shortly after this, consideration of the need to educate their growing families compelled the Salernos to put El Questro on the market and return to Adelaide, leaving Margaret assisted by Albert Gobius to run the property until a sale was completed.

By this time Emma Gorge was recognised as one of the local beauty spots and attracted campers and passing traffic. A string of caretakers lived in one of the caravans, collecting the camping fees and running a small retail shop. One of these caretakers was an Irishman who had a psychotic episode and when he was eventually arrested, he raved about the Salernos killing people.

The gorge was a popular recreational location with local folk, some of whom felt it should be named Mulaga Springs after Torrance MacMicking and raised the matter at a Shire Council meeting. Margaret presented her case to the councillors and it was decided that the Salernos, who were responsible for opening the gorge to visitors, were justified in naming it after Margaret and James's daughter Emma.

In Salerno days, visitors had the choice of hiring canoes or using their own boats on the Chamberlain River. Following the sale of El Questro in 1991, but prior to its handover to the purchaser, there was a dramatic crocodile attack on this river. Danny Waser having launched his orange canoe in the water at the Big Hole was gently paddling upstream with his wife Regula concentrating on her fishing when he noticed they were being stalked by a saltwater crocodile (*Crocodylus porosus*).

In an attempt to frighten the reptile Danny whacked his paddle on the water but it broke on impact and caused him to overbalance and fall into the river. Regula watched in horror as a surreal scenario unfolded. She saw the crocodile disappear with the broken paddle in its jaws and then, as her husband fell into the water, the croc launched itself partly into the canoe where Danny had been sitting only seconds earlier. The canoe rolled over, tipping Regula and all of their belongings into the water. Efforts to scramble onto the upturned canoe caused it to sink, leaving the couple no alternative but to swim frantically to the riverbank. Fortunately, the incident took place just before the entrance to the gorge, enabling them to reach the western bank. Once well clear of the water they said a prayer of gratitude for their lucky escape. News of the crocodile attack was reported in the media as far afield as the Wasers' homeland in Switzerland.

The Conservation and Land Management Department was contacted and after establishing the crocodile's location from a helicopter, a trap was set to capture it; but the fugitive reptile managed to remain at large until the wet season in 1992–93. It was eventually captured and taken to the crocodile farm at Wyndham where it was named Doc and remained as an attraction in the central lagoon for many years.

The Burrell era 1991–2005

Will Burrell and Celia Shelmerdine's first inspection of El Questro was in November 1990 at the beginning of the wet season. They found a property with spectacular landscapes on a vast scale, an outback homestead and outbuildings that were in every way a far cry from the prime farmland on which Will had been raised in England.

Nevertheless, at 23 Will was no stranger to Australia. After leaving school, 18-year-old William travelled to Australia during his Gap Year and followed his father's example of working for a short time as a jackeroo on cattle stations. Here he discovered his interest in the cattle industry and, with the knowledge of an inheritance from his grandmother, his dream of having a station of his own was not unrealistic.

The Burrell contact with Australia goes back three generations. Early in the 20th Century Will's great-grandfather Lord Thomas Denman, in his capacity as our Governor-General between 1911 and 1914, finally settled the dispute over the location of the future capital city of Canberra.

Additionally, Will's mother Margot Pearce was an Australian who during her first marriage had lived on a cattle station in northern New South Wales. She then married businessman Mark Burrell and moved to the 1,200-hectare Burrell estate in Sussex next to Knepp Castle, the family seat for 700 years. As a child Will had often travelled to Australia to visit his antipodean relatives.

In London in 1988 Will met a young Australian woman, with whom he shared his plans and ambitions. Celia Shelmerdine's father Peter was a well known Melbourne restaurateur and a respected real estate agent, and the family included entrepreneurs and winemakers. In 1987 Celia had graduated from the Royal Melbourne Institute of Technology with high distinction in Visual Arts and Communication and the next year she moved to London, working as a designer for an international advertising company and as an in-house designer for Terence Conran.

Will and Celia returned to Australia in 1989 and decided it was the ideal time to pursue Will's dream. Will set the purchase of a station somewhere north of the Tropic of Capricorn as his goal. Recognising that a cattle property would need a second income stream to protect it from the vagaries of the cattle industry, Burrell engaged pastoral consultant Philip Gibson to source a 'large property in a forgotten neighbourhood', stipulating that it should have areas of intrinsic and outstanding beauty of value to tourism.

Ownership of a vast tract of untamed country was a romantic notion and the young couple inspected 16 stations across tropical Australia before discovering El Questro. Will and Celia were immediately smitten by the diverse beauty of the burnished landscape and immediately recognised the potential for development in both cattle and tourism areas.

The Station was close to one million acres when in April 1991, 23-year-old William Burrell paid $1,000,000 to purchase it and the estimated 2,000 cattle from the Salerno syndicate. A decade later Will discovered that the mother of his great-grandfather, Lord Denman, was a family connection of an earlier owner of El Questro, Torrance MacMicking.

At that time there were few buildings on the vast property: the 1964 homestead, the rustic self-contained stone bungalow, the large workshop, and some random sheds and stables at Spurlings Pocket. Burrell's plan was to develop the cattle operation and support it with a low-key tourist venture. He planned to offer outback adventure with a soft place to sleep at day's end, and wanted the El Questro experience to be available to all travellers, regardless of their budget.

Queensland architect Geoffrey Pie was asked to design a new homestead and an environmentally sensitive resort at Emma Gorge. During the 14 months of planning and building, Pie travelled to the Kimberley monthly. Many days were spent in a 4-wheel drive or helicopter exploring possible locations for a new homestead and eventually the secluded cliff top location overlooking the Big Hole on the Chamberlain River was chosen.

Pie approached Alan Emblin, who was experienced at building modified prefabricated accommodation for the mining industry and whose construction company, Building Solutions, had an excellent reputation for work in remote areas. Pie and Emblin had collaborated successfully on projects in the past and both were captivated by Will and Celia's dream.

Initially Burrell's new home was to have four bedrooms and a large living area, but the costs of building and running it were unsustainable, so another three rooms were added to the plan to enable the house to be leased commercially. While attending a family wedding in Venice, Burrell was inspired by the dimensions of the Throne Room at the Doges's Palace, prompting him to instruct Pie to double the size of the Homestead's living room.

Celia Shelmerdine and Will Burrell with architect Geoffrey Pie (centre). Courtesy of the Burrells.

The Salernos' small campground at the entrance to Emma Gorge was replaced with a rustic, safari-style resort accommodating 54 guests in a lush woodland setting with little disturbance to the dense natural vegetation. The 27 elegant little twin-bed cabins were prefabricated in Queensland and along with all additional material and equipment for the station were transported across the continent to El Questro in 16 semi-trailers. Designed in the style of miner's tents with a central ridge pole and canvas fly over the top, the cabins were elevated on metal stumps some 30 centimetres or more for cooling purposes and to discourage termites and prevent flooding. In an evocation of outback radio communication, each cabin was named after the phonetic letters of the alphabet, beginning with Phonetic followed by Alpha, Bravo, Charlie, etc.

By April 1992 the construction was finished and Celia's marketing skills were rewarded by an enthusiastic opening of the resort at Emma Gorge. National media and representatives of the travel and tourism industry wrote glowingly of the setting close to a swimming pool on wide, shady, green lawns.

In the ensuing Burrell tenure El Questro was highly acclaimed and constantly recognised in the annual Western Australian tourism awards. In 1994 Burrell received Western Australian's Young Achiever of the Year award in recognition of his contribution to the development of the East Kimberley.

Development of Station infrastructure and guest and staff accommodation continued. At the Station centre, local contractors built the stone office block and modified the original homestead for use as management quarters. They extended the former stone stables, converting them into a small store called Doesn't Matter Shop that met most of the needs of the staff and the trickle of campers, who paid a daily rate of five dollars to utilise campsites along the Pentecost River.

The venture experienced remarkable development in the field of tourism under Will Burrell and his co-director Celia Shelmerdine.

The following is a summary of Western Australian tourism and hospitality awards during the Burrell tenure.

- *Sir David Brand award for Tourism Excellence 1995, 1997 and 2000.*
- *Unique accommodation 1998, 1999 and 2000.*
- *Luxury accommodation 1998.*
- *Major Tourist Attraction 1995, 2003 and 2004.*

On achieving three successes in a selected category, a contender is placed in the Western Australian Tourism Commission's Hall of Fame.

By March 1992, the store had become a bar where everyone gathered at day's end to slake their thirst and discuss their many and varied activities. The Swinging Arm Bar was named by Greg (Hairydog) Harman who for commercial reasons encouraged drinkers to keep their elbows swinging.

The *Doesn't Matter* shop. Photo courtesy of the Burrells.

The range of employees in the early Burrell era was as colourful as the landscape itself. There were several who would fade into the bush on learning the authorities were making a routine visit in search of illegal immigrants. One of these was a volatile machete-carrying foreigner, who entertained his workmates with tales of his time with the French Foreign Legion. He was a good worker and is responsible for some of the stonework around the Station Centre, however after a few ales he was inclined to howl at night. Then there was a New Zealander, a surly loner with a skull and crossbones tattooed on his forehead who slept apart from the others. Some months later a former employee claimed to have seen him on the police television show – *Australia's Most Wanted*!

Albert Gobius was a mechanic and general all-rounder who stayed on from the Salerno tenure. An aeronautic enthusiast, Albert had his own gyrocopter which he used for off duty jaunts around the property. Early one Sunday morning he took to the skies and staff were jolted from their slumbers when the distant drone of the gyrocopter suddenly cut out. Fearing the worst, a rescue team was hastily gathered and located the aircraft wreckage and the unconscious pilot suspended upside down in a tree. Fearing he had broken his back, Gobius's rescuers brought him back to the Station on a mattress. The Royal Flying Doctor, already engaged with a problem at Kalumburu Mission, was unable to come to El Questro so, since Gobius was still in a seated position, it was decided to strap him into a seat in the helicopter and transport him to hospital by air. With Richard Baillieu at the controls, flying low over a backup vehicle, the mercy flight set off for Kununurra. Gobius was treated in hospital and recovered but was left with a permanent mild disability, while Baillieu faced an enquiry into flying below regulatory height and for landing in the hospital grounds.

Within five years there was another aeronautical incident on the Station which ended in a tragedy on Mount Harrison – a low conical peak at the southern end of the Erskine Range – when one of three F18 airforce pilots was killed while hang-gliding. Because of the thermal updrafts associated with the peak, the summit known as Hanglider Hill, was a popular launching place for local enthusiasts. The Bastion peak with its Five Rivers Lookout at Wyndham was also an ideal area for hang-gliders.

Burrell's first aerial inspection of the Station led him to fear that the inclusion of 2,000 head of cattle in the purchase price had been optimistic. However, when he commenced mustering his cattle he was delighted when stockmen and friends working from several stock camps accounted for some 4,000 beasts.

Before any building could commence at the Homestead, 23,000 tonnes of soil had to be trucked from the banks of the nearby Pentecost River and spread over the rocky site to create a foundation for the buildings and garden. Following the completion of their work at Emma Gorge, the team of 30 builders from Queensland moved to the Station where they camped along the Pentecost River for six months while assembling the mostly prefabricated Homestead complex. El Questro's employees slept in swags under a truck tarpaulin on the riverbank adjacent to an open air kitchen, where Ronnie Atkins cooked for builders, staff and occasionally for campers.

The completed Homestead cost $1.9 million. Using a modular panel system, Pie designed the Homestead buildings on a metre grid with generous spaces. Set on a wide lawn extending to the cliff-edge, it provided accommodation for 12 guests and comprised four main buildings with spacious verandahs in traditional country homestead style, connected by covered pine walkways.

The cement-clad exterior walls were finished with a tinted lime wash echoing the colours of the surrounding escarpments.

The early colonial style living room is the central architectural feature of the house. Furnishings were sourced locally and from Indonesia by Will and Celia. The six en suite bedrooms have private verandahs with views to the expansive wilderness beyond; three of the cliff top rooms are partly cantilevered over the waters of the huge water hole below. The garden was planted with palms, a frangipani alley and other tropical greenery. Trellises of jasmine and bougainvillea were also established.

The Homestead was ready for accommodation in October 1992. A fly-in group from Skylink were the first commercial visitors to enjoy the 'home away from home' experience that became the hallmark of the Homestead with Celia and Will playing host to their many guests.

The next development was undertaken by Will Atkins and his family: Brumby Base on the Pentecost, five kilometres downstream from the Station Centre. In direct contrast with the Homestead, this rustic set-up accommodated 12 in dormitory accommodation, with an open-sided undercover kitchen and dining area, generated electric power, hot showers and a flushing toilet. A manager was appointed to operate the complex, and fully inclusive Station Camp Packages proved popular with backpackers at $130 a night, including transfers from Kununurra, all meals, accommodation and tours.

The Atkins family were deployed to the Wild Dog area to erect fences for a stock paddock one mile square (260 hectares) and on their return to the Station centre they took over the operation of Brumby Base. Ronnie ran a daily transfer service to Kununurra, ferrying backpackers and collecting supplies for guests and workers. Her husband 'Wild Will' was a popular tour guide and took guests on interesting horse rides. Under his supervision weekly rodeo competitions commenced at the arena near the new horse stables. They attracted interest from the locals but were discontinued due to the risk of accident.

Brumby Base, with its excellent meals and evening fireside entertainment, proved to be so popular that it began to eclipse Emma Gorge as an accommodation option and was eventually closed. It was later used intermittently by travelling adventure tour companies until 2000 when Kimberley Wilderness Adventure leased it exclusively and had a permanent cook-cum-caretaker on site for their regular tours. Although termites have taken their toll and Brumby Base has known times of serious dereliction, it had a renaissance in 2004 when it was used as a film location and featured as a homestead in the reality television series, *Outback Jack*.

At the Station, stones were collected and carted for the construction of four family bungalows that opened in May 1993. Bungalow guests shared a kitchen in the adjacent stone dwelling that had been constructed for Margaret Salerno. The latter was converted and reopened in June 1995 as the Steakhouse restaurant.

Celia's sense of style was reflected throughout all levels of accommodation. She was determined to offer the outback experience to all El Questro guests without sacrificing the normal comforts of life. Celia insisted on details like feather pillows, fluffy towels and good food. With levels of accommodation options ranging between secluded riverside campsites and exclusive packages at the Homestead, El Questro met the Burrells' objective of offering outback tourism experiences that were second to none, incorporating a degree of comfort and catering to all budgets.

Activities offered included horse and camel rides, gorge walks, bird watching, heli-scenic flights, fishing and canoeing on the Chamberlain River. Five camels and a helicopter were based at Emma Gorge, but the camel rides were not popular and the animals were subsequently released. There have been intermittent sightings of them around the Wilderness Park since. In deference to environmental concerns, silent and non-polluting battery powered boats with electric outboard motors replaced the canoes on the waterways; a catch-and-release fishing policy and the use of crushed barbs on fish hooks were introduced to protect fish levels.

A station manager was employed to oversee both the cattle and tourism businesses. Guests and provisions were transferred from Kununurra by Buddy Tyson or the manager's wife. Buddy came to El Questro in 1993 and until his death in 2011 he regarded the Station as his home. The son of a renowned stockman, Buddy was raised on a cattle station in central Queensland and grew into a competent horse-breaker, stockman and general all-rounder, who became well known on the national rodeo circuit. He was not sufficiently dedicated to win an Australian title; instead he made a living riding 'one out'; competing for prize money all over the country.

In his heyday he was the Open Champion at Central Australia's first organised rodeo, held at Aileron to the north of Alice Springs in 1963 and he also won a bull riding title in New South Wales. Always immaculately dressed, Buddy changed into a clean, well ironed shirt between each event at the meets, where he was known as The Black Prince. After his knees buckled, Buddy the showman was in his element as a clown in the rodeo ring where, as well as keeping the spectators amused, his principal role was to distract the enraged bulls and prevent them from goring fallen riders. His natural performing abilities earned him bit parts in films: *Eskimo Nell, The Silver Brumby* and *The Flying Doctor* series. At El Questro, visitors were magnetically attracted to Buddy's entertaining and easy going manner and he came to be recognised as the face of El Questro.

In 1994 All Seasons Hotels were contracted to handle tourism and hospitality, surviving the baptism of a flooding event shortly after taking over the reins.

Celia and Will were married the same year. Will's marriage proposal took place during the wet season when they were staying at the Homestead with the editor of one of the English glossy magazines and her husband. Celia, keen to share their exciting news, phoned neighbouring Carlton Hill Station on the Ord River and invited Susan and David Bradley to fly over and join them for dinner. David was mustering cattle when Celia phoned and was not expected home until late so Susan, unaware of the reason for the last minute invitation, asked for a raincheck on the dinner. Meanwhile, she took delivery of 250,000 dung beetles from a representative of the Department of Agriculture, destined for Carlton Hill and five other stations further up the track.

An average cow drops 10–12 dung pads daily, and a single dung pad can produce up to 3,000 flies within a fortnight. Dung beetles were introduced to reduce the fly problem. Carlton Hill had only been allocated 50,000 beetles but, as the access road to Rosewood, Argyle, Newry, Auvergne and Legune Stations was impassable due to recent heavy rains, Susan was given all the beetles. The Department staff directed that they should be out in the paddocks within 48 hours of their arrival in Kununurra if they were not to be wasted.

Susan recounts the events that followed:

> Celia called me again. This time she explained that Will had asked her to marry him so the dinner was actually their engagement party, and they

really wanted us to be there to help them celebrate. I again radioed David, who said he would be in, but to have a change of clothes and his wetpack ready as they would be chasing the last light arriving at El Questro.

I wondered what I could take them as an engagement present. Then I thought of the dung beetles. I raced down to our cool room, and took out one of the boxes of 50,000 which I wrapped in very shiny gold paper and tied with a huge gold ribbon. The card read: 'There will never be any flies on El Questro. Congratulations Will and Celia – an amazing couple in an amazing land.'

We flew to El Questro in the R22 right on sunset, me nursing the big gold box and David covered in dust. We landed on the front lawn of the not-quite-finished Homestead and the visiting English couple could not believe their eyes! Celia and Will of course were over the moon, idyllically in love and absolutely thrilled with their gold encased dung beetles.

The six of us then proceeded to celebrate with many bubbles on the verandah, a wonderful meal and great stories from Will as we watched a huge tropical storm descend over the Gorge. After dinner when the rain had cleared, we all piled into the clapped out old bull-catcher with the dung beetles, clutching our wine glasses and ready for action.

Will drove and the rest of us looked out for large wet cow pats. Bumping along over the rough ground, we would spy a Brahman bull in the distance and then follow him in the hope of finding his mark so the dung beetles could commence their work. Each time we made a deposit, we recharged our glasses, so by the time the 50,000 had been put out to settle on El Questro, we were a very happy little team.

We sang our way back to the homestead as another storm broke, and enjoyed a nightcap toasting the long and happy life not only of Will and Celia but also the dung beetles on El Questro!

It really was a great night and I will never forget the looks on the faces of the glamorous English couple.

When Will bought El Questro in 1992 he was mindful of his Station's early association with the struggling town of Wyndham and during race week in August he sponsored the Wyndham Cup.

An annual fishing competition was introduced to boost the dwindling visitor numbers at the end of the tourist season. The Barrafest, supervised by the Fisheries Department of Western Australia, was a popular event among the locals and attracted barramundi fishermen from around the North West. In 1998 the competition coincided with the federal election and a polling booth was set up at the Station Store. By 2001 tourism was operating at a profit so there was no longer a need to promote the property in this way and the fishing competition ceased.

Celia's ability with design and marketing was effectively utilised. Marketed initially as 'El Questro Station, East Kimberley', it was not long before the attraction was audaciously rebranded as 'El Questro, Australia' and later simply as 'El Questro Wilderness Park'. She was responsible for the production of quality merchandise and refined promotional material for purchase in the retail areas at Emma Gorge, the Station Store and in downtown Kununurra where El Questro maintained its Booking Office. She also published several children's books *Flora the Flowergirl* (1995), *Rosie and Mack Head Outback* (1995), and *Colour the Kimberley* (2001), and a pictorial souvenir book, *El Questro, A Million Acres of Outback in the Kimberley Wilderness.*

By 1995, within three years of opening, El Questro was recognised as one of the top small hotels of the world and was a finalist in two categories in Western Australia's tourism awards: the Major Tourism Attraction category and the prestigious Sir David Brand Tourism award for Tourism Excellence. In that year some 50 per cent of the visitors to El Questro were international.

Without attempting to meet the criteria required for Five Star rating, the luxurious yet unpretentious Homestead accommodation with its glorious setting and unique sense of remoteness offered a home-away-from-home experience with friendly and unobtrusive service. This successful formula combined with an all-inclusive room rate attracted regular repeat patronage and industry recognition. In 1999 the celebrated Homestead was included in the Tatler/Ritz-Carlton list of the top 50 hotels in the world. It has also enjoyed listing amongst '101 Best Hotels' and other accommodation guides to small luxury hotels.

By the time of my arrival in 1996 the infrastructure and seasonal tourist routine were well established and some 45 employees were involved in tourism and hospitality on the property. All were employed by and answered to All Seasons Hotel Management Group. Despite the challenge of distance from suppliers, the restaurant on the verandah at the little Emma Gorge resort was recognised as one of the best in the Kimberley and local folk happily travelled the 85 kilometres from Wyndham or Kununurra for a special dinner. Many stayed overnight to enjoy an early morning walk to the beautiful ferny pool and droplet waterfall at the end of Emma Gorge.

The alumininium 'tinnies' with their capacity of five to seven passengers met requirements for the popular Chamberlain Gorge cruise during the early years of tourism at El Questro, but by 1996 increased visitor numbers and coach traffic necessitated a larger boat. The arrival of *M.V. Wandjina* caused great excitement at the Station early in the season. The large shallow draught vessel licensed to carry 48 passengers was designed by Burrell and a naval architect and built at Hastings in Victoria at a cost of $70,000. It was transported across the continent to take up service on the Chamberlain River. The popularity of the tours it facilitated recouped the full costs of construction and transportation within a few months. The vessel was named in recognition of the spirit ancestor of the former occupants of the land. Images of the anthropomorphic Wandjina figures overlook rapids at the southern extremity of the cruise waters.

Without doubt a relaxing soak in the thermal pools at Zebedee Springs is the most popular of all the activities at El Questro. Conveniently located a short distance from the Station driveway, the 32°C spring water flows from the base of a burnished red cliff and tumbles through a series of intimate pools and small cascades in a forest of palms and other moisture loving tropical plants. The pockets of forested areas at Zebedee Springs and El Questro Gorge are amongst the Kimberley's diminishing ancient rainforests where the stately palms and other remnant vegetation are ecologically fragile and vulnerable to fire and human impact.

Beautiful walks along Emma and El Questro Gorges can be explored independently or in the company of an experienced Ranger and generally involve a refreshing swim in the pristine waters along the way. However, during the winter solstice the sun's oblique rays scarcely reach the pool at the base of the waterfall at Emma Gorge where the water temperature drops to a chilly 15°C, although elsewhere in the pool an infusion of warm thermal water raises the temperature by ten degrees.

The Kimberley is tough country and enjoyment of its beauty is often hard won. Over the years there has been a discernable increase in the number of visitors of retirement age, and it was often my painful experience to witness visitors facing the disappointment of being unable to manage the physical challenges encountered on walks such as these. To accommodate those facing this dilemma, a 20-minute video was made allowing them to enjoy the beautiful features of Emma Gorge from the comfort of an armchair. On one occasion a visitor to Emma Gorge suffered a heart attack and died at the droplet waterfall. The harrowing removal of his body was the fourth time Emma Gorge staff had made a stretcher evacuation using the rough and hazardously narrow 'goat track' along the floor of the gorge. Some weeks earlier it had taken 10 men three hours to carry a 110 kilogram visitor down the 1.6 kilometre track. Contrary to recommendation, the visitor had been wearing thong sandals when she fell and seriously injured herself.

The high cost of Public Liability Insurance caused many operators throughout Australia to cease offering horse riding and trail rides to the public. This was not the case at El Questro where more than a dozen retired stock horses were available and many guests seized the opportunity to explore the Station environs on horseback.

Trying one's luck at fishing for barramundi was a 'must do' activity, especially for the fellas. El Questro offered 4-wheel drive and 'heli-fishing' tours, the latter providing helicopter flights to remote fishing areas.

Despite good publicity and Will having invested four times the property's purchase price on infrastructure in the first five years, El Questro barely made an operating profit until 1998. Nevertheless, the Kimberley gained recognition as a remote destination and as visitor numbers increased additional accommodation was required for both guests and staff at Emma Gorge and the Station. Meeting the increased demand from the lucrative inclusive tour market was critical to El Questro's financial survival and during the 1998/99 wet season at Emma Gorge an additional eight deluxe cabins increased the guest accommodation to 35, half of them with en suite facilities. Extra staff quarters and a dedicated guest dining area were simultaneously constructed. At the Station eight new guest bungalows along the Pentecost River increased the number of commercial bungalows to 12.

In 1998, a second longer airstrip was constructed at the top of the Emma Gorge driveway to cater for the increased aircraft activity associated with guests participating in a range of regional aerial tours. A John Deere quad bike was purchased the following year and it became a useful workhorse around the resort, capable of towing a trailer with seating for 10 passengers.

To provide additional activities within walking distance of the resort an informative Nature Trail was formed through the woodland, and Boab Gully Ramble opened along the course of a creekbed lined with dozens of boab trees. Unfortunately both of these peaceful walks were lost to the ravages of Cyclone Ingrid in 2005. Bird watching was another passive activity at the Resort with the Great Bowerbird amongst the most conspicuous of the extensive range of birds found around the resort.

In 1999 the Wandjina-Wunggurr-Willinggin Aboriginal Land Claim was served on El Questro and other leases for the country on the south side of the Gibb River Road. The total claim exceeding 60,000 square kilometres of land between Wyndham and Derby, was the largest to come before a court in Australia. Statements were taken from parties in support of both sides of the case. To validate their claim, the Aborigines were required to prove a continuous physical connection with the land but, with their removal from their homeland and their traditional culture all but destroyed, this was challenging to say the least. Burrell understood that no valid claimants were found over El Questro's relevant country. In the main the pastoralists throughout the state were collectively represented by the Pastoralists and Graziers Association.

The determination of the claims was released in December 2003 when Justice Ross Sundberg in the Federal Court found the Wandjina-Wanggurr-Willinggin claimants had proved their strong links to the land along the Gibb River Road and Native Title was determined over 11 pastoral leases. The Aborigines were given a blanket right to access all of the claimed land for traditional use. However the pastoralists rights to conduct pastoral and tourism activities prevailed over the Aborigines.

ABORIGINAL RESERVE
WYNDHAM
Ord River
Great Northern Highway
Parry Lagoons Nature Reserve
Nulla Nulla
River
WEST ARM
Mt Cockburn Lodge
Diggers Rest
The Grotto
Home Valley Station
Lookout
Pentecost River
HOME VALLEY STATION
Bindoola Ck
COCKBURN RANGES
King River
Mt Rob
Gibb River Road
Emma Gorge Resort
Matteo Springs
Pigeon Hole
Amalia Gorge
Homestead
Branco's Lookout
Chamberlain Gorge
Saddleback Ridge & Lookout
EL QUESTRO STATION
Explosion Waterhole
Zebedee Springs
Champagne Springs
El Questro Gorge
Moonshine Gorge
PENTECOST RANGES
TIER RANGE
Salmond River
DURACK RANGES
Miri Miri Falls
SAW RANGES
Elgee Cliffs
Chamberlain River
Pentecost River
DOON DOON STATION
Dunham River
KACHANA
Kilometers
0
30

Previous page: A relief map of El Questro and its attractions. 2012. Design by Zak Dragic, Explorers Australia Pty Ltd.

Top: The Burrell's Homestead on the Chamberlain River. 2005.

Below: The exclusive Homestead and grounds. Photo by Peter Lloyd.

Top: Amalia waterfall. Photo by Darcy.

Below: Ochre Pool on the Amalia walking trail.

Above and opposite: The warm thermal pools at Zebedee Springs nestle amongst palm trees at the foot of rust coloured cliffs. Photos by Maria and David Wolfe.

Top: Champagne Springs.

Below: Looking north along the Station driveway. Photo by David Wolfe.

Top: Monika Taylor overlooks the site of the Pentecost shootings. 2005.

Below: Explosion Waterhole on the Chamberlain River. Photo by Brownpete.

Previous page
Top: The view from Brankos Lookout. Photo by Brownpete.
Bottom: The iconic Pentecost Crossing. Photo by Brownpete.

Top: Weekly delivery of supplies to the Station Store.
Below: The Store and Swinging Arm Bar. 2006.

Top: The Station Centre in 2005.

Right: David Byard, El Questro's artist in residence. 2008.

Below: The Steakhouse Restaurant. 2004.

Top: The Chamberlain River before the 2012 floods.
Middle: A Chamberlain Gorge cruise.

Opposite: The waterfall at Emma Gorge. Photo by Brownpete.

Top: Rain in the wet season. Photo by Darcy.

Left: Heliscenic flight over the dramatic Pentecost Gorge. Photo by Brownpete.

Opposite top: Hidden Falls. Photo by Brownpete.

Opposite right: Saddleback Lookout. Photo by Prownpete.

Fireside entertainment at the Station. Photo by Tobie.

Lunch on the mudflats.

The Saddleback Track. Photo by Brownpete.

Communications at El Questro were upgraded late in the 1999 season when Telstra contractors ran fibre optic cable from the Great Northern Highway and installed it to all Station buildings. This was the Burrells' first profitable year. Visitor numbers represented a 20 per cent increase on the previous season and the staffing level hovered around 50.

Burrell began to explore the possibility of developing the Station as a wilderness park and engaged Zak Dragic to draw up a management plan and compile a management manual. Tracks and walking trails were opened to new and existing attractions and appropriate interpretative signage, maps and fact sheets were produced for nine activities.

Fibre optic communication comes to El Questro in 1999.

The dawn of the new century saw the property moving away from its cattle station image and in 2001 it was officially opened as El Questro Wilderness Park. Visitors could no longer drive onto the property and explore the many attractions without a permit. Wilderness Park Permits costing $15 were valid for seven days and the revenue raised from the entry fee contributed to improvements and the general upkeep of attractions as well as the constant road maintenance. The development was so successfully accomplished that many visitors were unaware they were on privately owned property.

Responsibility for management of the Wilderness Park was handed over to Pete Guggisberg. Among his legacies is the creation of the acclaimed El Questro Wilderness Park Compendium, a comprehensive and informative manual covering all natural aspects of the property.

Having successfully negotiated the purchase of All Season's portfolio of managed properties, the French company Accor took over the tourism and hospitality side of El Questro. Although Accor was recognised as the world's largest hotel management company with assets in 90 countries, Burrell insisted the El Questro name continue to stand alone. His modus operandi also did not conform with Accor's conventional management procedures. There was no business plan for the hospitality and tourism operation, nor was there a master plan for services and developments which were undertaken on an ad hoc basis. However, to some degree this flexibility appears to have accommodated seasonal vagaries and other setbacks.

The Burrells appointed a dedicated marketing manager from within the Accor team. Working exclusively for El Questro, Christopher Fenech raised El Questro's profile and increased the revenue, predominantly through negotiating with major coach companies and encouraging them to schedule additional overnight stays on the property. During Fenech's term the number of accommodated guests and campers reached 11,000 and day visitors were estimated to be 40,000 for the season.

Shortly before the start of the 2000 season Tropical Cyclones Steve and Rosita deluged the region with heavier than usual rains. A total of 560 millimetres fell at El Questro in March, whereas only 205 millimetres were recorded in the same month of the previous year.

Cyclone Rosita was described as 'the most intense cyclone to strike the West Kimberley coast in 100 years'. Although its centre crossed the coast south of Broome and devastated the newly opened Eco Beach Resort, it also inflicted considerable damage to the town. Between 15 and 24 April, 191 millimetres of rain fell at Emma Gorge in association with Rosita's rampage.

The heavy rains from the cyclonic activity prevented the graders and other equipment from working on the Gibb River Road for weeks and the road remained closed to through traffic until June, meaning that, contrary to expectations, there was a reduction in visitors to the Kimberley region.

On the Station, El Questro's grader driver and a team of earthmoving trucks and excavators worked for six weeks rebuilding and repairing roads that had been washed away. Some $80,000 was spent with the earthmoving contractors on repairing the 18-kilometre driveway and reopening damaged tracks where possible. The property was not opened to public access until

1 May, a month behind schedule and, with the budget already blown, all costs were cut.

Over the years El Questro has hosted its share of celebrity guests. Entertainer Kylie Minogue was amongst those who chose to visit El Questro anonymously when she took time off from her very public appearances at the Olympic Games in Sydney. Travelling incognito with her partner, she arrived to spend a few days at the Homestead under the names Mr and Mrs Brown. Kylie has revisited the property several times since under her own name and, like other celebrity visitors, enjoys the escape from the media and the uninterrupted freedom of movement El Questro offers.

Similarly, Mary Donaldson and Denmark's Crown Prince Frederick slipped in unannounced in 2002. The reservation for the future royal couple was made in the name of Fred Jensen. Their visit was late in October when the temperature was in the high thirties and the humidity oppressive. Rain clouds filled the skies during the preceding week and during their stay the first rain of the season fell at the Homestead. At the Station Township the same thunderstorm produced less than a millimetre of rain but lightning started a small grass fire on Telecom Hill behind the stables. The gusty wind drove the fire over the ridge and out of sight where it was assumed it would burn itself out.

More than a day later the fire reappeared near the Chamberlain River and jumped the track, heading for the fuel supply beside the Homestead generator shed. An SOS to the maintenance department brought assistance rushing to the scene where they found the Homestead staff and guests – including the Prince – frantically engaged in holding the fire at bay until it could be brought under control.

Also seeking anonymity, film director Baz Luhrmann made his reservation in the name of Mr Lilly when he came to El Questro in 2005 to research locations for his romantic epic film *Australia*. He very quickly recognised there was no threat from the paparazzi at El Questro.

Most of the cattle scenes in the movie were filmed on El Questro's flat northern country with the Cockburn Range in the background and during the shooting, Jack Thompson, Nicole Kidman, Keith Urban and others socialised at Emma Gorge. The production of the film cost $130 million and it was recognised with three Australian Film Industry awards and was used by the Australian Tourism Authority for promotional purposes.

As a result of an injury sustained in 1996 during a skiing holiday in France, Celia was unable to travel to the Kimberley for several years. She remained in Melbourne while Will travelled back and forth to El Questro several times each year and rarely missed a cattle muster. Initially he had no permanent accommodation and for several years he stayed wherever a spare bed could be found until he took over a room in the old homestead where he stayed until 2004.

The cattle station operations at El Questro ran a herd of around 5,000 and endeavoured to turn off 600 steers annually. During the Burrell tenure the percentage of inbred Shorthorn cattle was gradually replaced by the more viable Brahman breed, better suited to the tropical environment and resistant to cattle tick. Burrell purchased an additional 360 breeding cows and around 24 bulls from Rockhampton in a concerted effort to improve the bloodline of his cattle, aiming to maintain a ratio of one bull to 20 cows. The change to the Brahman strain was well timed, for by the mid-1990s the original English Shorthorn breed was of little commercial value except as 'slush pack' for the American burger trade and consequently yielded little return.

Brahman cattle were introduced to Australia about the same time as the Zebu breed was imported from Pakistan in 1956, and many new breeds more tolerant to the cattle tick and the heat were developed from these two imports. Prices for the *Bos indicus* breeds remained steady with the Brahman and Brahman crosses dominating. Most East Kimberley cattle were destined for the live export trade and shipped from Wyndham to South East Asian and Middle Eastern markets. On El Questro, cattle sales earned around $250,000 annually and when costs were deducted they provided a tidy profit in the vicinity of $150,000.

The cattle figures during Burrell's latter years ran to around 6,500 head with approximately 2,500 breeding cows and around 1,700 calves branded, marked and weaned annually; the mature Brahman steers were taken to Wyndham for export. Any steers found to be underweight would spend up to six weeks on a nearby feedlot prior to being loaded onto the multi-level transport ships. The remnant Shorthorn cattle and any Brahman cows considered too old for breeding purposes were trucked to the meat works in Katherine until it closed around 2003. Afterwards all cattle were exported live.

Most of the pastoral improvements under Burrell focussed on the superior grazing area to the north of the Gibb River Road. In addition to creating dams to catch the seasonal run off from the Cockburn plateaux, Burrell installed three bores that fed water through five kilometres of underground polypipe to strategically located tanks and troughs.

Approximately 40 kilometres of additional barbed wire fencing was erected, increasing the total fences in the area to around 80 kilometres. Elsewhere rivers and ranges provided natural barriers and did not require fencing, as was the case with the Station boundaries.

The Kimberley is home to a wide variety of large and small frogs, and visitors to Zebedee Springs and other natural outdoor pools will notice numbers of small dark coloured frogs at the water's edge. Toilets and other domestic water appliances provide a useful home for the larger green tree frog *Litoria caerulea.* For more than three years, the staff quartered at the old homestead looked out for a large Splendid Tree Frog that divided its time between the bathroom and the adjoining toilet. Measuring up to 12 centimetres, the *Litoria splendida* is Australia's largest frog and its decorative golden spots on the upper part of its body makes the species outstanding amongst its many smaller cousins. Spot was no exception, and when relaxing on the toilet seat overhung both edges.

Snakes generally inhabit the same area as frogs and this was certainly the case at El Questro where the law prohibiting the killing of native fauna was respected wherever possible. Harmless pythons and tree snakes are common. It was Wilderness Park practice to relocate any wildlife that might upset visitors or residents. To facilitate this, snake catching devices were discreetly hidden around the buildings, including behind the door of the staff toilet. I recall finding a lovely banded tree snake entwined around the curtain rail of the shower cubicle in our bathroom – a gentle prod saw it slither out through the louvre window – and at the beginning of one season I found the skeleton of a medium sized snake in the bottom of my bedroom wardrobe.

The tree snakes were particularly partial to the colourful bougainvillea that softened the wide verandahs at the Homestead and for an entire season one small snake dwelled behind the bar in the large living room, frequently emerging at inconvenient times requiring the staff to divert the guests' attention.

Rangers were often asked to assist with the relocation of snakes from the luxury accommodation. On one occasion the housekeeper gave a colleague an errant reptile for a routine relocation. After driving several kilometres she stopped to drop the snake off but found to her dismay that it had escaped from the pillowcase in which it had been captured. A radio call to the boys in the maintenance department for assistance proved fruitless. No amount of searching uncovered its whereabouts in the vehicle and with time running short to meet guests from a flight into Kununurra, Simone had little alternative other than to be on her way. It was not until she was well along the return trip that she espied the snake coiled around the mounting of her seat belt on the floor beside her. Unflustered and without a word, Ranger Simone continued on to the homestead and delivered her unsuspecting guests.

Measuring more than a metre in length and often referred to as a goanna, the harmless Mertens water monitor *Varanus mertensi* is generally seen close to watercourses where it enjoys basking in the sun on rocks or other flat surfaces – such as the bench seats or covered bow of El Questro's small aluminium boats. There was an occassion when one appeared from under the seat of a boat that was half way along the Chamberlain Gorge. It was mistaken for a crocodile, causing hysteria and mayhem amongst those onboard the boat until the intruder was correctly identified.

Ten more cabins were constructed at Emma Gorge to cater to the increased coach market in the 2001 season, bringing the total to 45.

The seasonal nature of travel to the region made the North West an unattractive destination for airlines to service. In September 2001 Ansett Airlines collapsed, creating chaos across the continent, particularly in regions like the Kimberley where it had operated almost exclusively and was responsible for the carriage of more than half of El Questro's clients. Other carriers stepped in to bridge the gap for the following year and in 2003 the growing demand from tourists during the dry season led to an increase in seating capacity on air services to Broome and Kununurra. Direct flights were also introduced between Broome and Sydney and Melbourne.

Today as in former years, pastoral country in Western Australia is leased from the Crown through the state government. Almost 40 per cent of Western Australian landmass is held on a leasehold basis with a common expiry date of 30 June 2015. The years preceding this general expiration date provided the government with a rare opportunity to review the system for future land usage and make the adjustments they deemed appropriate.

On the 12 December 2002 the state government subsequently sent notices to 97 of the 527 Pastoral Leaseholders in Western Australia advising them of the changes to be made to their holdings. The intention was to forcibly acquire a total of two million hectares of land at the expiration of the leases. Most of this acquisition was earmarked for future nature reserves.

The affected pastoralists were given a two-year window of opportunity for limited negotiation. Conservation and Land Management earmarked 97,361 hectares of El Questro's land for exclusion from its 274,149-hectare lease. This area comprised the Cockburn Ranges and all the surrounding area on the north side of the Gibb River Road. The loss of this good grazing area would have seriously compromised the viability of the Station and put the tourism operation at risk. The Burrells negotiated with the Department of Conservation and Land Management (DCLM) to reduce the exclusion to 45,000 hectares, thereby retaining the grazing rights to the fertile flood plains north of the Gibb River Road in exchange for the release of the spectacular Cockburn Ranges for a future National Park.

Flood, fire and accidents are all part of the annual cycle of events at this tropical paradise and, from the outset of his involvement at El Questro, Will prudently did not economise on accident and public liability insurance coverage. His efforts to ensure that outcomes from all imaginable scenarios were covered proved to have been a shrewd move considering the number of times the insurance company financed El Questro's recovery from a wide variety of mishaps.

Over six days in February 2002, Emma Gorge recorded 543 millimetres of rain, and at the Station Township some 600 millimetres of rain caused the Pentecost River to rise well above any formerly recorded level. Flood debris was caught in trees throughout the Station Centre at heights not seen previously. Water from the swollen Pentecost River inundated the eight new riverside bungalows and reached the top of the dining tables in the Steakhouse. Black Cockatoo campground completely disappeared and the floodwater flowed through most other buildings at the Station and extended across the paddocks beyond the Station Store, sending the 20 horses and domesticated cattle onto higher ground.

The event cleared all of the understorey vegetation from beautiful El Questro Gorge. The large melaleuca trees growing along the bank of the Chamberlain River opposite the Homestead were uprooted and swept into the Pentecost River and many kilometres downstream. Trees growing along the Pentecost River at the Gibb River Road crossing were ripped up and swept downstream to the gulf where the tidal flats resembled a vast timber graveyard.

With the start of the 2002 tourist season imminent, replacement carpet and furniture were ordered. Fortunately most consequences of the flooding were superficial and only required a concerted clean up by staff as they returned to the Station for the start of the season.

The 1,500 metre station airstrip was an exception; it sustained heavy damage. In most places it was entirely washed away and elsewhere deep channels incised its gravel surface. The driveway was also badly damaged and required extensive restoration. One of many vehicle tracks needing repair was the rough 20-kilometre track to Explosion Gorge and beyond to Sandwich and Split Holes on the Chamberlain River. This old track had been reopened in the previous year and the memorable Explosion Gorge and Sunset Viewing tours commenced. Visitors who have taken this tour have been moved by the drama of Explosion Gorge and the sensational views over the timeworn landscape from Branko's Lookout in the late afternoon light.

Having a bulldozer on the property provided an opportunity to create access to new attractions. The groundwork for the last and most challenging task for the bulldozer was accomplished by Phil Slade who carved a route up Saddleback Ridge to a suitable lookout point. The resulting track with its steep hairpin bends is suitable only for experienced 4-wheel drivers and the warning notice at the start of the drive should not be taken lightly. Later a viewing platform was constructed and installed at the Lookout on Saddleback Ridge. It offered wonderful 360° views and was particularly popular on occasions for sunset viewing, star gazing and special dinners.

The year 2004 was an eventful one, starting with record rainfall and a mini tornado causing $140,000 of damage. Building Solutions constructed ten additional cabins at Emma Gorge, increasing the total to 55. On completion of this work the team moved to the Station Centre and added a new self-contained extension to the 1964 homestead, giving the Burrells and their rapidly expanding family permanent accommodation at El Questro instead of having to rely on vacant commercial accommodation.

The *Outback Jack* TV mini-series was filmed on location at El Questro from mid-March until 7 May. The associated crew utilised all 12 bungalows and 130 tents. These tents were hired from Central Australia and were equipped with generated power. Throughout the duration of the filming Black Cockatoo campground resembled a canvas city with neat rows of tents resembling a streetscape.

Despite the reservations of previous managers, Burrell's dream of a remote safari camp on the tidal section of the Pentecost River eventually came to fruition and Mount Cockburn Lodge was opened in 2004, utilising six fire-damaged twin-bed cabins from Emma Gorge. Most guests taking this safari option declared it to be the highlight of their stay at El Questro.

Nearby in the North Cockburn Range a panel of prehistoric rock art containing a Gwion Gwion figure approximately 1.5 metres in height was found by bushwalkers. It became the largest known Bradshaw period figure on El Questro.

On the plateau above El Questro Gorge a staff member found an interesting rock formation where, over millions of years, nature's forces had sculpted the sedimentary rock into an impressive outcrop of towering boulders divided by a labyrinth of caverns, tunnels and caves. Prehistoric rock paintings and accommodating shelters and recesses suggest this might have been a habitation site, and the location was accordingly named Lost City. Situated relatively close by is Hidden Falls, a spectacular waterfall at the end of a discreet valley.

The Old Saddleshed Gallery was opened outside the Steakhouse. This rustic little gallery was originally intended to display art that had been created by visitors to El Questro and given to staff members. The following year, 2005, the gallery area was expanded to accommodate works by David Byard, El Questro's first Artist-in-Residence.

The Taj Mahal was built to house the Burrells' assorted poultry. Yards and sheds were constructed to protect the laying fowl, ducks and turkeys from dingoes and the elements. The fence proved no barrier to a python which found its way into the yard and consumed a hen. By the time the snake was captured and had regurgitated its meal the unfortunate chook measured well in excess of 60 centimetres.

This eventful year also saw its share of tragedy. English couple Peter and Norma Quilliam bought their Cessna 421 aircraft in Switzerland and flew it in easy stages to Australia, intending to visit their daughter in Perth. After a two-night stay at the Homestead they were both killed when their plane crashed and exploded on take off from El Questro's airstrip.

Peter Birch, an Aborigine affectionately known to all as Black Pete, died during the year. As a teenager he had worked at El Questro for Torrance MacMicking and Morris Marshall and later as a grader driver and entertainer for the Burrells.

El Questro won Western Australia's 2004 award as Major Tourist Attraction for the second consecutive year and turned in a record profit. There were 89 staff on the payroll at that time and a remarkably low staff turnover. As a combination of cattle station, wilderness park and tourist attraction, El Questro during the Burrell era enjoyed a high profile, nationally and internationally. The tourism industry, despite its seasonality, grew to become the third highest income earner in the Kimberley, clearly outstripping pearling, pastoral and irrigated agriculture combined.

During Accor's management, most of El Questro's supplies were sourced through the company's purchasing department in Perth and each week an average of 7,800 kilograms of freight was hauled 3,455 kilometres by road from Perth to Kununurra where the supplies were stored awaiting delivery to the Station. Once a week on 'truck day' the goods were transferred to a refrigerated semi-trailer and transported a further 115 kilometres to Emma Gorge and the Station Township where the perishables were kept under refrigeration and the balance held in dry storage. Coca Cola claims the Kimberley is their world's longest delivery run. Annually there were around 33 deliveries between March and November and the logistics of supply and storage were complex. For example, during a typical season over 800 kilograms of laundry powder were required, and around 1.7 tons of locally caught barramundi were supplied by a company in Wyndham.

The corrugated roads and rough tracks of the area took their toll on motor vehicles. Seasonally each of El Questro's three Toyota Landcruisers travelled an average of 38,000 kilometres, mostly on trips to Kununurra. Instead of continuing to run the sedans for two or three seasons, a decision was made to start the season with new vehicles and resell them six months later while they still held some value.

Visitors and staff alike have reason to be grateful for the vision of Celia Shelmerdine and Will Burrell whose courage and energy have allowed others to share in the beauty of the area. Their legacy in establishing the combination of a cattle station and remarkable wilderness park and tourist attraction was recognised in January 2006 when the couple were made members in the Order of Australia for 'service to the tourism industry in the development and promotion of outback wilderness travel and raising awareness of the cultural significance of the Kimberley region'.

The popularity of the Kimberley region and particularly of El Questro put so much pressure on the Wilderness Park and its infrastructure that significant expansion became inevitable. Consequently in 2004, after 14 years of 'blood, sweat and tears' and millions of dollars expended in transforming a run-down cattle station into an internationally recognised tourist destination, Will made the decision to move on and leave the next phase of the development of their remarkable property to another party.

Negotiations for the sale of El Questro to General Property Trust commenced and by early 2005 agreement had been reached. With only ten days until the opening of the tourist season, the parties concerned were within hours of signing a contract when Cyclone Ingrid in its dying stage dumped 445 millimetres of rain at Emma Gorge. The plateau above the gorge provides a natural basin and any rain falling on the south-eastern corner of the Cockburn Range converges into a common watercourse on the plateau. This stream cascades down the escarpment as a split-level waterfall and flows along the floor of the gorge. When there is excessively heavy rain, the normally tranquil creek becomes a raging torrent and roars through the gorge, uprooting vegetation and relocating rocks and boulders. It is events such as Ingrid and other forces of nature that have over countless millions of years sculpted the 1.4-kilometre long gorge that we enjoy today.

The resort was devastated by the Cyclone. Conclusion of the sale was suspended until the damage was assessed and the contract could be renegotiated.

General Property Trust 2005–2010

The sale of El Questro to General Property Trust (GPT) was eventually completed later in 2005 at a renegotiated price of $17.4 million. GPT's large and diversified Australian property portfolio embraced retail, office, industrial and business real estate. In 1997 the company had begun to diversify into the hotels and tourism business and purchased Ayers Rock Resort. In due course their portfolio grew to include a total of 19 premier resorts including Queensland's Bedarra, Brampton, Heron, Hamilton, Dunk, Lizard and Wilson Islands. All of the resort properties in the portfolio were managed by their subsidiary travel company, Voyages.

The El Questro property now covering approximately 273,486 hectares in area, was a perfect fit with GPT's hotel-tourism investments which represented one of the largest portfolios of nature-based and environmentally sensitive assets in Australia. The overall value of this portfolio was $687 million and constituted approximately nine per cent of GPT's total property assets.

News of GPT's purchase of El Questro became official in June 2005 when the tourist season was at its peak. By this time most of the fallout from Cyclone Ingrid had been addressed under the management of Accor, and the routine operation of the Wilderness Park was well established under the respective department heads. To observers it would have been a seamless change of management from Accor to Voyages.

A condition of their purchase of El Questro was General Property Trust's insistence that Burrell obtain a special tourism lease in addition to the pastoral lease already held. The new permit was duly secured and amongst the associated provisions was a specification that no Aboriginal tourism could be undertaken on the property.

Over successive seasons the numbers of campers and visitors increased significantly, bringing additional pressure to bear on the already inadequate public amenities at the Station Township. One of the positive outcomes from the destruction of Emma Gorge was the salvage of seven of the en suite facilities formerly attached to the safari tents at the resort. These were relocated to the Township and went a long way towards easing the critical shortage.

Under Voyages, two highly acclaimed activities came to an end. All rock art tours including the Emma Dreaming trail were terminated pending approval from local Aboriginal groups. The accommodation at Mount Cockburn Lodge, or Club Mud as it was called by the staff, was closed and this unique overnight safari experience in the northern quadrant of the Wilderness Park ceased and was replaced years later by the Big Day Out – a full day tour around the Cockburn Circuit.

Probably the most significant change resulting from the sale was that the Station was administered from afar. It was still managed at a local level by a general manager who took up the position at the end of July and had to compete with GPT's 16 other hotel/tourism properties for capital expenditure.

Nevertheless, the Homestead was refurbished and new generators fuelled by bio-diesel were installed at Emma Gorge and the Homestead. Extra staff accommodation was provided at Emma Gorge and the Station. The Wilderness Park gained a much needed replacement grader and a new Manitou tractor with a bucket and lifting attachments. Additional plant included two new Safari wagons and a change to Toyota troop carriers as passenger vehicles. Guests' luggage trailers were purchased for use for transfers to and from the Station.

Pastoral leases in Western Australia are required to carry stock and Voyages having no stock management experience, had to decide whether to keep or sell the cattle. Keeping the cattle would necessitate employing a pastoral manager, while selling them meant Voyages needed to find a third party to agist cattle on El Questro in order to comply with pastoral leasing requirements. After some deliberation the second option was selected.

Will Burrell was among the applicants vying to purchase the cattle that had once been his, but the contract was awarded to Lindsay Ward's Five Rivers Livestock company, a Kimberley mustering contractor acting in partnership with Kerry Slingsby of Heliworks. A sub-lease agreement was struck with these partners to purchase the cattle and lease El Questro country on an agistment basis. The agistment agreement was deemed by those whose opinions were sought to be unduly generous in favour of the agisters. New cattle yards and fences were erected and a network of tracks graded to service the cattle operation.

Craig Lorimer was contracted to supervise and audit the muster of the cattle acquired by GPT when they purchased the million acre Wilderness Park. Craig, who had managed El Questro in the 1970s for the syndicate, was working as a stock agent in Queensland from whence his association with the Voyager-managed Wrotham Park Station led him back to El Questro.

Craig found a very different place from the one he had known more than 30 years earlier. Driving along the greatly improved Gibb River Road adjacent to the Cockburn Range, he would have noticed an unfamiliar turning to Emma Gorge Resort, where the Queensland building company was in the process of reconstructing the tented cabins and other infrastructure so badly damaged by Cyclone Ingrid earlier in the year.

At Spurlings Pocket, only the 40-year-old residence and nearby workshop remained to remind Craig of the 18 months he had spent at El Questro back in 1971 and 1972. The 'station look' had been displaced by developments befitting a tourist destination. He found tourist bungalows along the banks of the Pentecost River, a restaurant, a general store and information centre, a bar and a reception area, and a spectacular luxury homestead on a cliff top above the Chamberlain River.

The annual cattle muster was already late when Craig returned to El Questro in August 2005. The daily temperature was high and almost all of the water in the dams around the Karunjie Track had been lost when the retaining walls were breached by the cyclonic floods; consequently the cattle had to cover great distances between the water and grazing areas and were in critical condition. Calving had finished and the cows, already in poor condition, were struggling to support their progeny.

In 2006 Lindsay Ward purchased the heli-mustering business from Slingsby and established Ward's Heliworks. Later he was to come under criticism from the Agricultural Protection Board for running unsustainable numbers of cattle on El Questro. During Burrell's tenure it was generally agreed that without any pasture improvement the property had a limited carrying capacity of around 5,000 head of cattle. Ward is reported to have claimed that he had well in excess of that number on El Questro.

In 2009 Ward had a brush with the law and was required to answer charges of attempted murder. The following quotation was reported in the media on 21.10.2009:

Pastoralist accused of trying to run over campers

... Police alleged Ward, 41, lost his temper when he came across four men from the Oombulgurri community on a remote part of El Questro in June. It is alleged he set their car on fire and then tried to run over them. He pleaded 'not guilty'. The case is to be heard in December.

Ten months later the ABC *Rural Report* of 25 August 2010 stated:

Kimberley pastoralist escapes immediate jail term

An East Kimberley pastoralist has escaped an immediate jail term despite admitting trying to run over a group of Aboriginal men he found camping on El Questro Station.

Lindsay Wayne Ward has been convicted of three counts of wilfully and unlawfully causing damage by fire, and acting in a way that endangered the lives of the four men.

The incident occurred on El Questro Station last June, when he came across the Oombulgurri men illegally lighting a campfire. He set their landcruiser on fire and tried to run them over with his truck, leaving them with minor injuries. Ward initially denied the charges but later entered a guilty plea in Kununurra District Court. He's been sentenced to three jail terms, each suspended for two years.

Interestingly, Lindsay Ward was represented in court by Salerno Law, a legal practice established by family members of past owners of El Questro. The Salerno family also bought into a partnership with Ward's Five Rivers Livestock company and later bought him out.

Ward may loosely be described as a colourful character who allegedly grew up in his father's boxing tent. He shot a barramundi from his helicopter and unexpectedly found himself and his machine in the water and ended up having to fish his chopper from the swamp.

In accordance with Voyages' mission statement committing the company to operating in harmony with the environment and neighbouring communities, employment opportunities were made available to local Aborigines and several of them were put on the payroll. Voyages El Questro also became sponsors of local social events such as The Kimberley Moon Festival, the Dam to Dam Boatrace and the East Kimberley Football League. The Wilderness Park hosted Gravel Rush, the Gibb River Road bike ride for Police Legacy.

Voyages' environmental initiatives included the installation of eight composting toilets at various popular locations in the Wilderness Park. Designated rubbish bins were placed for the collection of glass, plastic and cans for recycling and arrangements were made for all used plastic, batteries and tyres to be taken to Kununurra. Containerised storage of bulk diesel and

The fishing mishap. Photo by Tobie.

Salerno cattle in the Canteen stockyards. Photo by Penney's Print.

gas replaced the drums and cylinders previously used, and a triple induction wastewater trap was installed at the Station's vehicle wash bay.

The expansion and rebuilding of Emma Gorge is undoubtedly GPT's most valuable legacy at El Questro. Once the plans for the Resort were completed, and after local earthmoving contractors JSW Holdings had prepared the devastated area, Alan Emblin and his building team were contracted to start work on reconstruction.

The decision to situate the new cabins on a tongue of land to the west of the Resort required the realignment of a creek and reinforcement of its banks. As a further safeguard against future flooding, the level of the cabin area needed to be raised in places and the cabins constructed on elevated pads. To accomplish this, truckloads of earth, rocks and shale were carted in from a quarry site at the far end of the Emma Gorge airstrip.

Voyages' first wet season at the helm of El Questro was uncoordinated to some extent, causing many of the preliminary annual preparations to fall behind normal scheduling. As a result, in 2006, the 1 April Wilderness Park opening was postponed until 11 April.

Having commenced late in the previous tourist season, the rebuilding project at Emma Gorge continued through the wet when it ran into various setbacks. A big dump of rain midway through March closed the Gibb River Road and prevented the delivery of the supplies and materials required to complete the reconstruction. With only ten days until the scheduled opening of the 2006 season, the construction, revegetation and pre-season set up at the Resort was hopelessly behind schedule. Wet season caretaker Phil Slade, with country common sense approach and logistic nous, was seconded to the Herculean task of pulling the job together.

The revamped Resort was reopened to wide acclaim. It offered an enlarged reception area, a second dining area backed up by a new and expanded kitchen with extra freezers, refrigeration and other amenities. In the grounds beyond the swimming pool, Philby's Footbridge gave access to the 60 deluxe cabins. The grasses, pandanus palms and young trees that were transplanted around the cabins and along the reconstructed creek responded well in the tropical environment and it took only a year for the vegetation to regenerate and restore the natural landscape theme.

The grazing rights Burrell had negotiated over the land along the lower King River (formerly designated as Water Reserve) were forfeited by Voyages and subsequently granted to the Darwalluh Aboriginal group, closing the King River track along the eastern side of the Cockburn Range to tourists.

Early in 2008, in response to the general economic downturn, GPT decided to liquidate its tourism and hospitality assets and concentrate its business dealings on its retail, office and industrial portfolios. Thus in 2009 El Questro, together with the balance of GPT's portfolio of resorts, was placed on the market as a package. Some months later the properties were listed individually and the Burrells, seeing this as an opportunity to return to El Questro at a bargain price, submitted an offer. However, once their identity became known the offer was rejected outright.

At the time General Property Trust put its resorts on the market, Delaware North was looking to extend its tourism business in Australia and the Pacific. El Questro was amongst the five remarkable properties they selected for purchase by its subsidiary company, Delaware North Australia Parks & Resorts.

Delaware North Australia Parks & Resorts Inc. 2010

In the United States of America in 1915, three enterprising brothers – Marvin, Charles and eight-year-old Louis Jacobs – sold popcorn and peanuts from a plank across two barrels outside a sports stadium in Buffalo, New York. It was the beginning of their sports concession empire: 'An empire built on peanuts,' declared a newspaper headline in 1968.

From this modest first step into the catering industry, the lads had their first breakthrough, signing a contract with the Detroit Tigers in 1927. Other ballparks followed and Jacobs Brothers became a fully fledged catering business at movie theatres, sports stadiums and airports throughout North America. In the 1930s the name changed to Delaware North, recalling an early company location on the corner of Delaware Avenue and North Street in Buffalo, NY.

International operations commenced at stadiums and airports in the United Kingdom in 1960 and now Sportservice provides catering at dozens of airports, sports and entertainment venues, railway stations and cultural and educational centres in the United States, Canada, and the United

Kingdom. The company expanded into Australia in 1988 and New Zealand followed shortly after. In 2009 Delaware North, together with Melbourne and Olympic Parks, was recognised with the award of National Venue Caterer of the Year.

Having all but saturated the catering market, the company looked to the tourism industry for diversification and Delaware North Parks & Resorts was established in 1992. The company won the contract to provide visitor services at Yosemite and Sequoia National Parks, the Grand Canyon and other state parks in the United States and Canada, as well as at major landmarks such as the Kennedy Space Centre Visitor Complex.

Today, still family-owned, Delaware North Companies are innovators in hospitality, entertainment, food service and retail. Employing some 50,000 personnel, it is one of the largest privately held firms in the world with annual revenues exceeding US$2 billion.

Delaware North Australia Parks & Resorts was incorporated in the second half of 2009 to facilitate the purchase of the five GPT properties: Kings Canyon in the Red Centre of Australia, Lizard, Heron and Wilson Islands on the Great Barrier Reef and El Questro Wilderness Park in the East Kimberley. These properties complemented their North American portfolio of recognised locations.

It cannot be an easy task to find a balance between capitalising on these remarkable assets and losing them to the ravages of overdevelopment. For as rugged and as resilient as the ancient Kimberley landscape may appear, it is not impervious to the impact of humans. It is fortunate therefore that Delaware North Companies has a sustainability action plan committed to best-practice environmental management. This is through their initiative known as GreenPath which focusses on protecting, conserving and restoring natural resources.

There remains a degree of irony in the fact that the increasing number of visitors coming to the Kimberley to appreciate its beauty and wilderness, also places pressure on the ancient landscape.

Human life evolved from the mists of geological time in relatively recent times and quickly rose through the order of life to become Earth's top predator. In only a few thousand years, we have upset the finely tuned balance of Earth's biota and become the significant agent of ecological change. In the brief period of European occupation of the Kimberley region, the human footprint across this formerly pristine wilderness and coastal fringe continues to increase at an alarming pace.

The arrival of pastoralists with their hard-hoofed stock heralded the beginning of human induced land degradation in the region. The loss of native grasses and overgrazing in some cases has resulted in the desertification of prime country. Inappropriate burning practices, unsustainable development, the introduction of exotic domestic and feral animals and plants continue to impact on the native flora and fauna. Roads, mining, pollutants and rubbish all take their toll on the Kimberley and its wilderness areas.

Thankfully today there is a realisation of the damage being done, and attempts are being made to arrest some of the avoidable destruction. It is within our power to halt the degradation by fostering cooperative land management practices in which pastoralists, traditional owners, mining companies, tourist operators and visitors work together to preserve the Kimberley's magnificence. Together with Delaware North and other custodians of the land, we must play a part in ensuring it will be enjoyed by generations long into the future.

Postcript

El Questro's Wilderness Park Manager, Pete (Brownpete) Guggisberg. Photo by Brownpete.

The following topics are in one way or another associated with El Questro. They have been included here for their general interest or simply for the records.

Bunnings

Because of its dealings with El Questro in the MacMicking – Marshall years, a brief outline of the development of this ubiquitous company is included.

The Bunnings Warehouses seen in many Australian cities today originated with a building company founded by brothers Robert and Arthur Bunning who arrived in Perth from England in 1886. They were carpenter-builders skilled in the new and intricate styles of Victorian architecture. Evidence of the excellence of their work may be seen in the Trinity Congregational Church and the Weld Club in Perth and the fine post office in Roebourne. Bunning Bros were acknowledged to be among the best builders in Perth and Fremantle. Trading as Bunning Bros Pty Ltd — Sawing, Planing & Moulding Mills, they developed timber, brick and firewood yards in Perth. They expanded further by buying a number of small sawmills throughout south Western Australia. Later as Robert and Arthur prospered and their sons entered the business, the company built larger sawmills in the lower south-west and by the end of World War II owned additional sawmills in Far North Queensland.

In 1952 Bunnings Limited was listed on the stock exchange. By 1955 it was one of the largest hardwood sawmilling companies in the country, and during the 1950s the company expanded into supplying the building industry with hardware as well as timber.

In order to supplement the timber resources available to them, in 1957 Bunnings diversified further into a *Pinus radiata* plantation at Boddington. During the early 1960s they continued to expand their milling operations and purchased additional sawmills in the south-west of the state. The trajectory of the company went from building to timber supplies to hardware, then returned to building in the 1960s, and by 1966 Bunnings was the largest supplier and builder of timber-framed houses in Western Australia. It was during this decade that Bunnings supplied all of the material required to build the first homestead on El Questro, at Spurlings Pocket.

Bunnings Manufactured Homes made an early entry into the transportable homes market and quickly became a major Western Australian supplier. The company continued to expand rapidly with the 1970 acquisition and merger of Hawker Siddeley Building Supplies, the old State Sawmills Company, and the acquisition in 1983 of the other major sawmiller in Western Australia, Millars Timber and Trading Company.

In October 1992, after 106 years, Bunnings Ltd was itself taken over by Wesfarmers Ltd, and the subsequent growth of the building supplies segment of the company has resulted in the Bunnings name becoming familiar throughout Australia and New Zealand.

Royal Flying Doctor Service

Recalling the services rendered to Kiwi Harrison after his accident on El Questro provides an appropriate opportunity to acknowledge Presbyterian minister Reverend John Flynn, whose drive and determination led to the establishment of the RFDS – a quintessentially Australian organisation that provides an invaluable service to the people of the outback. As Superintendent of the Australian Inland Mission branch of the Church, John Flynn saw the need for medical care in the outback and devoted his working life to providing it. In the process, he pioneered the world's first aerial medical service.

Flynn's dream of flying medical practitioners to where they were needed could not become reality until the problem of communication was resolved. At the start of the 20th Century very few outback homes had batteries or the means to charge them. A breakthrough came with Alfred Traeger's ingenious pedal-powered generator, which supplied sufficient direct power to operate a wireless transceiver. Using Traeger's invention, messages could be received and transmitted across distances of more than 500 kilometres. The first models used Morse Code.

On 17 May 1928, the first medical flight operated out of Cloncurry in Queensland and soon other outback bases followed; in the first year of operation they flew more than 30,000 kilometres. Despite the financial challenges arising from post-war austerity and the Great Depression, the fledgling service continued to expand and by 1934 there were bases in Western Australia, the first at Derby, and in 1936 a base was established at

Wyndham. By this time Alfred Traeger's transceivers were widely installed across the Kimberley.

About this time, technical advances in radio transmission opened the way for voice to replace the use of Morse Code. It was also possible for the pedal driven generator to be located a short distance from the set so the person talking did not necessarily have to pedal as well.

Having demonstrated the scheme's ability to provide medical and emergency care to remote areas, the fledgling service was ready to become a national operation. At the end of the depression in 1934, the energetic John Flynn and the Presbyterian Church were successful in persuading the government to fund and establish the Australian Aerial Medical Service as a national body. The name was changed to the Flying Doctor Service in 1942, and again in 1955 when it was awarded the prefix 'Royal'.

In 1960 the emergency call system came into operation. Meekatharra was the first place in Western Australia to have the emergency receiver installed, permitting daily 24-hour emergency contact. On stations where the airstrip was a considerable distance from the homestead, a small hut was built to serve as a consulting room for the visiting doctor to conduct emergency or periodic clinic flights.

More than 80 years after its modest beginnings, the organisation has a fleet of 60 aircraft operating from 21 bases, providing comprehensive aeromedical services to remote areas across 80 per cent of the continent. The RFDS covers approximately 22,000,000 kilometres per annum and attends to the needs of some 740 people daily. Demand for the service has increased by almost 50 per cent since 1998, endorsing the necessity for the organisation to keep pace with technical advances in medicine, aviation and communications. A new pure jet aircraft assigned to Western Australia in 2010 further enhanced the services offered to the people of the outback from the five bases throughout that vast state. In its first year of operation it was involved in several high profile rescues including coming to the aid of two ultra-marathon runners who were caught in a fire and critically burnt in El Questro's Wild Dog area during an international race in the Kimberley in September 2011.

The majority of funding for this not-for-profit organisation is provided by federal and state governments; 30 per cent is raised from the private sector.

With no outback service of its own, Victoria has been responsible for raising the private funding for the Kimberley region since 1934.

Within seven years of its foundation, this unique medical service had established a base at Wyndham with stations throughout the Kimberley. Traeger's pedal radio had given the people of the outback a voice to the outside world and allowed them to socialise locally over the airwaves. Telegrams and shopping were transmitted over the radio for all to hear and everyone knew everyone else's symptoms and business. In 1950 the first radio broadcast of School of the Air hit the airwaves from a base in Alice Springs.

Throughout the 1960s and 1970s the Flying Doctor Radio Base was the hub of communication for contractors, carriers, businesses and government departments across the vast Kimberley hinterland, enabling them to maintain contact and coordinate their various functions. With the decline of Wyndham in the 1980s, the RFDS Radio Base was moved to Derby in 1985 and the operations followed in 1990.

School of the Air

Until the 1950s the mail service was the only means by which children in the isolated communities of the Australian outback could receive an education. The service was unreliable and slow, and provided only those educative experiences that could be sent and received by mail.

Reverend John Flynn's Flying Doctor Service (FDS – later RFDS) had not only provided an invaluable medical service for these remote outposts, it had also revolutionised communications. In 1946 during a visit to Alice Springs, a friend of Flynn, Miss Adelaide Miethke, a distinguished educator and former inspector of girls' schools, noticed that lack of socialisation opportunities appeared to have made the children of the outback more shy than their contemporaries in the towns and cities. She noticed also, however, that the outback children were all taught to use the FDS radio service. Miss Miethke believed the network could bring them both the education and the social contact they lacked and described her mission as 'bridging the lonely distance'. She devised and set up the world's first School of the Air, operating as a branch of the FDS, which began broadcasting from Alice Springs Higher Primary School on 20 September 1950. On the remote homesteads of the outback children used individual, pedal-wireless sets to receive their lessons.

Three half-hour sessions were broadcast each week. At first lessons were a one way affair, but soon a question and answer time was added to the end of each broadcast. Sometimes a microphone was taken into one of the classrooms at the school and the outback children could listen to specially prepared lessons or dramatisations.

Modern technological developments have further revolutionised distance education to an extent that could never have been envisaged at the birth of the School of the Air. Equality of educational opportunity in the 21st Century knows no geographical borders and students who come under the category of 'travellers' have been enrolled in recent years. Programs are personalised utilising teacher/pupil and home supervisor interaction wherever possible.

Kimberley School of the Air commenced operation in 1960 at the RFDS base at the Derby Airport, transferred to Derby District High School for a time and in 1981 moved to its own building. Staffing for the school varies according to student numbers; in 2006 there was a principal, 11 teachers, a registrar, full-time school officer, support teacher, Information Technology teacher and Music teacher. The student population was around 58, although the enrolment fluctuates during the wet season. Aboriginal students represented 30 per cent of the 2006 enrolment.

Donkeys at El Questro

Visitors to El Questro will be familiar with Lucky and Jill, the two friendly donkeys grazing amongst their equine cousins in the Horse Paddock. Lucky and Jill joined the Station's menagerie in 1999 after their mothers had been shot as part of W.A. Agriculture Protection's feral donkey eradication program. Helicopter pilot Jack Larsen and marksman Derek Goddard, believing the foals would find a good home amongst the staff and guests at El Questro, dropped the lovable bundles of fur at the Station Centre. Lucky and Jill took no time to find their way into everyone's heart but, regrettably, nobody took responsibility for training them and they became quite unmanageable.

Simone Field with young Lucky and Jill in 1999.

Donkeys are not native to this continent and were introduced about 1866 for hauling produce and carrying packs for early pioneers. By the late 1800s and early 1900s, with the arrival of more efficient forms of transport many donkeys became redundant and were released into the wild.

Mules and donkeys are recognised as being more intelligent than their horse cousins. Mules are sterile and are generally bigger and stronger than donkeys. At Argyle, pioneer M.P. Durack introduced a breed of Spanish donkey that was superior to the norm and by crossing them with quality mares he produced a number of excellent mules. Torrance MacMicking recognised the superiority of the bloodline and acquired as many of these mules as he could purchase.

Donkeys are ideally suited to conditions in northern Australia. These hardy beasts can survive comfortably on a rough diet that would not sustain a horse, and they do not appear to be negatively affected by crotalaria. Without predators, disease or parasites the feral donkey numbers increased rapidly and their impact on the country was obvious. Given that a jenny donkey is capable of producing a foal annually for 40 years, there is little doubt the estimated donkey population exceeded 500,000 in the Kimberley, parts of the Pilbara and farther south.

Most of the Kimberley stations were overrun by feral donkeys and El Questro was no exception. In 1958 an organised donkey-shoot in the Kimberley killed 10,000 in only a few weeks.

Aerial shooting is recognised as the most efficient and humane way of controlling numbers. In 1978 the first of the annual aerial helicopter shoots in the Kimberley took place, jointly funded by pastoralists and the state government. Initially these organised culls netted in excess of 150 animals per helicopter hour but by 1994 this number had dwindled to below 20 per hour and a new technique was required to achieve complete eradication.

With the use of a tranquiliser gun, collars fitted with radio transmitters were placed on female donkeys of breeding age. These are known as Judas collars because they effectively betray the location of the rest of the mob. Aerial shooting on El Questro commenced in April 1999. Over a five-year period there were 41 eradication runs over the Wilderness Park, netting a total of 1,441 donkeys. In 2005, El Questro joined dozens of other Kimberley stations declared to be free of feral donkeys.

ORIA: The Ord River Scheme

The idea of damming selected Kimberley rivers and watering their rich flood plains had been mooted since 1909. Government agents sent to investigate this potential reported merit in the scheme but, apart from the establishment of the North West Department, little action was taken. Cotton was perceived to have value and in 1923 Hay and Overheu trialled cotton crops at Nulla Nulla on the western side of the Gulf. However, despite considerable funds being allocated to this industry it was soon abandoned and the North West Department abolished.

Apart from the interest shown in the area by Dr Steinberg on behalf of the Freeland League for Jewish Territorial Colonisation, the scheme lay dormant until the Western Australian government sent (Sir) Russell Dumas – accompanied by Kim Durack – to evaluate the feasibility of irrigating the fertile plains along the Ord River. The outcome of their survey was the establishment of an experimental plot at Carlton Reach on the Ord River.

Having graduated with honours from Western Australia's Muresk Agricultural College in the 1930s, young Kimberley Durack could see the merit in developing pasture improvement in the cattle industry as an alternative to the overgrazing practices of the day. By 1942 Kim and his brother Bill Durack had cleared and irrigated a small area and two years later successfully tested a range of grasses. Their results led to the state and federal governments in 1945 jointly funding a new research station on the Ivanhoe Plains. The Kimberley Research Station was duly established and from the experiments conducted, sugar and rice emerged with commercial potential.

By 1958 researchers were convinced of the viability of an irrigation scheme, and plans were laid to dam the Ord River and irrigate its black soil flood plains exclusively for agriculture.

This engineering project was to become the largest in Australia since the Snowy River Hydro Scheme which commenced in 1949. The federal government contributed around $20 million and the state $12 million towards the ambitious project. It was completed in two stages: Stage One commenced in 1959, damming the Ord River to form the Diversion Dam. From there the majority of irrigation water was fed by gravity into an extensive system of channels extending across 12,000 hectares of laser levelled flood plain. The balance was pumped to the adjacent higher land.

At that time Wyndham was the administrative centre for the East Kimberley with the meatworks and port the centre of activity. Kununurra was little more than a large works headquarters, however, very soon a carefully planned township was created adjacent to the Diversion Dam on land formerly part of Ivanhoe Station. Following the town planning model of Canberra, the streets in the central area of the rapidly expanding town were given a semi-circular layout and named after the tree species of the area. With no alternative at the time, the cement and all other building materials were shipped to Wyndham, then trucked along the upgraded Parry Creek Road to the dam site. This route traversed the Ord River using a new concrete crossing at Ivanhoe.

Kununurra is an incongruously modern town set in an ancient land. It was founded in 1961 and formally established in 1971. The first stage of the ORIA project was completed in 1963 and opened by Prime Minister Robert Menzies. The first farms were allocated for cotton farming in 1962 and the final allocation was in 1966. By then water supplied by the Diversion Dam was already irrigating 31 farms.

In the same year, construction commenced on Stage Two: the Ord River Dam, or Lake Argyle as it is generally known.

The purpose of the Ord River Dam, located 55 kilometres upstream from Kununurra, is to hold and regulate the huge volume of water collected by the river during the rainy seasons. Working during the dry seasons, the construction process took three years. The course of the river was diverted to enable construction of a dam wall across the southern end of the Carlton Gorge where the Ord River commences its course through the Carr Boyd Ranges.

Prior to the completion of the barrage and the inundation of Argyle Station, the Public Works Department dismantled Argyle's pioneer homestead, stored it for two years, then reconstructed it above the new dam some 16 kilometres from the original site. It is now a museum and a tribute to the early pioneers of the region. The Ord River Dam was officially opened on 30 June 1972. Usually covering 741 square kilometres, the lake is the largest man-made body of water in Australia.

Twenty-five years later, after adding a six-metre weir to the height of the spillway, Ord Hydro Pty Ltd completed construction of a 30-megawatt hydro-power station at the base of the Ord River Dam. In 1996 it began transmitting hydroelectricity to Argyle Village, Kununurra, Wyndham and the Argyle Diamond Mine. Displacing the fuel hungry generators in Kununurra, hydroelectricity reduced the consumption of diesel fuel in the East Kimberley by some 60 million litres annually.

When Kununurra was proclaimed Western Australia's newest town late in 1961 it was still heavily populated with government officials and their vehicles. Prior to the establishment of the Hotel Kununurra the working public slaked their thirst at the Thiess Bros camp canteen where, in a large tin shed with a bar on three sides, beer was served for two hours each evening and at closing time experienced barmen used a hose to fill all containers presented, ranging from a flagon to a jerry can – provided it could carry the liquid gold away.

The early cotton farmers faced their first major challenge when caterpillars developed a resistance to pesticides. Later, low yields and a drop in world prices resulted in a cessation of this industry; however, in recent years genetic modification has replaced the environmental fallout from the use of harmful insecticides and cotton is now one of the 60 agricultural crops growing in the 14,000-hectare irrigated area. Rice, chia, sorghum, pumpkins, melons, mangoes and sandalwood are just some of the other products. With some 45 per cent of the land under sandalwood production, the area currently has the largest commercial Indian Sandalwood plantations in the world.

After many years of negotiation with the traditional owners and concerns over environmental and funding issues, work has begun with the development of the next stage of the scheme. Known as Ord River Irrigation Expansion Stage 2, the planned area will extend along the Ord River flood plains and into the Keep River plains in the Northern Territory. Presently the focus is on developing 16,000 hectares to the north-east of the existing irrigation area. With growing concerns worldwide over food security, it is hardly suprising there has been investment interest shown by China and Malaysia.

Salerno's Ideal Human Environment

The origin of James Salerno's commitment to a search for peaceful mediation to resolve conflict may be traced back to his army experience in Vietnam where he found himself participating in a foreign conflict that had no relevance to his adopted country of Australia. Witnessing the suffering and atrocities inflicted by fellow human beings on one another, while risking his life and the lives of others for a cause in which he had no ideological belief, led James to seek a better way of resolving conflict. Commencing in 1968, this search for peaceful mediation of disputes became his life mission and it has taken him and his followers on a journey of commitment.

James has researched ways to resolve issues and create an ideal human environment within family units. His dream is to progressively introduce his methodology into schools and ultimately into the workplace. Ahead of his time to some extent, James the idealist saw the potential in exploring and developing strategies utilising the concept of emotional intelligence. He believed that an ability to identify, assess and manage one's emotions and the emotions of others is an important step in the process of resolving conflict. In the early days of his study there was little psychological research in the field of emotional quotient. Today the merit of developing a child's emotional competencies is seen as improving their academic abilities as well as their inter-personal skills.

In 1999, several years after relinquishing ownership of El Questro and after 30 years of social research, it was time to test his theories. From his home near Adelaide Salerno called for volunteers and selected 70 adults and children from diverse cultural and socio-economic backgrounds. With the new millennium fast approaching, the experiment was coded PR2000 and conducted in a secluded section of his former property at the foot of the Tier Range on the eastern boundary of El Questro.

The group established a basic camp in this remote area and lived together isolated as a community for almost six months. Life in a tent far outside of their normal comfort zone with a small generator as their only luxury was challenging to say the least. Unsurprisingly, conflicts constantly arose, providing plenty of opportunities to utilise Salerno's resolution formula. Although not all of the participants stayed the distance, the large majority who remained claim to have returned home from their experience greatly changed and far better equipped to deal with the trials of life.

The project had constant media coverage throughout its duration and many domestic and international journalists visited the temporary campsite at the entrance to picturesque Tier Gorge. Alert visitors may still discover remnants of the camp scattered throughout this popular vicinity.

Today the Salerno concept and practice of conflict resolution is gradually expanding amongst families and finding application amongst family and associated businesses.

Cyclone Ingrid

Across the seasons employees come and go. Timeless El Questro provides a unique work environment together with challenges and experiences for management and staff that are out of the ordinary. Floods, fires, mechanical breakdowns and accidents certainly test the mettle of all concerned. This is the account of Lizzi Capewell who was a staff member at Emma Gorge at the time of Cyclone Ingrid in March 2005.

Lizzi had enjoyed working at Emma Gorge Resort throughout the 2004 season where she had been in charge of housekeeping. When the season finished at the end of October, she opted to stay on as caretaker through to the beginning of April. Her duties during the wet season mostly involved attending to the grounds. During this period of prolific growth, lawns require mowing every five or six days and, in the event of extended periods without rain, the gardens need watering.

In general terms the rainfall at Emma Gorge during the 2004/2005 wet season had been relatively light, with around 365 millimetres of rain recorded from the begining of December to the end of February. But the arrival of Cyclone Ingrid in the middle of March pushed the total for that month alone to a record 578 millimetres.

Lizzi had worked long hours preparing the resort for the coming season. She had realigned the rocks bordering the paths throughout the grounds, the lawns were looking magnificent and the gardens and staff quarters were groomed and ready to impress Emma's new managers. By the time they arrived on 13 March Cylone Ingrid was impacting the Timor Sea to the north.

Employees Tahran and Stu arrived a couple of days later and were followed the next morning by Mick and his mate John on their bikes. It had been raining steadily for two days and by 5.00pm on 16 March the gauge registered 125.6 millimetres. Another employee, Robert, monitored the progress of Cyclone Ingrid on the internet and gave news of its approach.

After starting as a tropical low to the north of the Gulf of Carpentaria, Cyclone Ingrid had been drifting around Northern Australia since 3 March, travelling east into the Coral Sea, briefly turning south before reversing direction and heading west, developing into a Category 5 Tropical Cyclone – the most destructive category – before crossing Cape York Peninsula on 10 March. It travelled across the Gulf of Carpentaria, along the coast of the 'Top End' and continued west into the Timor Sea to the north of the Kimberley. On 14 March it turned south-west and crossed the Kimberley coast, again as a Category 5 cyclone, extensively damaging Faraway Bay Resort. On making landfall, by 16 March Ingrid had begun to weaken as it struck the Aboriginal community and mission at Kalumburu and was in its dying stages by the time she impacted at Emma Gorge.

By 9.00am on 16 March, 45 millimetres of rain had fallen and, with the cyclone approaching, the staff spent the day out in the rain securing loose articles, cleaning gutters and generally preparing for the unknown.

Over at the Station Township preparations were also underway. Eric Siewert, the General Manager, invited the Emma Gorge staff to evacuate if they wanted. But no – Lizzi and the others did not feel sufficiently threatened to warrant moving out. Around 4.00pm Lizzi ventured out with her new video camera to try to capture images of the many waterfalls thundering down from the escarpment on both sides of the gorge. By then water was streaming through the guests cabin area and car park in river-like quantities. The two Causeway creeks had become one, the swimming pool was already overflowing and water covered the lawns right up to the verandahs of the resort. The cabins were still intact at this stage.

After dinner the rain increased in the darkness and by the time the staff retired for the night it was bucketing down. At about 10.30pm, water started to enter the staff quarters and the team commenced putting equipment and belongings up onto beds and tables. Fearing further developments, and knowing that water and electricity are not good bedfellows, the generator was shut down. Using the headlights of a vehicle, the three men drove around the car park in an attempt to assess the situation and consider alternative accommodation. Even in the darkness it was obvious there would be extensive flood damage to the resort.

The group collected torches, food, dry clothes, a camping stove and other emergency supplies and moved into Lizzi's elevated room, one of the highest above the constantly rising water level. With the phones out of commission they used the El Questro radios to keep Eric informed of events throughout the night.

The six employees later admitted to feeling a certain amount of apprehension, but there was no fear or panic. From the window in her room Lizzi could vaguely monitor the water level outside and noted with some relief that it peaked and started to recede sometime after midnight. The rain gauge, which had been emptied during the afternoon, was read again twice during the night and overflowed once. By 9.00am the following day 445 millimetres of rain had been recorded for the preceding 24 hours.

It was drizzling slightly at first light when Lizzi and Tahran set out to inspect the damage. They were shocked by the devastation they found. Logs, sand, mud and rocks were strewn everywhere. Bedside chests, mattresses, pillows, sheets and other items from the cabins were scattered through the bushland and found in the most unlikely places. Much of the vegetation had been uprooted or swept away and any remaining trees were draped with pandanus leaves, broken branches, grass and other material swept downstream by the raging torrent during the night. Deep channels had been gouged throughout the grounds, laying bare broken electrical conduit and plumbing pipes. Foundations of the restaurant and main building were undermined and sections of wrecked cabins were scattered throughout the grounds and along the banks of the swollen creeks. Later, all 55 cabins were written off by the insurance company.

With the overall clean-up job too huge to contemplate, the team directed their attention to their own wellbeing and began shovelling mud out of the staff quarters. They also cleaned out a dinghy and used it to catch fresh rainwater for drinking. With little food, no power and limited fresh water, it was a morale booster for the group when Eric arrived by helicopter late in the morning, accompanied by an electrician from Hotwire in Kununurra. They had flown over the flooded King River and Cockburn Plateau above Emma Gorge but nothing had prepared them for the devastation they found at the resort.

Eric's face was ashen when he returned from inspecting the damage. With less than two weeks to the beginning of the tourist season, it was painfully obvious the resort would be closed for several months. During his visit, Tony the 'sparkie', restarted the generator and restored power to the refrigeration, lights and telephones. Later in the day the chopper returned with food and further morale boosting supplies of beer.

Road access into the resort was impossible for the next couple of days due to the height of the water and the submerged rocks at the creek crossings. On 19 March Phil Slade drove in from the Station accompanied by Don and Clint from the maintenance team. With the road washed away in many places and rocks strewn across most of the floodways it had taken them more than two hours to cover the 28 kilometres between the two premises. They set up a pump to supply water from the creek and, with the main underground tank full of silt, it was necessary to bypass it and utilise the smaller tank on the hill above. The staff at the resort enjoyed their first shower since the drama began. However it was not until 24 March that they were able to leave Emma Gorge and visit the Station Centre for their first outing in eight days.

The heavy dump of rain on the Cockburn Plateau turned placid Emma Creek into a raging river that roared through the gorge. All of the vegetation and topsoil was stripped away leaving the floor of the gorge from the falls to its mouth as a wide swathe of exposed rocks.

Although countless events have sculpted the gorge over millions of years, this was the first time the material trappings of modern day man had been seriously affected. The closure of Emma Gorge put the sale of El Questro to general property trust in abeyance while the damage was assessed and insurance matters attended to. Meanwhile prospective guests needed to be contacted and bookings rearranged wherever possible. Tents were purchased and erected at Black Cockatoo camp ground at the Station where they were offered as alternative accommodation.

Eight of the en suite facilities were salvaged from the resort and installed alongside the amenities block at the Station – providing a long overdue and much needed backup to meet the additional demand.

The luxury coach operators, Australian Pacific Tours, AAT/Kings and Australian Scenic, having been so loyal to El Questro over the years, were seriously disrupted by the closure of popular Emma Gorge and were obliged to change their itineraries and find alternative accommodation.

This loss of potential revenue was a huge financial setback for El Questro, and faced with this, and the uncertainty of the sale of the property, all but the most essential capital expenditure was suspended.

Many kilometres of tracks across the Station required repair, and damaged cattle yards and kilometres of demolished fences needed to be re-erected. A group of farmers from New South Wales with a connection to an employee, came out of retirement and had the fences and yards in working order in a matter of weeks. They were known as Dad's Army.

Following a $4-million agreement, a renegotiated sale to General Property Trust was effected at the end of the financial year and the Wilderness Park joined GPT's impressive portfolio of Australian tourist destinations.

Tropical Cyclone Ingrid, although relatively small, was intense and is on record as the only cyclone to have a severe impact on the coastline of three states or territories.

The devastated walking track at Emma Gorge.

Cyclonic damage to the cabins at Emma Gorge Resort. March 2005.

Photos courtesy of Brownpete.

On Staff at El Questro

The services – and service – at El Questro are provided by a team of more than 100 employees working under the respective department heads in hospitality, tourism, clerical, mechanical, food and beverage, maintenance and activities.

It was a happy team of employees at El Questro during the 11 years I was privileged to work there and on any subsequent visits I have made, it is apparent that little has changed.

Employees came from all walks of life, many far from their original calling. With the exception of a handful of staff members who lived in Kununurra and worked in the town office, board and keep was provided throughout the season to those based at the Wilderness Park. At the end of October all but the caretaker staff left the property.

A fellowship soon developed amongst the team accommodated on-site. Unlike most resorts where it is customary for staff to stay only a few weeks or months before moving elsewhere, employment at El Questro was remarkably stable with many returning each March to work additional seasons.

Staff accommodation was very ad hoc. Initially, dedicated quarters were constructed at the Station and at Emma Gorge Resort where employees had an air conditioned room and shared bathroom facilities. As additional accommodation became necessary, the easy option of installing demountables became the norm. This popular form of transportable outback accommodation is commonly known as a 'donger'. It resembles a shipping container externally, with the interior fit-out varying between basic and deluxe. With air conditioning installed, they made a very comfortable dwelling. Iron roofs and shade-cloth further reduced the effects of the hot Kimberley sun. Caravans scattered throughout the staff residential area supplemented the accommodation.

For many employees it is the first experience of working outside their familiar urban environment. After the initial shock of the remoteness and the realisation of their deprivation from city conveniences and the perceived necessities of life, most soon fall under the spell of the new-found freedom of the outback. Those who do not simply move on.

Going to town, fishing, and for the more energetic and adventurous – exploring, were popular pastimes for off duty staff. It is fair to say that despite the long hours and sometimes arduous work, the staff love their time at this unique workplace. Inter-staff relationships both fleeting and enduring provide grist for speculation amongst colleagues and visitors alike.

Feedback from guests and visitors over my 11 years unanimously expressed their appreciation of the friendliness of the staff and of the happy atmosphere amongst the team – possibly a factor contributing to the number of visitors of international and domestic origin who, despite the distances and travel expense, returned for multiple visits and continue to do so. However the clear leader amongst returning guests is Monika Taylor, an Australian who, after her first visit in 1996, holidayed at El Questro for 15 years and came to regard the Homestead as her second home.

Although significantly higher now, the staff level was approaching 90 when I left the Station at the end of the 2006 season. During the Burrell years employment constituted the major operating expense, and only three salaried staff were retained when tourism operations closed for the wet season at the end of October. And with no income from this source, all related costs were necessarily reduced to a minimum. This included the large fuel-hungry generators which were turned off for four to five months. Instead a 5 kva generator was used at Emma Gorge in the evenings to power the lights and fans, and the Station Centre cut back to a 26 kva unit. When power was required to run the irrigation pumps it was temporarily diverted from the large refrigerators and cool room.

Fuel, transport and establishment costs are high in such a remote and rugged area as this, and the window of trading opportunity in which to recoup outlay – let alone turn a profit – is small. Climatic conditions dictate that despite being open commercially for seven months, the peak period is less than three months in the coolest season when the property operates at close to capacity. The consequent need to set pricing for goods and services at an economically viable level may cause comment, but visitors would do well to remember that without those natural forces that limit the duration of the season and necessitate high prices, there would be no magnificent environment to visit.

Top: Staff canoeing in the Pentecost Gorge. Photo by Tobie.
Below: Staff exploring on the Cockburn Plateau.

Overleaf
Staff overlooking Caroline Valley. Photo by Tobie.

Top: Staff netting and relocating stranded fish in the channel country.
Photo by Maria.

Below: Camping out. Photo by Tobie.

Top: Staff horseriding and morning feed time. Photo by Nigel the farrier.

Below: Staff fishing at Brankos Hole.

Top: A fireside singalong with Blackpete c.1995. Courtesy of the Burrells.

Middle: Staff relaxing by a tranquil pool on the Dreaming Trail.

Below: Staff on the platueau above Emma Gorge.

Birds of El Questro Wilderness Park

Birds are certainly the most conspicuous of the fauna on El Questro Wilderness Park.

The diversity of landform and vegetation throughout the wilderness park provides habitat for a range of bird species from a variety of family groups. Many are yet to be recorded. The following compilation of 176 birds begs for review and expansion:

Brown Quail

Magpie Goose

Plumed Whistling-Duck

Wandering Whistling-Duck

Radjah Shelduck

Green Pygmy-goose

Darter

Little Black Cormorant

Little Pied Cormorant

Pied Cormorant

Australian Pelican

Cattle Egret

Great Egret

Intermediate Egret

Little Egret

Great-billed Heron

Pied Heron

Rufous (Nankeen) Night Heron

Striated Heron

White-faced Heron

White-necked Heron

Black Bittern

Royal Spoonbill

Australian White Ibis

Glossy Ibis

Straw-necked Ibis

Black-necked Stork

Brolga

Sarus Crane

Osprey

Black Kite

Brahminy Kite

Whistling Kite

Letter-winged Kite

Square-tailed Kite

Black-breasted Buzzard

Wedge-tailed Eagle
White-bellied Sea Eagle
Little Eagle
Spotted Harrier
Swamp Harrier
Pacific Baza
Collared Sparrowhawk
Brown Goshawk
Grey Goshawk
Nankeen Kestrel
Australian Hobby
Black Falcon
Brown Falcon
Peregrine Falcon
Purple Swamphen
Eurasian Coot
Australian Bustard
Comb-crested Jacana
Bush Stone-curlew
Black-winged Stilt
Australian Pratincole
Oriental Pratincole
Pied Oystercatcher
Black-fronted Dotterel
Masked Lapwing
Silver Gull
Common Bronzewing
Flock Bronzewing
Crested Pigeon
Spinifex Pigeon
White-quilled Rock-Pigeon
Bar-shouldered Dove
Diamond Dove
Peaceful Dove
Red-tailed Black-Cockatoo
Sulphur-crested Cockatoo
Little Corella
Cockatiel
Galah
Rainbow Lorikeet
Varied Lorikeet
Red-winged Parrot
Northern Rosella
Budgerigar
Brush Cuckoo
Horsfield's Bronze-Cuckoo
Little Bronze-Cuckoo
Oriental Cuckoo

Pallid Cuckoo
Common Koel
Channel-billed Cuckoo
Pheasant Coucal
Barking Owl
Barn Owl
Grass Owl
Southern Boobook
Australian Owlet-nightjar
Spotted Nightjar
Tawny Frogmouth
Fork-tailed Swift
Azure Kingfisher
Red-backed Kingfisher
Sacred Kingfisher
Blue-winged Kookaburra
Rainbow Bee-eater
Dollarbird
Black-tailed Treecreeper
Purple-crowned Fairy-wren
Red-backed Fairy-wren
Variegated Fairy-wren
Black Grasswren
Red-browed Pardalote
Striated Pardalote
White-throated Gerygone
Weebill
Little Friarbird
Silver-crowned Friarbird
Banded Honeyeater
Bar-breasted Honeyeater
Black-chinned Honeyeater
Blue-faced Honeyeater
Brown Honeyeater
Grey-fronted Honeyeater
Rufous-throated Honeyeater
Singing Honeyeater
White-gaped Honeyeater
White-lined Honeyeater
White-throated Honeyeater
Yellow-tinted Honeyeater
Yellow-throated Miner
Mistletoebird
Yellow Chat
Hooded Robin
White-browed Robin
Grey-crowned Babbler
Black-capped Sittella

Rufous Whistler
Grey Shrike-thrush
Sandstone Shrike-thrush
Leaden Flycatcher
Lemon-bellied Flycatcher
Restless Flycatcher
Shining Flycatcher
Grey Fantail
Northern Fantail
Willy Wagtail
Spangled Drongo
Magpie-lark
White-winged Triller
Varied Triller
Black-faced Cuckoo-shrike
Ground Cuckoo-shrike
White-bellied Cuckoo-shrike
Cicadabird
Yellow Oriole
Olive-backed Oriole
Figbird
Black-faced Woodswallow
Little Woodswallow
White-breasted Woodswallow
Grey Butcherbird
Pied Butcherbird
Australian Magpie
Torresian Crow
Great Bowerbird
Australian (Richard's) Pipit
Singing Bushlark
Crimson Finch
Double-barred Finch
Gouldian Finch
Long-tailed Finch
Masked Finch
Star Finch
Zebra Finch
Chestnut-breasted Mannikin
Fairy Martin
Tree Martin
Clamorous Reed-Warbler
Golden-headed Cisticola
Rufous Songlark

Place Names and Their Origins

Over the years many of the features of the land have been known by a variety of names. With no long lasting tenure or enduring association with the country, most of the unrecorded names on El Questro have undergone changes over past decades. The following compilation may help to add some permanency to the current place names on the property.

Amalia Gorge: This deep valley was named by the Salernos after James's niece.

Amaroo Falls: This waterfall was brought to general attention in 2010 when it was uncovered by the local Fire and Emergency Services Authority during their annual aerial burn off on the Wilderness Park. Initially named FESA Falls in recognition of the work done by the government agency, the name was changed by Delaware North in 2011 to Amaroo, a generic Aboriginal term for 'a beautiful place'.

Big Hole: A large hole on the Chamberlain River some 500 metres before its confluence with the Pentecost River. In 1992 Will Burrell built his cliff top homestead overlooking the Big Hole.

Burrells Bluff: A fiery red bluff dominating the horizon from Brankos Lookout and overlooking the Homestead. Named in recognition of Will and Celia Burrell who developed El Questro as a Wilderness Park and tourist destination between 1992 and 2005.

Brankos Hole and Lookout: Before and during the Salerno years, this waterhole on the Pentecost River was one of the favorite fishing locations of Branko Raicevic, a resident of Wyndham. Branko served as a councillor and shire president with the Shire of Wyndham and East Kimberley (SWEK).

Canteen Waterhole: Metal canteens were an essential piece of equipment used to transport water in the early days of travel with pack animals. Mules and horses carried a pair of canteens with a capacity between 16 and 20 litres and those carried by camels were much larger. Perhaps it was so named after the discovery of a discarded canteen in the vicinity.

Caroline Valley: This v-shaped valley incises the Cockburn Range approximately 4 kilometres to the west of Emma Gorge. During the

MacMicking–Marshall partnership the area was known as Donkey Yard Flats. The name appears to have been lost and the locality gained its present name during the Salerno tenure, after the wife of James's nephew, Jonathan.

Chamberlain River: Named by Brockman who travelled its length during his 1901 expedition. The origin of the name is uncertain, however English politician Joseph Chamberlain held office at the time of the expedition. He served as Secretary of State for the Colonies between 1895 and 1903. Another likely candidate is William Alexander Chamberlain a shipbuilder in Fremantle who built at least 100 pearling luggers between 1870 and 1900. At 220 kilometres the Chamberlain is the eighth longest of the 109 Kimberley rivers.

Champagne Springs: Named by the Burrells, a bubbling thermal spring pool along a watercourse that feeds into the Pentecost River.

Diggers Rest (The): Adjacent to El Questro, this area was part of the Government Water Reserve. The name is shown on maps before the turn of the century, suggesting that miners on their way to the gold diggings passed this way as an alternative to the route that became the Halls Creek Road. Years later a pumping station was built on the river here to supply fresh water to the meatworks and the citizens of Wyndham. This was superseded in 1971 by the Moochalabra Dam.

Diggers Rest Station: A small ranch style holding a short distance from the former pumping station on the King River. This country is not part of El Questro.

El Questro: In 1958 Torrance MacMicking applied to name his station 'El Questro'. There is no translation of this name; to Torrance it meant 'the hills'. It is possible that he was referring to the cuesta formations on El Questro, as seen in the Nimberline Range to the south of Emma Gorge.

El Questro Gorge: A marked trail extending for 3.4 kilometres along a deep fissure in the Durack Ranges to MacMicking Pool and waterfall. This beautiful gorge was named during the Burrell era.

Emma Gorge: Named during the Salerno tenure after the daughter of Margaret and James Salerno. In the 1960s, the locality was known as Mulaga Springs after Torrance MacMicking who was called *Mulaga* by the

Aborigines as a term of respect. In the 1980s David Selleck and his family were amongst the earliest of the owners to make their way into the gorge. Selleck named the pool and falls area Kingdom Cathederal and Frith Falls, Frith being the name of his daughter.

Explosion Gorge: Copying an earlier method of fishing, Burrell and pilot Richard Baillieu threw explosives into the water from the heli-fishing ledge in the gorge.

Flagstaff Falls: Midway along the west side of Emma Gorge there is a split level seasonal waterfall. It was named in 1997, following the incongruous sight of an enormous Australian national flag hanging over the ledge of the lower fall, placed by a bushwalker who later revealed the flag came from the flagpole on Parliament House in Canberra.

Gap Creek: The valley between the North and South Cockburn Ranges provided the way for an early stock route between Wyndham and Mt Barnett and other stations in the 'high country'. The watershed in this valley was known as Sahanna's Jump-up and the small southbound creek flowing from this point was shown on early maps as Cattle Creek. From 1915 on it is called Gap Creek. It crosses the Gibb River Road to join Nimberline Creek to the west of the El Questro driveway.

Goodluck Hill: This hill offering excellent views over the Pentercost and Champagne watercourses was one of the way points on the marathon footraces held during the 1980s. It is located on the same ridge as Telecom Hill.

Gningling Rock: This unusual rock outcrop, located approximately 8 kilometres from the eastern end of the Gibb River Road, was named Waltja Rock during the Salerno tenure – Waltja meaning 'play' in the Aboriginal Pitjantjatjara language. It was called Emby Rock during the early Burrell years; *MB* being the initials of an employee who researched the Aboriginal cultural sites associated with the rock. Burrell later changed the name to Gningling, believing it to be an Aboriginal word for 'galah'. These pink and grey birds are frequently seen by the roadside in this vicinity.

Hang-glider Hill: During the 1990s local hang-gliding enthusiasts from Kununurra found the thermal currents at Mount Harrison on El Questro's eastern boundary suitable for their recreational sport, and the peak became known locally as Hang-glider Hill. A plaque at the summit has been erected to the memory of a visiting pilot who crashed to his death from the peak in 1997.

Hidden Falls: These permanent falls at the head of a discreet valley were brought to general attention in 2003 by a staff member who discovered them while seeking a way down from the surrounding plateau. Because of their beauty, the manager of the Wilderness Park at that time named them Eden Falls, however his Swiss accent misinterpreted it as *'idden falls* and Hidden Falls they became.

Homestead: Designed by Geoffrey Pie and built for Will Burrell in 1992. Additional rooms were added in 2012.

Jackaroos Waterhole: This name was awarded to the location on Moonshine Creek by Burrell, because of its proximity to the nearby bronco yards.

Janies Hole: Located on the Pentecost River only a short distance from the Gibb River Road, this fishing hole was named by the Burrells who fished there with their friend Janie.

Killing Tree (The): A tree on the bank of the lower section of the Pentecost River was reputed to carry the bullet marks from the shocking Pentecost murders in 1987. The name remains despite the tree being swept away in the 2002 floods.

King River: The King River is named after Lieut Phillip Parker King, the coastal explorer who recorded the lower reaches of the river in 1819.

Moonshine Creek: Named by Will and Celia Burrell after seeing the moon reflected in the water. This watercourse, which flows through Jackaroo's Waterhole, was named Cattle Creek during the MacMicking-Marshall tenure.

Matteo Springs: For many years this spring, close to The Rock of Gibraltar in the historic Wild Dog area, has provided a useful supply of water for stockmen and travellers. It was named after the son of James Salerno.

Maze (The): A spectacular and complex gorge system in the Cockburn Range created over millennia by a north-flowing watercourse.

Memorials:

- **Birch**
  A plaque to Peter Birch is mounted on a rock beneath a boab tree close to the main station driveway. It reads: Peter Birch, 'Black Pete' 2/1/1950–3/8/2004. Stockman, singer and soul mate to many'. Born at neighbouring Durack River Station into a respected aboriginal family, young Peter accompanied his brothers to work on El Questro for Morris Marshall around 1964. He returned to the Station in 1993 to maintain the roads and tracks and entertain visitors during the Burrell era.

- **Bowring**
  A small cylinder containing the ashes of Mavis Bowring is discreetly located just off the Karunjie Track, approximately 10 kilometres north of the Gibb River Road behind the Pentecost Dam at Philby's Flats. It is engraved: 'Mavis Emma Bowring. 30/11/1936 – 23/9/2003. Husband Phil.' Mavis and Phil Bowring lived in Perth where they owned a SupaValue store in High Wycombe. During their holidays they regularly visited the Kimberley. Before her death Mavis requested her ashes be scattered in her favourite places along the outback tracks of the Kimberley.

- **Conlan**
  John Paul 'JP' Conlan; born 13 February 1962, died in an accident while hang-gliding from Mount Harrison on 29 March 1997. There is a plaque to his memory at the summit of the mount.

- **Johnson**
  An iron monument to John Mangus Johnson who died on 25 May 1907 may be found beneath a boab tree in the Wild Dog area. An early leaseholder in the East Kimberley, Johnson's holding included the land where the monument is located.

- **Marshall**
  Morris Leslie Marshall joined Torrance MacMicking on El Questro Station between 1962 and 1966. He died on 8 August 2005 aged 81. Morrie's ashes were buried beside the grave of his son in accordance with his wishes.

- **Marshall**
  Michael Gary was born 9 July 1955 and came to live at El Questro with his family in 1963. He died of leukaemia on 23 October 1964 and was buried on the property.
- **Tyson**
  Describing himself as a bushman, Buddy was born in Queensland 24 March 1942. During his colourful life he was a drover, rodeo champion, horse breaker and actor. He came to El Questro in 1993 and worked as a tour guide and entertainer until his death in October 2011. During these years, he was the face of El Questro.
- **Quilliam**
  Peter, born 28 April 1944 and his wife Norma, born 24 April 1940, died on 30 August 2004 when their aircraft crashed on take off from El Questro Wilderness Park. A plaque to their memory is mounted at the airstrip.

Miri Miri Falls: An Aboriginal-sounding name created for the popular falls by Will Burrell. It has no translation or significance.

Moonlight Valley: The most western lease of El Questro. Part of this area is now incorporated into neighbouring Kachana Pastoral Company.

Mount Cockburn Lodge: The opening of rustic Mount Cockburn Lodge was the fulfilment of a dream that Will Burrell held since 1999. Despite the lack of enthusiasm from any of his general managers, Burrell went ahead with the venture and in 2004 the Lodge with its six cabins opened commercially as part of a unique tour. In 2007 under Voyages management the Lodge or 'Club Mud' as it was affectionately known to El Questro staff, was closed and utilised as a stockman's camp for the nearby Yarrabar cattle yards.

Mount Margaret: Named by James Salerno. This solitary feature is located on the southern side of the Gibb River Road near the King River. It reminded James of his strong and independent first wife Margaret.

Orchasm: A spectacularly deep and narrow chasm created by water flowing into The Maze area of the South Cockburn Range. It was brought to the attention of the Wilderness Park by bushwalkers in 2003.

Pentecost River: Named after John Pentecost, the surveyor and geologist who accompanied Stumpy Michael Durack on his expedition from the Cambridge Gulf to Beagle Bay in 1882.

Philbys Flat: In order to counter the shortage of fresh water in the northern sector of El Questro, Burrell had several dams built to capture the run off water from the Cockburn Ranges. The construction of a bank across a gully by Phil Slade in 2003 created a wetland alongside the Karunjie Track that became known as Philby's Flat. (It is shown on some maps as Morris's Flat.)

Pigeon Hole: Named by Burrell after the white-quilled rock pigeons that frequent the area.

Popies Hole: During the early Burrell years this fishing hole on the Pentecost River was named for an employee known as Popie by his father, a Bishop and passionate fisherman.

Prison Tree: This large hollow boab tree standing on the western bank of the King River was used to temporarily imprison Aboriginal detainees being taken to Wyndham. Laurie Shaw in 1958 was the last trooper to be based in Wyndham and to use the tree for this purpose. In the early days of pastoral settlement the tree was known as the Hillgrove Lockup.

Rock of Gibraltar: Situated close to El Questro's eastern boundary in the Wild Dog area, this rock outcrop rises abruptly from its surroundings, as does its namesake in the south of Spain.

Saddleback Ridge and Lookout: A track and viewing platform established by Will Burrell in 2002 on the ridge overlooking El Questro's operational centre at Spurlings Pocket.

Sahanna's Jump-up: The saddleback/watershed in the valley between the North and South Cockburn was named after the Afghan from Moonlight Valley who used this section of the Barclay Stock Route to drove his cattle to the meatworks.

Salmond River: Although his name was not given to the river until sometime later, the exploration of the river was accomplished in 1903 by the surveyor Alexander Salmond while on his way to survey the country farther west. It may be a strange coincidence that the upper section of the Salmond River flows through adjoining Karunjie Station which was taken up in the names of James A. (Scotty) Salmond and Dave Rust in 1926.

Sandwich Hole: Named by Will Burrell who walked to this location on the Chamberlain River and, while enjoying his lunch, reflected on the origin of the sandwich. The name of this universal snack came into use in 1762 when John Montagu, the Fourth Earl of Sandwich, considered to be the most immoral man of his time, was playing cards and called for some roast beef between two slices of bread so he could satisfy his hunger without getting his fingers greasy or having to halt the game.

Scotties Yard: So named before the Burrell era. The remnant ironwood yards with the old bronco panel and surrounding holding paddock were called Cattle Creek Yards at the time of their construction in 1960–61.

Spurlings Pocket: Today the operational centre of El Questro's tourism activities is located on Spurlings Pocket. This fertile pocket of land extends east along the Pentecost Valley from the Chamberlain River, and beyond towards the King River. It was named after Jack Spurling a leaseholder in 1906. Prior to this it was briefly called Limerick Park Station. This area, where Morris Marshall built El Questro's first homestead in 1963, was known as Spurlings Pocket until recent years.

Station: Macquarie Dictionary gives the origins of the Australian usage of this word as 'a privately owned rural establishment for raising sheep or cattle; a sheep-run or cattle-run; a government run agricultural or pastoral establishment employing convicts'.

Sydney Harbour: A large dam along the Karunjie Track, one of seven created during the Burrell years.

Telecom Hill: When the telephone line was installed at El Questro during the Salerno tenure, a microwave station was established on this hill. In 1999 it became obsolete and was removed when optic fibre lines were introduced. The walk to this point where only a concrete pad remains offers excellent views over the valley and Station Centre.

Tier Gorge: This little gorge with a delightful spring-fed pool is named after the range it dissects. In earlier days it was known as Billy Goat Springs, named by George Sullivan whose goats escaped and made their way up there. For several years it was called Salerno Gorge after James Salerno and a small community who camped there in 1999 as part of Salerno's social research program.

Tombstone Creek: Crossing the station driveway is a watercourse with many large boulders. In 1973 a grader driver clearing a particular rock from the creek bed, jokingly declared 'this rock will be my tombstone'. He died unexpectedly three months later and Morris Marshall named the creek in memory of him. Unfortunately the colourful story of the original name has been largely forgotten since it was renamed Amalia Creek by the Salerno family.

Veranda Falls: After heavy rain in the wet season, this seasonal waterfall on the east mouth of Emma Gorge offers a spectacular view from the verandah of the Staff Quarters.

Wandjinas Window: This is a spectacularly framed outlook from the top of the principal waterfall in Emma Gorge with views down the gorge to the Nimberline Range and beyond. It is named in recognition of the mythical Wandjina's association with water.

Wild Dog: This name pertains to El Questro's first leased area on the headwaters of the King River. It is shown on an early map and has been used ever since. It incorporates Matteo Springs and the Rock of Gibraltar.

Yarrabar: The name almost certainly would have been given by Reverend Ernest Gribble of Forrest River Mission following his involvement with an Aboriginal mission established by his father at Yarrabah on Cape Grafton, Queensland. The meaning is uncertain, however a similar word used by the Kungangee Aboriginal people near Cairns means 'a coastal meeting place'.

Zebedee Springs: The Salernos called these thermal springs Bens Springs, after El Questro's co-owner Ben Salerno. The name was changed to Zebedee Springs by Will Burrell after a character in a television program called The Magic Roundabout. The almost human wizard known as Zebedee wore a yellow jacket and had a coil spring for feet facilitating movement by bouncing.

The Chronology of El Questro

Since the granting in 1879 of the first leases on part of the country known today as El Questro Station, boundaries have changed many times as subsequent owners added or released acreage according to the demands and perceived opportunities of the day.

The maximum area held in the name of El Questro was 404,686 hectares. The following chronology commencing early in the 19th Century summarises the European history of the country located within this larger area of El Questro Station.

1819	Lieutenant Phillip Parker King in the *HMS Mermaid* enters and names the Cambridge Gulf. He explores along the King River and names the Cockburn Range.
1879	Eight adjoining 50,000-acre allotments are speculatively reserved on 'El Questro country' along the 'conjectured' course of the Ord River.
1882	The Durack expedition arrives in the Cambridge Gulf and traverses the conjectured course of the Ord River, the Pentecost River is named. On completion of their expedition they release their speculative allotments in favour of more fertile country to the east.
1887	William Henry Osmond and Joseph Anderson are granted 50,000 acres at *Wild Dog* in conjunction with 300,000 adjoining acres to the east. Lease unpaid 1888.
c. 1894	P.M. Durack takes up the 50,000 *Wild Dog* lease held in association with Dunham Station.
c. 1894	Charles Nelson and John Mangus Johnson on 36,000-acre *Mount Rob* lease in conjunction with nearby *Hillgrove Station*.
c. 1894	Charles Nunn Kidman is the first pastoralist on the 87,000-acre *North Country* lease.

1897–98	C. Nelson and J. Johnson take up the *Wild Dog* lease adjoining *Mount Rob*.
1901	The Brockman expedition traverses the northern reaches of the Chamberlain River and names the river.
16.11.1903	Favell & Co. applies for 25,000 acres – received 50,000 acres at *Spurlings Pocket*. He names his country Limerick Park.
29.3.1906	Lease of Limerick Park is transferred to John Spurling & Joseph Wills. It is known as *Spurlings Pocket* or *Paddock* thereafter. Rent unpaid second half of 1909 and the land reverted to vacant Crown Land.
1908	C. Nelson and J. Johnson holding *Mount Cockburn* lease in addition to *Mount Rob* and *Wild Dog.*
1915	Connor, Doherty and Durack holding the 75,000-acre *Wild Dog and Mount Cockburn* leases.
c.1915–20	Leonard R. Overheu on 87,000-acre *North Country.*
1921	James Ebenezer Davidson, *Wild Dog and Mount Cockburn. Leases* combined in 1923.
1925	Edmund Harold Brennan. *Wild Dog–Mount Cockburn.* Lease shown as vacant in 1927.
15.10.1925	George James Williams, *Mount Rob.* Rent 10/- per 1,000 acres = 250 pounds p.a.
1927	Oswald Threckeld Siddons holds *North Country* and later the *Wild Dog–Mount Cockburn* leases.
1929	Jack Follocks Paddock. *(Conjectured) Spurlings Pocket.*
1.08.1930	Lease cancelled.
1930	Sir James Mitchell, *North Country.*

18.5.1931	George James Williams on *Mount Rob* 50,000 acres. Rent 10/- per 1,000 acres then 5/- per 1,000 acres (17.11.1931) and further reduced to 3/- per 1,000 acres (19.7.1933).
1935	*North Country, Mount Cockburn–Wild Dog* leases totalling 138,000 acres are designated as Aboriginal Reserve 21422.
12.9.1938	*Mount Rob* lease transferred to William Stuart Gordon, Douglas Joseph Durack Davidson and H.M. King George VI for issue of a new lease in Davidson's name.
1938	Philip Collier MLA, *North Country, Wild Dog–Mount Cockburn.*
30.1.1940	Frederick Edgar Bahr *Spurlings Pocket,* about 141,500 acres. Lease cancelled 19.10.1945.
16.12.1948	Lancelot Henri Hughes. Reduced to 159,300 acres by boundary survey, 15.5.1954. Lease cancelled 7.1.1955.
Mid-1950s	Aboriginal Reserve 21422. The *Wild Dog, Mount Cockburn* and *North Country* is returned to pastoral classification.
28.8.1957	Charles Torrance MacMicking completes an application for pastoral leases totalling 165,951 acres.
1.7.1958	Lease: P/L 396/812 District King is approved. 159,300 acres. 5/- per 1000 acres – 40 pounds p.a.
30.7.1958	MacMicking writes to Lands Dept in Perth naming the country between the Pentecost and King Rivers *'El Questro',* he requests their final notice on his allotment so he can register his brand and earmark. The application for a Pastoral Lease is approved by the Minister for Lands 22.8.1958.

8.1962	MacMicking meets Morris Marshall at the Wyndham races. Marshall learns of MacMicking's financial difficulties and subsequently becomes involved in El Questro. A bank loan is applied for.
1964	The first house was built at Spurlings Pocket on the river flats of the Pentecost River and was occupied in August. (1,000 acres around the homestead is surveyed for freehold title. Lands Dept has no record of this.)
21.8.1964	After two years of bargaining, P/L 396/812 was transferred and registered to Charles Torrence MacMicking and Morris Leslie Marshall as tenants in common in equal shares. The holding was still 165,951 acres. P/L 398/421 was also acquired adding 463,010 acres. This area was recalculated on 5.9.66 bringing it to 464,172 acres. Both leases were surrendered in accordance with the Land Act, for P/L 3114/921 containing 623,172 acres.
1965	Equal pay is granted to Aboriginal stockmen throughout Australia, but the Kimberley was slow to adopt this. Financial and family issues led to the property being put on the market.
29.8.1966	Transfer of land registered to David Millard Pty Ltd on behalf of Helen and Gordon Ohrt. 3114/921. *(Lease documents for 324/1968 and 398/564 not issued.)*
16.10.1966	King Loc 275 excluded from lease, further reducing holding to 464,174 acres. Ohrt built station workshop, airstrip, horse yards, generally improves existing plant and yards.
22.7.1968	Lease 3114/921 issued in lieu of Lease No: 396/812 (C.L. 437/1964) 398/421 (C.L. 452/1966) Area: 623,272 acres. Rent $312.50 p.a.

14.11.1969	Transfer (A232979) registered to El Questro Pty Ltd. representing a syndicate from Victoria and NSW.
1973 or 1974	Yarrabar area also leased to El Questro Pty Ltd.
	(Lease Districts: King Omalinde and Marndoc.)

Lease documents now registering in hectares rather than acres.

1985	Lease is released by the consortium.
11.4.1985	Mortgage transferred to brothers James and Ben Salerno in Frank Salerno's name as Centaninti Pty Ltd.
	P/L 3114/1075 = 351,335 ha or P/L 3314/1080 = 351,662 ha.
1987	Murder of three campers at Pentecost River.
2.8.1988	P/L is in excess of 1,000,000 acres. An allotment of 77,513 ha is released in accordance with government maximum acreage requirement and sold to Katchana Pastoral Co.
2.7.1991	Lease transferred to William Westray Burrell. Cost $1m includes estimated 2,000 cattle – a general muster of cattle the following year yards more than 4,000 head.
1992	Official opening of Emma Gorge Resort, attended by media and travel industry.
	27 tented safari-style cabins and restaurant. Rates $70 twin $40 single.
	Riverside camping available. Rate $5 p.p. Campers shared the stockmen's shower.
	Brumby Base built for backpackers. Offering electric power, hot showers and flushing toilet. The fully inclusive rate for Station Camp package – $130 p.p.
10.1992	Homestead opened. Rate $25,000 p.week for 12 guests.
1992 or 1993	Four stone bungalows each offering four bed family accommodation are opened for guests at the Station.

6.1995	Steakhouse opens at the Station.
1999	Wandjina–Wunggurr Aboriginal land claim lodged over 60,000 sq km northern Kimberley leases including El Questro.
2003	W.A. Dept. of Lands declares their intention to resume one-third of ELQ country on expiration of lease in 2015.
10.2003	Agreement reached with Conservation and Land Management over the exclusion of the Cockburn Range from the El Questro pastoral lease, to take effect in 2015.
12.2003	Settlement of Wandjina–Wunggurr Aboriginal land claim, giving pastoralists rights to control their leases over the rights of traditional owners.
7.2005	Ownership of El Questro Wilderness Park passes from Burrell to General Property Trust. El Questro's grazing rights along the King River Road are forfeited and the country is returned to the Aborigines.
4.2006	Emma Gorge reopened with 60 cabins and additional dining area. 82 staff on payroll.
2008	GPT puts El Questro and the balance of its portfolio of 17 resorts on the market as a result of financial difficulties arising from the Global Financial Downturn.
8.2009	El Questro is sold to Delaware North, a large American provider of hospitality and food service. The sale is finalised in March 2010.

Some of the above chronology has been compiled from a variety of unsubstantiated sources and discrepancies may be found.

Bibliography

An Unpromised Land. Leon Gettler. Fremantle Arts Centre Press. 1993.

Australian Dictionary of Biography. Melbourne University Press. 1974.

Boundary Lines. Charlie McAdam and family as told to Elizabeth Tregenza. McPhee Gribble Publishers. 1995. ISBN 0 86914 355 7

Bradshaw Diary Notes. Records on microfiche held in the Battye Library in Perth.

Brockman Diary Notes. Records on microfiche held in the Battye Library in Perth.

Bulls and Boabs. Athol Thomas. Rigby Limited. 1977.

Dating Rock Art. Alan L. Watchman. School of Anthropology, James Cook University.

Geology and Landforms of the Kimberley. Ian Tyler. Department of Conservation and Land Management. 2000.

Images of Power. Aboriginal Art of the Kimberley. Judith Ryan with Kim Akerman. National Gallery of Victoria.

Kidman. The Forgotten King. Jill Bowen. HarperCollins.

Kimberley. Dreaming to Diamonds. Hugh Edwards. Published by Hugh Edwards.

Kings in Grass Castles. Mary Durack. Corgi Books.

Luminescence Dating of Kimberley Rock Art. Richard G. Roberts. School of Earth Sciences, Latrobe University. Contribution to Walsh's *Bradshaw Art of the Kimberley*.

More Lonely Graves of Western Australia. Yvonne and Kevin Coate. Hesperian Press.

Pioneers of the Kimberley. The Maggie Lilly Story. Anne Marie Ingham. Halstead Press. 2000.

Plants of the Kimberley Region of Western Australia. R.J. Petheram & B. Kok. University of Western Australia Press. 2003.

Qantas Rising. The Autobiography of the Flying Fysh. Sir Hudson Fysh.

Rhythms of the Kimberley. Russell Geyer. Freemantle Press.

Rivers of the Kimberley. Their discovery and naming. Kim Epton. Hesperian Press.

Rock Art of the Dreamtime. Josephine Flood. Angus & Robertson.

Sons in the Saddle. Mary Durack. Corgi Books.

The Art of the Wandjina. I.M. Crawford. Oxford University Press.1968.

The Big History Question. Snapshots of Australian History. Frank G. Clarke. Kangaroo Press.

The Kimberley. Horizons of Stone. Alastair McGregor & Quentin Chester. Pub1992, New Holland Publishers (Australia) P/L.

The Man from the Sunrise Side. Ambrose Mungala Chalarimeri. Magabala Books. 2001.

The Riches of Ancient Australia. Josephine Flood. University of Queensland Press.

The Rock and the Sand. Mary Durack. Corgi Books. 1970.

The Timber People. A history of Bunnings Ltd. Jenny Mills. Bunnings Ltd, 1986.

The Vital Link. The history of the Main Roads Department. Leigh Edmonds. University of Western Australia. 1997.

The Unambal. A tribe in northwest Australia. Andreas Lommel. Takarakka Nowan Kas Publications.

Wanamurraganya. The story of Jack McPhee. Freemantle Arts Centre Press.

Western Australia's Tempestuous History. Vol 1 & 2. John Nairn. North Stirling Press. Revised edition 1978.